THE
VOYAGE

Johnny Duhan

Life is an ocean, love is a boat,
in troubled waters it keeps us afloat.

To my mother I owe the heart-
felt beat of my purest aim
that puts spirit in the word and
soul in the air; and from my father,
the steady note that carries
the melodious theme of
compassionate love in my song.

A special thanks to Paddy Houlahan
for suggesting that I write this book and
for advice and encouragement along the way.
Thanks also to John MacKenna, Francis Kennedy,
Dave O'Connell, Willie Kealy, Sylvie Simmons,
Jerome Taheny, Kevin McNicholas, Tom Carter,
Victor Caprani, Des Kenny, Paul Charles,
Alba Esteban, Patrick O'Donoghue, Ollie Jennings,
Ronan McGreevy, Ronan Collins, Pat Egan,
Michael Clifford and Declan Lynch.

Not forgetting my first mate & crew.

Published in 2018 by Bell Creations,
110 Liosmore, Barna, Galway, Ireland.
belljohnny@eircom.net

The author has asserted his moral rights.
ISBN 978-1-9164963-0-9

Design and layout: Shane Foley, Limerick.
Printed by Alma Pluss, Salamandras iela 1, Vidzemes priekšpilsēta,
Rīga, LV-1024, Latvia.

Front photograph: Kevin Byrne
Back photograph: Ray Ryan

The Voyage

I am a sailor, you're my first mate,
we signed on together, coupled our fate;
hauled up our anchor, determined not to fail,
for the heart's treasures together we set sail.

With no maps to guide us we steered our own course,
weathered the storms when the winds were gale force,
sat out the doldrums with patience and hope,
working together we learned how to cope.

Life is an ocean, love is a boat,
in troubled waters it keeps us afloat,
when we started the voyage there was just me and you,
now look around us we have our own crew.

Together we're in this relationship,
built with care to last the whole trip,
our true destination is marked on no chart;
we're navigating for the shores of the heart.

Life is an ocean, love is a boat,
in troubled waters it keeps us afloat,
when we started the voyage there was just me and you,
now look around us we have our own crew.

Contents

Contents

A "T" SHORT OF THE WORD

*For each pleasure you've paid double
in tears and trouble.*

When You Go

Entering the main grey building of St Joseph's, I made my way through a maze of hallways till I reached St Camillus' locked ward. As I rang the bell at the side of the glass-panelled door a male patient with glazed eyes shuffled past me in the narrow corridor mumbling to himself. The translucent glass I was facing turned wavering white and a key turned in the lock inside. As the door opened a middle-aged nurse leaned her head forward and squinted through a pair of thick-lensed glasses. 'How can I help you?'

'I'm here to see my mother, Chris Duhan.'

The nurse stepped to one side. 'Come in, Mr Duhan. She's sitting at the front of the office. I think she's sleeping. But go on, you can go down and sit with her. I don't think she'd be up to going to the visitors' lounge in her present condition. She's been finding it hard to walk these past few days; she's on strong medication.'

Following the nurse, I glanced at a framed picture of Our Lady on one of the pale green walls above a line of seated elderly women with grey impassive faces. A pungent smell of disinfectant fused with urine and ordure made me wince and wonder why some windows weren't open.

The nurse pointed towards the slumped figure of my mother in a corner and kept walking towards the office. 'If you need me, just tap on the glass.'

Though my sister, Kay, had warned me on the phone a few days earlier that my mother was in a poor condition, I was shocked as I approached her. Slouched over the arm of her metal chair, she was nothing but skin and bone. Since I'd last seen her, she'd lost two or three stone in weight.

I sat beside her and touched her shoulder. Her eyes opened briefly and closed again. I tapped her arm. She pulled away and groaned, shifting her frail body slowly back in the chair. Her eyes opened again. She gave me a blank look and started shaking her head. 'It's no good; no good I tell you. No good.'

'Mam, it's me, Johnny. What's no good?'

She stopped muttering and sat forward, looking into my eyes. For a moment I thought she recognised me but then her pupils retracted and she started groaning, as though in great pain.

Other patients sitting around the ward were gazing in our direction, some with irritated expressions, annoyed by the disturbance my mother was making. One old woman sitting close by gave me a sympathetic smile and turned away bobbing her head and squeezing her hands.

I looked towards the glass office. The nurse who had let me into the ward was sitting at a desk with a mug in her hand talking to another nurse reading a file. I thought of questioning them about my mother's condition but decided to put it off till the end of the visit.

I took my mother's hand and started rubbing it. I could feel the hard bone through the withered skin. The back of her hand was a mass of bulging veins and wrinkled, prune-coloured tendons. I noticed that her marriage ring was loose on her nicotine-stained finger.

'Mam, can you hear me? It's me, Johnny.'

Her eyes opened and she started getting to her feet. Before I could stop her she moved away from her chair and took a few shaky steps in the direction of the door. I followed and tried to take her arm as she mounted a step near the visitors' lounge. She pulled away from me in a sudden jerk, lost her balance and toppled over and fell on the floor. I bent to pick her up, but she resisted. The nurse came up behind me. 'Here, Mr Duhan, I'll get her.' She leaned down to take her arm but my mother pulled away.

'Come on now, Chris; you can't act like this, it isn't fair. Stand up, dear. Come on!'

My mother started kicking and flailing. 'Leave me alone! Leave me alone!'

The nurse forced a smile. 'I'm not doing anything to you, dear. Come on now, please, get up. Your son is here. You're upsetting him with this carry on.'

My mother stopped kicking and laid back with both her arms extended as though she was about to be crucified on the floor. I bent down and started rubbing her shoulder, asking her to get up. Her eyes opened and for a moment I thought she knew who I was. She smiled and closed her eyes.

The nurse spent a minute or so trying to rouse her but then gave up. 'I think she's asleep. I'll phone for one of the male nurses and we'll put her to bed. You have no need to worry, Mr Duhan; she'll be alright now. We'll look after her. You should go. You can call again tomorrow, if you wish.'

Outside the hospital, I stood in a daze gazing at the cars going by on Mulgrave Street. Without realising what I was doing, I started walking towards the city cemetery, the opposite direction to home. Near the entrance to the graveyard I sat on a bench and started crying, rocking backwards and forwards on the wooden seat. I looked over my shoulder to see if there was anybody watching me and noticed a line of grey headstones beyond the main gate. My brother John was buried in the graveyard with my grandfather. It had been his death that had caused my mother's first breakdown before I was born. Tears kept flowing from my eyes. I could feel my face growing contorted from the intensity of my sobbing. A car driving by slowed down and the driver stared in my direction. I got to my feet and started making my way home.

Turning into Bowman Street, the bells of St Joseph's chapel started chiming the six o'clock Angelus. I dropped into the church to let the God I didn't believe in have a piece of my mind. The church had the same name as the hospital I'd just come from and St Joseph was one of the saints my mother was most devoted to.

Without dipping my fingers in the holy water font, I pushed open the door. The six or seven years that had elapsed since I'd last been in the building seemed less than a day. Little or nothing had changed. The confessionals that had echoed with my earliest sins still had the same framed Stations of the Cross above them, and on either side of the main altar life-sized statues of Christ and Our Lady still looked down from their high marble pedestals.

I walked up the centre aisle and stood defiantly before the tall statue of Christ. 'I just dropped in to let you know that I'm glad I no longer believe in a God who makes people suffer endlessly for no reason.' I went on glaring at the white figure with my lip curled down and began to feel silly. My mother, lying on the floor of St Camillus' ward with her arms outstretched, came into my head. It occurred to me that her Christian name, Chris, was only a 't' short of the word Christ and that the letter t was shaped like a cross. This association of useless information had come to me before. I dismissed it, left the church in silence and made my way home.

My brother Michael opened the front door of our small terraced house on Wolfe Tone Street. Surprised to see me, he flicked a strand of long, wavy hair out of his eyes and smiled. 'I didn't know you were coming.'

Following him through the narrow hallway, I explained that I'd phoned our sister Kay the day before. 'I came on the afternoon bus and went straight to the hospital to see Mam. She's in a bad way. I don't think she recognised me.'

In the kitchen, Michael closed some books lying on the dining table and put his fingers through his hair. 'Strange how Mam hijacks the conversation every time we meet. Eric and myself were up with her yesterday. She didn't speak a word the whole time we were there, just looked at us with dead eyes. They have her doped up to the hilt.'

I took a seat at the table. 'How long's she been like that?'

Michael sat opposite me. 'Since she got back from Canada. She had to be carried off the plane on a stretcher. I thought you knew?'

I shook my head. 'I had a letter from her six or seven weeks ago from Montreal. She seemed to be fine then. She sent me a photograph of herself in a swimsuit, sunbathing by her cousin's pool with a tall glass in her hand. She was boasting about the bar they have in their living room. She seemed to be having a ball.'

Michael smirked. 'The peak before the trough. She'll come out of it soon.'

I glanced at the books on the table. 'And you, how are you? How's college?'

Michael tossed the books into a shabby canvas satchel. 'Lousy. I'm thinking of dropping out next year and going to Berlin. You learn nothing about art in college. It's a waste of time, unless you want to be a teacher, which I don't.'

'You might be glad of the security to fall back on.'

Michael grinned. 'Like you! How are things in the music biz? Any news about this famous record deal you've been writing home about?'

I sat forward. 'That's part of the reason I'm here, to break the good news. My manager finally clinched the deal last week. I fly to London on Monday to sign the contract and to talk to some big-shot record producer.'

Michael shook his head. 'Any moolah in it?'

I hesitated, smiling. 'The deal in total's worth half a million, but recording and PR costs for three albums come out of that. Along with a regular allowance for three years, I get an advance of twenty-five thousand sterling when I sign the dotted line. My manager gets twenty percent of that.'

Michael gasped. 'Twenty-five grand! He deserves it. Who is he?'

'Ruben Singer, a New Yorker living in London. I met him by chance when he came along to a demo session with one of the musicians I was using. He worked as a photographers' agent before he became involved in the music business. He has a terrific flat in Hampstead and a gorgeous girlfriend, a top model.'

'What're you going to do with the dosh?'

I smiled. 'Joan and myself are thinking of buying a house in Galway. We'll soon be needing a place of our own, anyway. That's the other reason I'm here, to tell Mam and Dad that they'll soon be grandparents.'

'Joan's pregnant?'

'Confirmed the other day.'

The front door could be heard opening. Michael glanced over his shoulder. 'That'll be Da.'

My father came into the kitchen, slightly stooped, his hair frizzled and grey. When he spotted me he straightened up and smiled. 'Kay said you might be coming.'

I glanced at my watch. 'Still getting the bit of overtime in, are you, Dad?'

Michael laughed. 'No no, he drops into St Joseph's on his way home. He's become a right Holy Mary in his old age, haven't you, Da?'

My father smirked. 'You know me, I've always been a gambling man. I'm just hedging my bet on the off chance that your mother might be right.' He took off his overcoat and hung it neatly on a hanger at the back of the kitchen door.

Michael broke the news to him that he was about to become a grandfather. My father glanced at me for confirmation and smiled. 'You're mother'll be delighted.'

I picked up a spoon and put it down again. 'I was up to see her at the hospital. She hardly recognised me.'

My father filled the kettle. 'This news might bring her out of herself.'

'I've never seen her so bad.'

My father plugged in the kettle. 'She'll be alright in a few weeks.'

'Michael was telling me that she had to be carried off the plane when she got back from Canada?'

My father moved towards the bread bin. 'That bloody holiday was the cause of it all. I didn't want her to go, but you know your mother when she gets a thing into her head. She kept on and on about it till she convinced your sisters that she was up to making the trip.'

'You should have gone with her.'

My father shrugged. 'Do you think I'm made of money or what?

Do you know how much it cost for her flight alone? Over three hundred pounds! And three more for spending.'

Michael chuckled. 'Dad sewed two fifty pound notes into the cups of her bra as an emergency fund.'

I laughed. 'Her bra?'

My father took some beef from the fridge. 'You know how money burns a hole in your mother's pockets. She's like a sieve. I had to make it hard for her to get at.'

I watched my father cutting the meat. 'I still think you should have gone with her. Surely with all the money you've saved over the years you could afford one holiday in your lifetime?'

My father's face grew rigid. 'Anything I have in the bank is for your mother, for when I'm gone.'

'How do you know you'll be gone before her?'

My father took a bite from his sandwich and muttered something incoherent. I looked at the flaccid skin around his jaw, which had a yellow pigment. 'How's the prostate problem?'

My father shrugged. 'The water works are still slow, but I'm fine otherwise.'

'You haven't seen a doctor about it?'

My father sneered. 'All doctor's are interested in is emptying your pocket. I'll be alright. How about yourself? Making any money from that mug's game yet?'

I'd been waiting for this chestnut to crop up ever since my father's arrival but Michael got in with an answer before me: 'Actually Da, he's just about to sign a record deal for half a million quid.'

My father gave a false laugh.

I smiled. 'It's true, really.'

My father stopped chewing. 'I'll believe it when I see the cheque.' He got to his feet and went and filled a saucer with milk and headed for the back door. 'I'd better feed the cats before it get's too late.'

THE DEAL

I'm in two minds about where to go,
the church on the hill or the harbour below

Two Minds

While the dealer was spreading cocaine on the glass coffee table, I moved closer to the lamp to get a better look at the photograph chosen for the cover of my forthcoming album. The photographer who had taken the shot tore his eyes away from the white powdery lines and glanced at my manager, Ruben. 'I like the one where Johnny's smiling but Arista prefer this moody one.'

Ruben took the snap and scrutinised it. 'This is the one alright. The serious expression is in keeping with the mood of the album.'

Ruben's partner, Alma, sitting slightly removed from the rest of us, held out her hand for the photograph. After poring over it for a few moments she smiled at me. 'You could escort me down any catwalk in the world looking like that, Johnny.'

I laughed. 'I might take you up on that if the album doesn't take off.'

The dealer made his way around the coffee table and glanced at the photo in Alma's hand. 'He looks sharp alright, but not very rock'n'roll.'

I noticed a dark stain on the narrow lapel of the dealer's tight-fitting mohair jacket. I had been in his company once before in his Knightsbridge flat while Ruben was transacting a drug-deal. In the middle of the proceedings a knock came to the door and the dealer went to answer it. When he returned he had a grin on his face. "That was the ex-wife of a once famous rock star. The poor bitch is really strung out. Wanted to know if I'd accept a coloured TV for some *Charlie*. Would I fuck! You wouldn't believe some of the things I get offered when people hit the skids."

I thought of going to my room, but felt obliged to stay for the photographer's sake.

The dealer took a thin metal cylinder from his inside pocket and handed it to the photographer. 'Try this, it's a lot better than sticking a tenner up your nose.'

The photographer took the tube and snorted one of the lines, then smiled. 'Good toot.' He pinched his nose and handed the cylinder to Ruben. 'How're the recordings going?'

Ruben sniffed a line and turned to me. 'You don't mind if I play them some of the rough cuts, do you?'

I glanced at the dealer and shrugged. 'If you like.'

The dealer snorted a line and held out the cylinder to me. 'What kind of music do you play, man?'

Ruben turned to the dealer. 'Johnny doesn't do drugs. He's as clean as a whistle. His music's kinda clean too, but not middle-of-the-road clean. I'll put the tape on and you can hear for yourself.'

While Ruben was regulating his hi-fi system, Alma got to her feet and stretched her arms. 'I'll leave you boys and go to bed. I fly to Milan early in the morning for a shoot, so I need my beauty sleep.'

The photographer turned to Alma. 'What's the commission?'

Alma yawned. 'Cosmetics, for *Vogue*. The pay's good. And we need it, now that one of us has changed professions.' She threw Ruben a look, then went and kissed him on the cheek. 'You'll probably be up till all hours again. Try not to wake me when you come to bed. Good night Johnny. Good night everyone.'

After Alma left the room the dealer grinned at Ruben. 'She's a peach. Where'd you meet her?'

Ruben hesitated. 'When I moved here from New York Alma was the first model I commissioned. She'd just come from Munich.'

The dealer smirked. 'It's kind of an odd combination, a Jew and a German, if you get me?'

Ruben raised an eyebrow. 'Yeah man; it's a gas.'

The photographer laughed and turned to me. 'Rube gave me my first break too when I moved here from Australia. That's why I agreed to do your shoot.'

Ruben grinned. 'That and the fat fee Arista are paying you, plus all the perks you've been getting from me on the side.'

The photographer took up the metal cylinder and grinned. 'You don't mind if I take one more of those perks before I go, do you?'

Ruben put my tape in the cassette deck. 'You're not leaving till you hear some of these songs.'

I looked through the glass patio door at the night sky above Hampstead as my voice came through the speakers.

I can hear sirens down in the harbour,
I can hear chapel bells ringing louder,
I'm back many years ago on a street I know by a corner,
my thoughts in disorder.
I can see the chapel's tall steeple
On the hill like a phallic symbol,
Or like a rocket to be launched to heaven
If I step aboard at seven
With the people heading for the steeple . . .

The dealer glanced at me and grinned. 'Phallic symbol! Great stuff.'
Ruben put his finger to his mouth. 'Shhhh. Listen to the chorus,
man.'

And the congregation going up the hill
Are all dressed up for the invisible saviour.
The countdown is ringing in my ear,
A choir is waiting to sing there for the saviour,
And I'm in two minds about where to go
The church on the hill or the harbour below.

The dealer smirked. 'I can't get that phallic line out of my head.'
The fact that the dealer had honed in on the most dubious line in
the song began to bother me. I shifted on the couch.

I can see a ship coming up the river
With a halo of gulls squealing overhead her;
It's just back from some paradise,
All the sailors will be singing tonight in the harbour;
I'm in a fever,
Cause there's prostitutes coming down the street
All dressed up for the sailors they'll meet in the harbour.
Sirens are ringing in my ear
Soon the sailors will be drinking beer in the harbour bar,
And I'm in two minds about where to go
The church on the hill or the harbour below . . .

As the last notes of the song began to fade the dealer shook his
head. 'That brings back memories. I'm from Dublin originally. Been over
here more than twenty years, but I still go back occasionally. You've
really captured all that shite we were brainwashed with growing up.

It's a great anti-Catholic song.'

I glared at the dealer. 'It's nothing of the sort. It's about the choice between the road to pleasure and the spiritual road.'

The dealer squeezed his nose and laughed. 'No contest there, man.'

Ruben glanced at me. 'I thought it was about losing your faith?'

I hesitated. 'It's more than that; there's regret in it too.'

Another song started playing.

O Mary it's true I loved you
but it's been so long I'd forgotten you . . .

I wondered if I should explain that the Mary in question was the Virgin Mary and not some girlfriend. I glanced at the dealer's crooked mouth and decided against it.

The photographer turned to me. 'You've a very unusual style. That's almost like a hymn. I'd love to be able to write songs. Do you find it difficult?'

I thought back on the bumper months on Joan's parents' farm when the inspiration for a couple of dozen songs came to me effortlessly in the space of a few months. 'These ones came like apples to the trees. But sometimes it can be a struggle. I worked for years before I wrote anything that I could sing without blushing.'

The photographer laughed. 'How'd you meet up with Rube?'

I explained how Ruben and I had met by chance in a recording studio. 'The session was financed by a small independent label but Ruben won me over by telling me that he could get me a deal with one of the majors.'

Ruben cleared his throat: 'Clinching Johnny's deal with Arista wasn't easy. Singer-songwriters aren't exactly the flavour of the month. It took a lot of tootin' around before I managed to get a few of the biggies nibbling. RSO really wanted him but we went with Arista 'cause they offered the best package. The deal in total's worth somewhere in the region of half a mill. Johnny got himself a nice house back in Ireland with the advance.'

The dealer shook his head. 'A half million quid! Shit, I'm in the wrong business.'

The photographer got to his feet. 'The album sounds great, but I'm going to have to blow. I have an impatient girl waiting at home. I'll be on the lookout for the launch invite. When's it due for release?'

Ruben got to his feet. 'Tomorrow's Johnny's last day in the studio. Then Arista'll decide. It shouldn't be long. Two or three months, max.'

While Ruben was showing the photographer to the door the dealer came and sat closer to me. 'That guy sure likes his toot. Did you see the way he was hogging it?'

I looked away and said nothing.

Ruben returned, clicking his fingers. 'You don't know how lucky you are, Johnny. That guy's one of the most sought-after photographers in London. He normally charges a fortune for a shoot.'

Another song started on the hi-fi. Ruben and the dealer started talking in low tones. The dealer took a plastic sachet from his pocket and placed it on the table. Ruben went to a drawer and took out a small weighing scales and weighed the sachet, then he handed the dealer a wad of notes. 'Count it, if you like. It's all there.'

The dealer put the money in his pocket and grinned. 'I trust you, man. Are you not going to try the stuff?'

Ruben dipped a silver blade in the sachet and scooped a small quantity of its contents on to the glass tabletop. The substance was more the colour of pepper than salt. While Ruben was chopping up the golden grains he noticed me looking at the lines. 'Don't worry, man; I told you before, this stuff's not so dangerous when you sniff it.'

A few minutes after they snorted the heroin Ruben went to the bathroom and could be heard retching through the open door. A few moments later the dealer followed him and he too could be heard getting sick. When they returned to the room they sat in silence staring at the carpet as though there was something interesting going on in the grey fibre. I got to my feet and announced that I was going to bed. Ruben raised his hand slowly, as though lifting a great weight, and wished me good luck in the studio the following day. 'I probably won't be up when you leave, so see you when you get back.'

In bed I started imagining a wild scenario where the apartment was being raided by a drug squad. At a deeper level my conscience started pricking me for remaining in the room while drugs were being consumed. Since teaming up with Ruben this was a constant issue I grappled with, but, given the proliferation of drugs within the music industry, I couldn't see a way of operating outside the culture. After a lot of tossing and turning, I fell asleep.

I woke before dawn and spent a couple of hours reading in bed. When I got up I found Alma in the kitchen. 'I thought you'd be gone by now?'

Alma smiled. 'A taxi's on its way. Get yourself some breakfast and sit.'

I smiled at her curt German manner and filled myself a bowl of muesli. 'How long'll you be away?

'Two days, possibly three. You'll be gone when I get back, yes?'

'My flight's in two days' time, an early flight.'

Alma smiled. 'Your wife will be glad to see you after all this time. Your baby too. How old is he now?'

'A little over three months.'

I chewed on some muesli, thinking back to a night a week earlier when Alma had come into my room looking for some item of clothes in her underwear while Ruben was out of the apartment. The fact that she had little on didn't surprise me, as I knew that models were in the habit of strutting around half naked. But as she rooted in drawers and presses I began to sense a shy flirtatiousness in her movements. While she was stretching up towards a high shelf, I couldn't stop myself from staring at the arc of her behind. She turned and smiled. The nipple of her right breast was exposed above the low neckline of her white vest. I was tempted to move towards her, but held back. Moments later the sound of the front door could be heard opening and Ruben called out Alma's name.

Alma took an apple now from a bowl and started squeezing it. 'I'm worried about the amount of drugs Rube's been talking. I'm sure you've noticed?'

I swallowed some cereal. 'He seems to think he can stay on top of it.'

Alma twisted the apple. For a moment I thought she was going to cry but then her expression hardened. 'He'd better stay on top of it! I have no intention of nursing a junkie. I have my career to think about.'

The intercom started buzzing. Alma put the apple back in the bowl and got to her feet. 'My taxi. If you get a chance, try and talk some sense into him before you leave.' She kissed me on the cheek and was gone before I got a chance to thank her for putting me up for the past five or six weeks.

Ruben was still in bed an hour later when I left the apartment.

Later that evening I returned to the flat and found Ruben in the living room with two young punks with spiky hair. Ruben introduced one of them as a member of Johnny Rotten's new band. 'We've been listening to your rough cuts.'

The two boys looked me up and down. One of them started scratching his head. 'Your songs are great, mate, but the production's poxy. You should get rid of your producer.'

Ruben laughed. 'I told them Paul's one of the top five producers in the UK but they think he sucks.'

I stared at the boys, wondering what they were doing in the

apartment. They looked to be no more than seventeen or eighteen. I waited for Ruben to inquire about the mixing session I'd just come from, but he didn't broach the subject.

I went to my room. Twenty minutes later I made my way to the kitchen to make a mug of coffee and found the two boys bent over a spoon at the sink, melting heroin.

THE LONG ENDURING

*There was a rat in the attic polluting our home;
it sent shivers down my backbone*

We Had Our Troubles Then

I knew I was truly lost when a car pulled up beside me seeking directions and I hadn't a clue where I was. After the vehicle drove away I started crying. I walked on, taking deep breaths, trying to get my bearings. Recognising a petrol station on the other side of the street, I came back to myself. It occurred to me that I might be having a nervous breakdown. This fear had been growing in me for some time, but I kept telling myself that my confusion wasn't as bad as it seemed. A few days earlier I had thought of going to our GP, but then recalled my mother's lifelong dependence on medication and changed my mind.

I forgot to take a right turn for the river, my usual destination after my day's work. Galway Cathedral loomed in the twilight before me. I focused on the cross at the top of the dome – my eyes drawn to it like a magnet – but then I turned away.

Rather than retrace my steps I made my way to a bar on Shop Street. Though it wasn't yet eight o'clock, the place was buzzing. I ordered a pint of Guinness and took it to a table facing the bar. While sipping, the thought struck me that it had been months since I'd been out for a night's drinking. I gulped back some stout and lit a cigarette. After a few puffs I felt a sharp pain in my stomach below my ribcage. I gritted my teeth and cursed. One of my old road wounds, a duodenal ulcer, was acting up, brought on by the smoke and drink on an empty stomach. I stubbed out the cigarette and gazed around the bar. A group of young students at a table close by were laughing and joking. I tried to remember how long it had been since I'd laughed like them. I couldn't recall. For the past six or seven months most of my waking time had gone into the writing of an autobiographical story based on my time spent on Joan's parents' farm before I got my recording contract.

I sipped some Guinness and found myself thinking about my former manager, Ruben, whom I'd split from nine months before, after the collapse of my record deal. The last time I saw Rube he was strung-out on heroin. I recalled the dilapidated state of his apartment during my final visit to see him and remembered bloodstains on the walls and carpets. Because of his condition, I didn't inquire at the time about the origin of the stains but every time he came into my head since then I remembered the blood. I shuddered now thinking about it and felt another stab of pain in my side. Without finishing my drink, I got to my feet and left the bar clutching my stomach.

During the two mile walk to the housing estate where Joan and I lived I started throwing up on the pavement. When I reached our semi-D, the house was in total darkness. Joan and our child, Ronan, were away in the country, staying at her parents' farm.

I turned on the kitchen light. Three days' dirty dishes faced me in the sink. I took a bottle of Maalox from a press and had a quick swig. Within seconds the pain in my gut was gone.

As I hadn't eaten since breakfast, I prepared an omelette. Half way through the meal I began to feel nauseous. The butter I'd fried the eggs in was irritating my stomach. I pushed the plate aside and drank some more Maalox.

Glancing at my watch, I realised that I was way behind in my work schedule. Usually after dinner I concentrated on songwriting for an hour before going back to work on my autobiographical story. Though I had absolutely no inspiration now, I got my songbook and guitar and started plucking out a bit of a melody. I tried to think of a few words to go with the air but nothing occurred to me. While I was humming, the melody began to remind me of a recent pop song I'd heard on the radio. 'Jesus, is this the best you can do!'

I put down the guitar and located a cassette copy of the album I'd recorded in London almost a year before to remind myself of what real songs were like. I switched on the tape and sat down as the first track began to play:

> I'm up here where the night is star-freckled,
> The moon on my head is a lily petal;
> And a thousand eyes are looking up at me,
> Will I stay alive, that's what they're waiting to see.
> I'm employed in a carnival . . .

Not having listened to the tape in several months, the slick production values began to grate on my ear. I recalled the countless battles I'd had with the producer over musical differences during the recording sessions. Not only had I compromised on the use of harmony on several of the tracks, but the choice of material chosen for the album had been taken out of my hands. One of my best songs, *Just Another Town*, hadn't made it onto the record, simply because the producer felt that the lyrics were "too raw" for commercial consumption.

I knocked off the machine and went upstairs to the toilet. While washing my hands, I took a long look at myself in the mirror above the sink. Over the past six months I had lost a lot of weight. My jaws were caved in. I looked like a famine victim. 'Dear God, please pull the wool back over my eyes so that I can go on for a while longer.'

I went back to the kitchen and made myself a mug of strong coffee and took it upstairs to my workroom. I sat in front of my typewriter and placed the mug beside my manuscript – a fat bundle of A4s with the title *THE LONG ENDURING* printed in bold capitals above my name on the top sheet. The idea for the story had come to me during the days following the discovery that my recording contract was put in jeopardy by the merger of my record label with another bigger company. While Ruben and I were awaiting the fallout from the bombshell, I killed time by filling up two copybooks with reflections on my struggling years spent on the farm searching for the songs that had got me the deal in the first place. When the worst happened and I was dropped by the revamped record company, I put the copybooks aside and didn't read them again until two months after I arrived home to Ireland with my tail between my legs. Since then I had been working flat out trying to knock the first draft into shape for possible publication.

I took a sip of coffee now and started reading the page inserted in the typewriter:

I was just leaving the bathroom when I noticed
a large spider on the floor. As I watched it scuttling across
the lino I wondered was it the same spider I had seen earlier
in the day, trapped in the bathtub . . .

I picked up the manuscript from the desk and located the earlier connecting incident:

While sitting on the toilet I noticed a fat black spider
trying to crawl out of the bathtub. As I watched it

slipping and sliding on the enamel surface I wondered
would it ever get out. Robert the Bruce in his Scottish cave
came to mind. I remembered how a simple spider had
inspired him to go back into battle. I watched the spider
in the tub with deep concentration as though its fate was
tied up with my own.

A scraping noise above my head interrupted my reading. I looked
up at the ceiling and shuddered. For the past few weeks the intermittent
sound of this scratching had been playing on my nerves. At first I
suspected that it might be a mouse but lately I was beginning to think
that it was more likely a rat, judging by the level of noise it was capable
of making. The scraping stopped. I waited for a few moments for it to
start again then went on reading.

I watched the spider in the tub with deep concentration . . .

A tremor in my hand interrupted my train of thought. At the same
time a nerve started twitching at the side of my eye. I put the page down
and started crying, bawling my eyes out. The intensity of my weeping
began to frighten me, but I couldn't stop.

A sudden noise downstairs grew louder. I froze, thinking that an
intruder had entered the house. Moments later the room door opened
and Joan stood before me with our son, Ronan, asleep in her arms. A
look of alarm came over her face. 'What's wrong? Didn't you know we
were due down tonight?'

I tried to stop crying but the tears kept coming. 'I forgot.'

Joan came towards me. 'Why are you crying?'

'I'm not sure.' I touched Ronan's little forehead, then looked into
Joan's frightened eyes. 'I think I might be cracking up. I can't seem to
get a handle on anything. I can't work on the book; I've been stuck on
the same page for days. And I can't write songs anymore either. I'm lost.'

Joan touched my arm. 'You're not lost; you're just exhausted. You've
been cooped up in this room night and day, seven days a week, for six
or seven months. Is it any wonder you're the way you are? You've run
yourself into the ground. I've been telling you for months to take it easy
but you wouldn't listen.'

'I was trying to finish the story.'

Joan shook her head. 'From the looks of it, the story's finished
you. What the hell's so important about a story about living on a farm,
anyway?'

'It's not just about living on a farm. It's about survival.'

Joan shifted Ronan in her arms. 'If you're not careful, you won't survive the writing of it.'

I glanced at the manuscript. 'I'm nearly finished. I just don't know how to end it, that's all.'

Ronan's eyes opened. Noticing me, he smiled and stretched and went back to sleep. Joan watched him. 'I'd better get this lad to bed. You should come to bed too. You're not going to finish the book tonight, that's for sure.'

After Joan settled Ronan in his cot we turned out the house lights and went to bed. Under the covers the sole of one of Joan's feet touched my leg. It was ice-cold. I thought of moving closer to her, to warm her, but held back. A few nights earlier I had tried snuggling into her but she'd pulled away from me under the sheets. In the morning when I asked her why she'd done this, she couldn't remember the incident but she did recall a disturbing dream in which an old man had tried to rub himself against her in a queue.

In bed now Joan's breathing grew calm and even as she drifted into sleep. An hour went by and I was still awake, my mind grinding away on a range of unsolvable issues. For three or four months now it had been like this every time I went to bed. I couldn't remember when I'd last had a full night's sleep.

The scraping in the attic started again. I looked up at the shadowy ceiling and began to shudder. I stuck my fingers in my ear but could still hear the scratching faintly above my head. For five or six minutes it went on, then suddenly it stopped. While I was waiting to see if it was going to start up again my stomach started acting up. In frustration, I slipped out of bed and tiptoed down stairs for a swig of Maalox.

The medicine relieved the pain, but I felt too irritated to go back to bed. In an attempt to tire myself, I decided to read for a while. In the living room I took down the first paperback that came to hand from the bookshelves beside the fireplace, *The Bhagavad Gita*. I opened it at random and read: 'Of the ten thousand thousands of those who seek the way only a few will find it.' I started crying. I closed the book and put it back on the shelf. Still weeping, I stood looking at the rows and rows of books, pondering on the fact that a high proportion of them dealt with spiritual subjects, even though I considered myself an atheist. I reached for the *Collected Poems* of T.S. Eliot and read a few flat lines from *The Hollow Men*, then put the book back on the shelf and went to the window.

A pedestrian going by at the bottom of our garden glanced in my direction. I turned out the light so that I couldn't be seen through the glass and went back to the window. Above the rooftops of the houses across the street nothing was visible in the night-sky except dense cloud. The line I had read from *The Bhagavad Gita* went through my head again: 'Of the ten thousand thousands who seek the way only a few will find it.' I shuddered at the seeming injustice of this, then remembered a similar passage from one of the Gospels: 'Many will seek the way but few will find it.' Again, the seeming injustice of this made me shake my head in anger and frustration. I looked up at the dark ceiling and started cursing the God I didn't believe in. In the middle of my rant I found myself on my knees, crying out the opening line of the Lord's Prayer: 'Our Father, who art in heaven, hallowed be thy name, thy Kingdom come, thy will be done on earth as it is in Heaven, give us this day our daily bread . . .'

The Blight

With the blight on my mind the poison ran straight to my heart.
Then I couldn't find courage to make a fresh start.
I had worked many years on my own,
clearing deadwood in a western zone,
but for all of my effort my brain turned to desert
where the buzzards wouldn't leave me alone.
I lost almost three stone,
eaten with worry, I was picked to the bone.

For six months or more I was consumed with despair.
I locked my front door and wouldn't go out anywhere.
At night I was tossed in my bed
by a fever going on in my head;
I was famished and weak and I found little sleep
and the little I found full of dread;
my dreams were all fed
on that terrible blight that wanted me dead.

With my eyes dripping tears, I knelt down one day and I prayed.
I hadn't done this in years and it made me no less afraid;
that night was no better for me,
No let up in anxiety,
but at dawn in the sunlight
someone called me outside
And out there I started to see, in a mist from the sea,
Among my own neighbours, there were others like me.

CHRISTY

I sing for the lonely souls
who haunt this world with unearthly goals

My Gravity

Clutching my guitar case, I came to the terraced house on Mountshannon Road and rang the bell. Moments later the door opened and Christy Moore stood before me, a little smaller than I was expecting but with the same whimsical smile I was familiar with from newspaper photographs and TV.

'Bejaysus, Johnny Duhan. Thanks for comin', man. Come in, come in.'

In the kitchen he introduced me to his wife, a soft-spoken, raven-haired woman with gentle eyes. 'Val was a big fan of yours back in the '60s before I met her. I knew of you too but I was more into The Clancy Brothers. When I got your tape a few weeks back I was surprised. You've turned into a balladeer.'

A wall phone started ringing. Christy cursed and went and lifted the receiver. After listening for a moment he drew a loud breath. 'I'm busy now; can't talk. I'll call you later.'

Val went to the kitchen to make coffee. Christy started talking about Galway. 'Great town, love giggin' there. The locals have a sense of humour all their own. I have a gig comin' up there soon, in Oughterard.'

The phone started ringing again. Christy cursed and called Val. 'Unless it's really important, tell whoever it is that I won't be taking calls for a few hours.' He turned to me. 'That fuckin' instrument! I swear I'll get rid of it one of the days.'

When the coffee arrived Christy gave me a nod. 'Come on, we'll drink it upstairs. Get your box there. I have a little cabin at the top of the house where we won't be disturbed.'

The room we went to was small, with just a long plain wooden desk and a couple of hardback chairs. Above the desk a single wooden shelf held a row of cassette tapes and little else. On the desk a cheap looking cassette tape recorder stood beside an open copybook with a biro lying on a half-written page. An acoustic guitar stood against the wall near a curtainless window.

Christy glanced around the bare room and smirked. 'A home studio for a one-track mind. The only thing that's important to me is the song. Take a seat.'

A recollection of the only time I'd seen Christy perform live came to me. He was with Planxty, in a support role to Donovan at the National Stadium. The moment he stepped up to the microphone and started singing *The Raggle Taggle Gypsy*, the audience was gripped, including myself. I glanced at the copybook. 'You're working on something?'

Christy looked at the page. 'I've been sweating over it for more than a week. It's the first serious song I've attempted. Been having nightmares over it.'

'What's it about?'

He hesitated. 'The hunger strikers. I'm writing it for the families of the men. Very close to the bone stuff. I find the whole writing thing very difficult anyway; how to know if what you're putting down on the page has the right to be there, if you know what I mean?'

I sat forward. 'I struggled for years writing half-baked songs that were more an echo of other people's ideas than my own. It's only lately that I've managed to tap into my own real feelings.'

Christy looked at me. 'How do you know when they're real?'

I hesitated. 'By the way the words flow. Inspired lines have an individuality about them. Often they come almost subconsciously as though something outside yourself is doing the work. But I don't think that's the full case. Usually I'll have thought long and hard on a subject – sometimes for years – and often I'll have written little prose pieces, trying to tap into the flow. Eventually these rough fragments germinate and become songs. Melody, for me, is almost always the catalyst.'

Christy's eyes brightened. 'You come up with the melodies first?'

I swallowed some coffee. 'Often I'll have airs going around in my head for years before they become songs. Often, too, I might write a second set of lyrics for the same melody, if the first don't work. Getting the two separate things to gel is the difficult thing. And the stronger the melody, I find, the harder it can be to come up with words that sound natural with it. I read this interesting thing by Tolstoy where he points out that melody and lyrics are two totally different art forms and that quite a few classical composers often make a mess out of bringing them together. He maintained that folk song is the most natural expression of art we have, in all cultures.'

Christy nodded. 'Fair play to Tolstoy.'

I leaned forward. 'I read somewhere else that Russian folk music comes directly from Russian Orthodox Church music. The peasant musicians down the centuries speeded up the rhythms in the same way that Gospel was jazzed up in the States at the beginning of our century.'

Christy scratched his forehead. 'I've often thought myself that sean-nós is a direct lift from plainchant. Taken out of the hands of the tight-fisted clergy, ordinary punters gave it the human touch. Then fiddlers and other musicians added the jilt it needed to dance.'

A knock came to the door. 'Phone, Christy! It's Donal.'

Christy got to his feet. 'Sorry about this, I won't be long.'

With Christy out of the room, I went to the window and glanced out at the back garden. A black cat sitting on a red brick wall was staring at a small bird foraging in the grass below it. I thought of my Tolstoy remark and felt embarrassed, thinking that Christy might have felt that I was showing off.

The door opened and Christy reappeared. 'I have a gig with Moving Hearts in the Baggot tonight. You can come along, if you like. You're staying overnight, aren't you?'

'With my brother Michael, in Rathmines. I'd love to go to the gig.'

Christy picked up his guitar. 'Will we sing something?'

I took out my old Yamaha and tuned it to Christy's Martin. Christy looked at the worn body of my instrument and nodded. 'Well seasoned. The dents and cracks show it's been through the wars. What'll we play?'

'You decide.'

Christy started picking. 'I really like the last song on the tape you sent me; the one you didn't finish. It breaks off in the middle of a verse after a chorus.' He started singing:

One hundred miles from his home,
Through a lonely city he roams,
Till he finds a bed he doesn't own,
In a house for rolling stones.
There he can lay his head down;
There he can relax his frown;
There he can dream of his hometown,
In his sleep his troubles drown.

But when he wakes up and takes his first look
At his tattered surroundings,
When he awakes, when his dream breaks
he asks himself, 'How can I survive
another day of being alive
till the evening comes.

Christy stopped singing. 'There's another couple of lines after that but then it suddenly stops.'

I cleared my throat and started singing the missing verse:

One hundred miles from his home,
He has nothing left to call his own,
just the rags for his bones
and the memory of his home.
And as he gets out of the bed
sadness starts to cloud his head;
His heart fills with dread,
He almost wishes he were dead,

For when he wakes up and takes his first look . . .

Christy joined me in repeating the chorus. When we got to the end of the song he shook his head. 'That refrain sends shivers down my neck; the melody as well as the words. It nearly had me in tears the first time I heard it and by Jaysus it nearly has me the same way now. I keep thinking of an uncle of mine – my only uncle, Jimmy Power, from the banks of the Boyne. He died on a lonely street in Birmingham, God rest him. He was a lovely oul' fella but he had a fatal craving for the gargle. Where did the idea for the song come from?'

I related my experience of staying in a St Vincent de Paul's night-shelter when I was fifteen. 'It was a real eye-opener seeing so many tramps and down-and-outs all grouped together in one place. The memory stayed with me, probably because deep down I have a fear that I might end up like that myself one day.'

Christy nodded. 'Haven't we all. But tell us, how come you didn't put the full song on the tape?'

I hesitated. 'I was on edge the day I put it down. I've never been a hundred percent happy with the words; they're a bit clumsy here and there. While I was recording it I lost confidence. I planned to rework it and rerecord it at a later stage but it went out of my head. The past year has been a bit shaky for me. A record deal I had in London fell through last year and my health took a nose-dive, mentally as well as physically.' I forced a smile. 'I'm okay now, but I'm still not fully happy with the song.'

Christy laughed. 'You wouldn't make a great car salesman. I'm thinking of recording it.'

I smiled.

'There's another song on the tape I'm also thinking of doing, *El Salvador*. Tell us about that?'

I sat forward and explained that the idea for *El Salvador* had come from a TV documentary I'd seen some months before. 'I was so disturbed by the injustice of the situation there, I picked up my guitar and wrote the song in a couple of hours.'

'Sing it.'

I played the intro and launched into the song.

A girl cries out in the early morning,
woken by the sound of a gun.
She knows somewhere someone is dying
beneath the rising sun.
Outside the window of her cabana
the shadows are full of her fear.
She knows her lover is out there somewhere,
he's been fighting now for a year
to heal the soul of El Salvador.

The moon like a skull is over the country,
the sky to the east is blood-red.
A general wakes up and takes his coffee
while he sits on his bed.
Outside the barracks soldiers are marching back
with their guns in their hands.
The general goes out, salutes his army
and issues new commands -
he makes the guns roar in El Salvador.

Bells ring out in a chapel steeple,
a priest prepares to say Mass.
A sad congregation come tired and hungry
to pray their troubles will pass.
Meanwhile the sun rises over the dusty streets
where the bodies are found;

flies and mosquitoes are drinking from pools of blood
where a crowd gathers round -
They cry for the soul of El Salvador.

Out on a rancho a rich man's preparing
to go for his morning ride.
They've saddled his horse out in the corral,
he walks out full of pride.
He looks like a cowboy from one of those movies
Regan made in the past.
Peasants in rags stand back for El Rico,
they know he gallops real fast
over the soul of El Salvador.

Christy smiled. 'It's like a film rolling inside my head. How do you come up with them?'

'I had the melody for that one knocking around for years.'

Christy sang part of the opening line of *El Salvador* at a different tempo than mine. 'I haven't learned all the words yet, but they're the real thing. You'd swear it was written by someone who had real experience of the events.'

Another knock came to the door. 'It's Mattie, Christy. He just wants to talk to you for a minute. It's important.'

Christy cursed. 'I'm going to leave it off the hook altogether after this. I won't be a minute.'

While he was gone I took a packet of Bisodol tablets from my pocket and put two in my mouth. My ulcer was acting up.

Christy returned. 'That was my manager, wanting to know if I'd do an interview on RTE radio early tomorrow morning.'

'You're kept busy.'

'Like a horse-fly on shit.' He sat and picked up his guitar. 'I'd like to sing you a bit of that song I was telling you about, the one that's giving me the nightmares. Donal Lunny gave me the air, but it's not finished; I just have a few verses. He started singing.

The time has come to part my love, I must go away;
I'll leave you now my girl, no longer can I stay.
My heart like yours is breaking but together we'll prove strong,
The road I take will show the world the suffering that goes on.
The gentle clasp that holds my hand must loosen and let go,
Please help me through that door though instinct tells you no.

Christy wiped some perspiration from his forehead. 'I have another few lines that I'm thinking of changing. I have to tread lightly. It's a sensitive issue. Some of the families of the men may not want such a song written.'

'I like the last line about the loosening handclasp and the instinct not to let go. It's a huge sacrifice they're making.' I scratched my neck. 'I've been thinking of writing a song on the North myself; about the suffering that the violence has brought to both sides of the divide.'

Christy looked at me but didn't say anything.

I looked away. 'I have mixed feelings about the whole political situation there. I remember my father being picked on by an IRA sympathiser in a bar in Limerick when I was a kid simply because he was wearing a poppy on Commemoration day, in memory of his father who had been in the British army. I wrote a piece on the incident, *Two Lapels*. It's in my copybook. Will I read it?'

Christy hesitated. 'Fire away.'

I got the book and found the page.

An Easter lily on a thin steel stalk yellowed each year
a spot on Joe's lapel, and on Remembrance Sunday a
poppy reappeared in John's buttonhole, as though last
year's artificial flower had left seed in the tweed.
Joe often called his neighbour "John Bull". The double
joke of it was, John was Taurean, though he rarely showed
his horns. On the days they wore their emblems both men
drank an extra pint or two (as though their paper flowers
needed nourishment) and respectfully kept the peace.
But on other occasions Joe would start on about Pearse
and Connolly, John about the Munster Fusiliers.
On one St Patrick's night, while drowning the shamrock,
Joe called John's old-man a traitor and pulled the green
weed from his lapel. John drawled "Come outside!"
Joe launched the first blow. John saw stars. The stars
brought out the bull in him. Joe stood his ground like a
matador and ended up with a rosy mouth. John was left
holding his snout that dripped poppies at his feet.
After the fight John walked off in a huff. Joe, still stunned,
noticing some shamrock on the ground, bent to pick it up,
but changed his mind when he saw that the green
trifoliates were poppy-red with blood.'

Christy smiled. 'You have a way with words. I like the bit of humour too. You don't get that in your songs.' He looked at his watch. 'Will we go down for a sandwich and a cuppa tea?'

While we were having lunch Christy put on a cassette. 'Have a listen to this song. I'm thinkin' of recording it as my next single.'

'Don't forget your shovel, if you want to go to work . . .'

THERE IS A GIRL

There is a time in life, it seems,
for believing in dreams, for me it's gone

There is a Time

Having finished an encore, I was stepping back from the microphone, soaking up the applause, when the silhouette of a female figure approached the low stage and handed me a slip of paper, which I thought was a song request. Before I had a chance to get a look at her face she disappeared back into the audience, pressing towards a side exit. I glanced at the note and instantly recognised the signature at the bottom of the scrap of paper, though I hadn't seen it for many years. I got off the stage as quickly as I could and pushed through the crowd to the side door.

In the street just up from the club entrance, I spotted a young woman in a black leather coat opening the door of a white Mercedes. I came up behind her and touched her shoulder. 'Helen?'

She turned and smiled. 'I didn't think you'd come after me. I shouldn't have scribbled that note. An impulse. I just wanted to set a few things straight.'

'A ghost from the past.'

Helen brushed back a strand of hair. 'I'm real enough. I saw you on *The Late Late Show* and bought your LP. I was very hurt by one of the songs. I think it's about me.'

I laughed. 'Which one's that?'

'Did you not read my note?'

I still had the scrap of paper in my hand. By the amber light of a street-lamp I could just about make out the writing:

Dear Johnny,
If I'm the girl in your song *There is a Girl*, I just want to say that
I would never be as callous as that. You're very clever with words,
but I think you've taken too much of a poetic license here.
I enjoyed your show tonight, and I hope you receive the
success you deserve. But try and be more sensitive to the
feelings of those you write about in the future.
Regards,
Helen

I smiled. 'Which part of the song did you find hurtful?'
'The second verse.'
The verse came to mind:

In my dream I always end up repairing a run-down room,
it's the run-down room where she left me; I am that room.
She stands over by the window while I make repairs;
she smiles over at my progress and like a fool I care.

I laughed. 'It's just a dream.'
Helen looked me straight in the eye and her lower lip quivered. 'I
don't like what it implies.'
'Sorry. Come back to the club and I'll buy you a reconciliation drink.'
Helen glanced towards the club. 'It's very noisy back there. Can
we go somewhere else? There's a quiet pub down here just around the
corner.'
I hesitated. 'OK, but the club closes soon. I'll have to get back to
meet up with my manager and get my guitar. I'm staying at his place
tonight.'
As we moved away I glanced back at the Merc. 'You've done well for
yourself, by the looks of things. Married?'
Helen shifted the strap of her shoulder bag. 'My partner Jim and I
run a stud in county Kildare. We've done well, financially.' She glanced
at me. 'And you? I read in some newspaper that you're married, with
two kids?'
'A boy and girl. Joan and I have been married for five or six years but
we've been together for more than ten. We live in Galway.'
Helen smiled. 'Happy?'
I nodded. 'We have our ups and downs like most couples. I'm
difficult to live with. You're lucky you got out when you did.'
Helen gave a wry smile. 'The bar's just here on the right.'

The lounge was half empty. While I was ordering drinks at the counter Helen found a table. I glanced back at her. She had taken off her coat and was tugging at the ends of a short leather mini skirt. I recalled the knee-length polka-dot dress she wore on the night I first met her and smiled. When I rejoined her with the drinks I found it hard keeping my eyes away from her knees. 'I hope you're not just having the beer for old time's sake. You look more like a G&T lady now?'

Helen sipped her drink. 'I have beer occasionally. I'm not a big drinker; wine with meals. I never drink gin.'

'Tell us about your stud.'

Helen laughed and looked away. 'There's not much to tell. Jim and I raise horses and sell them all over the world; Europe mainly, but the Middle East and Japan too. There's quite a lot of travel involved.'

'Sounds exciting.'

Helen took another sip of beer. 'It can be. It can be boring as hell too at times.' She paused and drew a long breath. 'Jim and I have our . . . tensions.'

'You don't get on?'

She shifted her legs. 'Like you said, all relationships have their ups and downs. Jim and I have more downs than ups. He keeps himself busy; likes socialising with his old college friends. When he's away on the Continent or in Asia, God knows what he gets up to. I have my suspicions but I don't pry.' She paused. 'And you, you seem to be doing well? I hear your songs on the radio all the time. Ronan Collins played *Girls in my Memory* today.'

I swallowed some beer. 'The album's getting a lot of airplay, but the sales figures won't make me rich. We're hoping a record company will finance the recording of a new album soon.'

'We?'

'I have a kind of manager. I say "kind of" because he keeps telling me I'm unmanageable. His name's Red Murphy. He used to work as a PR agent for Granny's Intentions back in the day. He reckons I have a subconscious will to fail. And he may be right.' I took a notebook from my pocket and read a recent entry: 'We Irish are suspicious of success, knowing there's a lot more of the infinite in its opposite'.

'A strange adage.'

'I found it in a newspaper article by Ulick O'Connor. I'm always jotting things down.'

'You read a lot?'

I smiled. 'You should know, you got me into the habit. *The Castle*, remember?'

Helen gave me a quizzical look. In the glow of the wall-lamp above her head, I noticed a small zigzagging vein at the corner of her left eye. Ten years earlier I had found this blemish highly attractive. She leaned forward. '*The Castle* by Franz Kafka. The novel I gave you on our first date.'

'Our second, actually. But, yeah, I have you to thank for one of the greatest loves of my life.'

Helen's eyes twinkled and she laughed. 'Kafka?'

'Literature in general. Before I met you I hardly read a book. In fact reading *The Castle* was as onerous as the task the main character, K, has in the story of reaching his illusive goal. I think it was that unresolved struggle that got me hooked on the never-ending literary search I've been on ever since.'

'What kind of books do you read now?'

'*The Charterhouse of Parma* at the moment, for the fourth time. I'm also rereading *The Four Quartets* by T.S. Eliot as a kind of antidote to Stendhal's high romanticism, and atheism. I'm a practising Catholic.'

Helen raised an eyebrow. 'You were always so anti Christian. What brought about the sea change?'

I hesitated. 'The return was gradual; no Road to Damascus stuff, just a slow-growing realisation that I couldn't go through my life any other way. I still have my doubts, just as I had doubts in my unbelief in the past. The difference is subtle, but I believe it will make all the difference in the end.'

Helen smiled. 'When the last trump is called?'

'You're taking the piss.'

'Not at all. I lost my belief in such certainty long ago but I admire people who hold on to theirs.'

I drank back my beer, trying to think of something to say. I finished the glass and glanced at the clock behind the bar. 'I'm going to have to get back to the club. They'll be closing up.'

During the short walk back to the venue Helen started reminiscing about the lanes and alleyways we used to meander through in our heyday. 'Remember the dilapidated house that almost became our love nest?'

I laughed. 'Almost.'

'Seems only like yesterday, doesn't it?'

I shook my head. 'More like a lifetime to me.'

As we approached the white Mercedes I spotted my manager, Red, coming out of the club down the street. He was carrying my guitar case. I called to him. He came towards us, eyeing Helen. 'I've been looking for you everywhere. Where'd you go?'

I introduced Helen. 'We used to go out together back in the late '60s. She came along to the gig tonight.'

Helen held her hand out to Red. 'I think we met a few times, years ago.'

Red handed me the guitar and shook Helen's hand. 'I remember you well. A lot of the songs on Granny's album were about you, if I'm not mistaken?'

I laughed. 'If you could call them songs.'

Red smiled at Helen. 'You're welcome to come back to my place in Rathgar for coffee, if you want to carry on your trip down memory lane with his nibs?'

Helen glanced at me. 'If it's okay with you?'

I hesitated. 'Fine.'

Red gave me a wink. 'You go with Helen. I have to drop off something at a friend's on the way so I might be delayed for a bit.'

During the drive I filled Helen in on how Red had helped me secure an Irish record deal for the album I'd recorded in London over a year before, and had put me in touch with Christy Moore and Freddie White, as well as acting as my booking agent. 'He's sound and has some great insights into PR.'

When we arrived at the apartment building in Rathgar, I suggested waiting in the car park till Red arrived. For five or six minutes we chatted about old times but then the conversation became strained. As a distraction, I suggested turning on the radio. Helen leaned forward and hit a switch. The low sound of Nina Simone singing *I Put A Spell On You* filled the car. The red glow of the radio-light lit up Helen's knees. I tried not to look at them. Helen became aware of my embarrassment. She glanced at me and smiled.

I laughed. 'What?'

Helen leaned across the gear pad and touched my leg and kissed me. For a few fitful moments I went with the flow, but then I thought of Joan and pulled away. 'I don't think this is such a good idea.'

Helen sat back in her seat and readjusted her clothes. The headlights of Red's station wagon flashed across the windscreen. Helen turned to me. 'Maybe I should go?'

'No no, come in for a few minutes.'

In the apartment, Red made coffee and the three of us sat around making light conversation. Red showed Helen a copy of a review of my album from a recent newspaper. 'John Boland is one of the finest popular music critics in the country, so this is quite an accolade for Johnny.'

After reading the article Helen turned to Red. 'If the album's this good, how come it's not selling?'

Red shrugged. 'The record company failed to live up to its commitment to promote it properly. Without proper advertising, you're dead in the water. We're hoping to get another company involved in recording a new album soon. But most of the bigger companies here are just offshoots of international companies, so they're limited in who they can sign.'

Helen sat forward. 'What's to stop you setting up your own company and bringing out an album yourselves?'

Red laughed. 'Recording and PR can be very costly.'

Helen smiled. 'How costly?'

Red hesitated. 'You could be talking twenty grand easily, just to get one album off the ground.'

Helen sipped her coffee. 'Do a thorough costing and get back to me. I've been thinking of investing in a business for some time. Setting up a record company might be just the kind of thing I'm looking for. I know a few people in the business myself; famous people who have bought horses from us over the years. I'll make some inquiries.'

I gaped at Helen. 'You can't just set up a record company on a whim!'

Helen raised an eyebrow. 'I don't do anything on a whim. Did you not hear what I said: I'll make inquiries.'

Red beamed. 'I'll phone around in the morning.'

Helen got to her feet. 'I'll call here tomorrow evening, if that's all right?'

I stood up. 'I won't be here. I'm heading home to Galway in the morning.'

Helen shifted her shoulder bag. 'That doesn't matter. Red and I can go over the details without you.'

I laughed. 'You'll see sense in the morning.'

Helen smiled but said nothing.

Red stood up, smiling at Helen. 'How does six suit you?'

'Six is fine.'

I walked Helen to her car.

As we strolled across the small car park I told her that she was mad to even think about becoming involved in the music business. 'If you're doing this in any way for my sake, I'd strongly advise you not to. You could end up losing a fortune.'

Helen opened the car door. 'I told you earlier, I'm bored with our equestrian business. There are no more challenges in it for me. This might give me a new lease of life.' She sat into the Merc and started the engine.

I gripped the side of the car door firmly. 'There's one thing I need to get straight with you: What happened between us in the car earlier will never happen again!'

'Why, because you're Catholic?'

'Because I'm married.'

Helen smiled and went to close the door. I kept a straight face and held the door open. 'I'm serious. The only thing I can see coming from this reunion is a song.'

There is a Time

There is a time in life, it seems,
for believing in dreams; for me it's gone.
And though I realise today,
dreams are empty anyway, I still feel wrong.

I felt cheated when you went away,
but not as defeated as I felt the day
you came back and we found so little to say.

There is a time in life, I know,
when we all must outgrow our young ideals,
but the wisdom that we gain
is paid for with the pain I now feel.

I felt cheated when you went away,
but not as defeated as I felt the day
you came back and we found so little to say.

SANCHO & DON

He keeps on going, carries on, and tries to find a way;
keeps alive a light that shone on him in better days

This Time

As I turned into our housing estate a man in a white shirt and floral tie approached me with his hand extended. 'I'm Peter Harkin, a neighbour of yours. Been a big fan for years. Loved your last single. It should've been a hit.'

I swapped my guitar case to my left side and shook his hand. 'Nice to meet you, Peter.'

'Call me Pete. Everyone does.' He glanced at my guitar case. 'Back from a gig, are you?'

'No no, I was demoing some new songs in a studio in Renmore. Tony Maher's place.'

Pete's eyes widened. 'I'd love to hear them. Any chance?'

I went to move away. 'Sure. Call around some time and I'll play them for you.'

'How about this evening, half seven?'

I smiled at his persistence, trying to think of some excuse to get him off my back. His eyes were bubbling with enthusiasm. I laughed. 'Sure. Seven thirty'll be fine. My wife's at her mother's with the kids, so there'll be no disturbance. But they're only demos, remember, not finished recordings.'

As I walked away I glanced back. 'I'm number 99, by the way.'

Pete nodded. 'I know.'

At a quarter to eight the doorbell rang. It was Pete, with two six-packs of Heineken and the same bubbly smile. He had changed into more casual clothes, a navy sweater and denim jeans. As he followed me into the living room, he glanced inquisitively around the place. 'Your house is a lot bigger than ours. We live in one of the two-bedroomed ones.'

I sat on the couch. 'Take a seat.'

Pete sat on an armchair opposite me and pulled two cans from the six-pack. 'I prefer Bud, but we had this left over after a party.' He handed me one of the cans, opened one himself and took a long swig. 'Maybe you should put these others in your fridge till we're ready for them.'

When I returned from the kitchen I found Pete on his feet looking at a large framed print of Don Quixote on the wall. He glanced at me and looked back at the picture. 'Picasso!'

'You know your art.'

He offered me a cigarette and lit one himself. 'I went to art college in Dublin for three years. Taught it too for a while back in the '70s, till they wised up on me.' He laughed and glanced at some shelves of books at the side of the fireplace. 'You read?' He went and looked at the spines of a few of the volumes. 'Homer, Virgil, Plato, Sophocles! Heavy stuff!'

'That's the classical section. The other shelves have contemporary novels and poetry. Do you read yourself?'

'Me!' Pete sniggered. 'I tried reading Joyce's *Ulysses* when I was in college but got bogged down in the first chapter.'

I smiled. 'You should have started with *Dubliners* or the chapters dealing with Bloom and Molly in *Ulysses*.'

He went back to his chair and gulped back some beer. 'What's your favourite book?'

I glanced towards the book shelves. 'That's a tough one. *Don Quixote* would be high on the list. I'm trying to put together a kind of modern version of the story in song, roughly based on my own experience in the music business. That's what I was demoing today – songs from the collection.'

Pete took a deep pull from his cigarette. 'Don Quixote was mad, wasn't he?'

I went and took down a book from one of the shelves. 'The guy who wrote this – Unnimuno, a Spanish poet and philosopher – believed that Don Quixote was the sanest and purest man since Christ. I agree with him.'

'I thought it was a humorous book?'

I smiled. 'One of the funniest I've read, but like all good humour, it's serious too. Sancho Panza, Don's squire, is great craic. A bit of a cute whore, while Don is an idealist, a dreamer with his head in the clouds.'

Pete took a long swig from his beer. 'How about hearing some of the songs?'

I located the demo tape and placed it in my old dented cassette player. Pete eyed the battered machine with a look of bemusement. 'It's seen better days.'

'The sound's OK.'

The first song began to play.

There is a time in life, it seems,
for believing in dreams, for me it's gone.
And though I realise today
dreams are empty anyway, I still feel wrong.
I felt cheated when you went away
but not as defeated as I felt the day
you came back and we found so little to say . . .

As the last notes were fading Pete smiled. 'Lovely words, but what's the connection with Don Quixote?'

I put the tape on pause. 'Don Quixote's main aim was to become a famous knight so that he could impress his lady in waiting, but she turns out to be just a figment of his imagination in the book. I had a similar wake up call with a girl I once went out with. The song's an ode to romantic disillusionment. And you can include in that my attitude to pop culture in general.'

Pete scratched his head and looked at his can. 'I'm almost ready for a second and you've hardly touched your first. Drink up.'

I picked up the can, took a swig and let go the pause button on the tape machine. An uptempo song began to play:

The whiskey didn't kill the pain,
so I walked and walked in the rain . . .

Pete gulped back the last of his beer and belched. 'I know the feeling! Nice beat.'

I stood up. 'I'll get you another beer.'

After the demos ended we talked about the vagaries of my musical career and Pete told me something of his own colourful history, going back to his seventeenth year when he ran away from his family farm in Co. Donegal after a row with his father. 'I really wanted to become an artist but got diverted into teaching after college. After I jacked that I worked at a whole series of casual jobs. I married Vicky in '76 and, when our daughter Laragh arrived, we moved to America and got involved in all sorts of hippie shit; drugs, booze, the works. In the late '70s we settled in Amsterdam. The next few years are a bit of a haze.'

He gestured towards his nose. 'Vicky wised up in the end and came back to Ireland with Laragh. That brought me to my senses. I cleaned up my act in '81 and followed them here to Galway.'

I smiled. 'And I thought I'd lived on the wild side.'

By ten thirty the room was clouded in tobacco smoke and the beer was gone. I suggested making a pot of tea. Pete baulked. 'I have some more beer back at my place. Why don't we go round there. Vicky would love to meet you.'

I hesitated. 'I'm an early bird, usually in bed by eleven and up at six.'

Pete got to his feet. 'You needn't stay long. I have to be up early myself tomorrow. I'm back on the job trail.'

Pete's house was just around the corner. We entered by a side door, straight into his kitchen. Two young women were seated at a table in the glow of a low-hanging red and blue stained-glass lamp. Pete introduced one of them – a good looking girl with long blonde hair – as his wife, Vicky, and the other as a friend, Carol. While I was shaking Vicky's hand Carol got to her feet and started to leave the room in a hurry. 'I'll call you tomorrow, Vic, and let you know how I get on.'

Vicky watched her friend moving towards the door. 'Whatever you do, Carol, don't be worrying. That'll only makes things worse.'

The door closed. Pete looked at Vicky. 'What was all that about?'

Vicky groaned. 'You know Carol; a bag of nerves. I pity her so much.'

Pete gave a false laugh. 'What's there to pity? She has a great career, a lovely house and a healthy bank balance.'

Vicky frowned. 'Money isn't everything.'

Pete went to the fridge. 'I must tell that to our bank manager the next time he calls me in.' He took out a few cans of Heineken and brought them to the table, offering one to me. 'Let's move into the living room. We'll be more comfortable there.'

The living room turned out to be an Aladdin's den of trinkets and baubles: stained-glass lamps, coloured candles, bronze and wooden sculptures, framed photographs and oil paintings, kettle drums, guitars, and rows of albums and tapes. While Vicky was directing me to the most comfortable couch in the room, Pete went to the row of albums and picked one to play. As he placed it on the deck of an elaborate hi-fi system, Vicky asked him to keep the volume down. 'I don't want you waking Laragh.'

Pete adjusted the controls. 'How is she?'

'Fine.' Vicky slid onto a fawn-coloured couch and tucked her bare feet beneath her, glancing at me. 'Our daughter Laragh suffers from asthma, nothing chronic.' She turned to Pete. 'She was asking for you when I put her up, but don't wake her or we'll never get her down again.'

Pete snapped open his beer and kicked off his shoes. 'Have you heard this new Dylan album? It's his best in years.'

I shook my head. 'I lost track of Bob after *Wesley Harding*.'

Pete sang along with the record, then glanced at Vicky. 'You should hear Johnny's new songs; they're terrific.' He turned to me. 'Maybe you'll sing one before you go, on my guitar?'

I glanced at an acoustic guitar leaning against the window frame. 'You play yourself?'

Pete laughed. 'I try.'

I looked towards the record player. 'Dylan's on tour in Europe at present, I believe.'

'He's always on tour.' Pete swallowed some beer. 'Vicky and I met him once in Chicago, didn't we Vic?'

Vicky laughed. 'I wouldn't say we met him, exactly. It was embarrassing.'

Pete chuckled. 'We were in this hotel having a drink. Vicky had Laragh on her lap. She was only a baby at the time. Bob walked in and sat at a table right opposite us. I tried to pluck up the courage to go over and ask him for his autograph but I couldn't do it. For about ten minutes I kept gaping at him while he was sipping a coffee. I couldn't believe that I was in the same space as him. He was my God at the time. Still is. Anyway, after he finished his coffee he got up to go. I panicked at that stage, realising that if I didn't act straight away I was going to blow my chance of being able to say that I met him. While he was passing our table I grabbed Laragh from Vicky's lap and held her out. "Here" I said, "Hold our baby, will you, Bob?"'

I broke into a fit of laughing. 'Did he take her?'

Pete's eyes started bubbling. 'Did he fuck! He looked at me like I was a madman and did a beeline for the door.'

Vicky sniggered. 'I'll never forget the look he gave us. But it must be awful always being pestered by people everywhere you go.'

I looked from Pete to Vicky. 'How long were you in the States?'

Vicky hesitated 'We were into a lot of dope while we were there, so things became very confusing.' She glanced at Pete. 'We must have been there over a year, were we?' Pete nodded. Vicky turned back to me. 'We moved to Amsterdam then, from the kettle into the frying pan.' She looked at Pete. 'Get the photo albums and show him some of the shots you took on our travels.' She turned back to me. 'Pete's a keen photographer. It's his first love, really.'

Pete left the room and came back with a couple of hardbound photograph albums. One contained a series of black and white family portraits going back to the beginning of the century. While browsing through a few of these dog-eared snaps Pete informed me that Vicky's family were related to Major John MacBride. 'You know the guy who married Maude Gonne; the fella she ditched W.B. Yeats for.'

I looked at Vicky. 'That's a coincidence. I'm reading Yeats's poetry at the moment. I don't think he had a lot of time for the Major, but that was probably jealousy on his part.'

Vicky smiled. 'Our family were down a few pegs on the social scale so we had no contact with the MacBrides, but my mother remembers going to their house for tea and cucumber sandwiches when she was a girl.'

Pete opened another album and showed me some coloured shots of himself with long sideburns and a few of Vicky with a beehive hairdo. Vicky laughed. 'Will you look at the head of me. I was a show, wasn't I? And to think I was a hairdresser then!'

Pete skipped to their wedding snaps. In these Vicky had a fringe and Pete's hair was shoulder length and wavy. Pete pointed to the wide collars of the suit he was wearing and chuckled. 'Look at the size of them lapels! Isn't fashion ridiculous too when you think about it.' He turned to some photos of their hippie phase in America and Holland. In several of these Pete looked totally bewildered. Vicky pointed to one shot of the two of them in caftans and beads. 'I remember the day we had that taken. Pete was so spaced we had to carry him home. How we ever survived them days I'll never know.'

The phone started ringing in the kitchen. Pete went to answer it and came back almost immediately. 'It's for you, Vic. Kay from Australia. I told her you'd ring her back.'

After Vicky left the room Pete handed me another beer. 'If you ever want to make long distant calls you can do it from here. We haven't received a phone bill in over a year. The phone company seems to have forgotten about us.'

The Dylan record came to an end. Pete put on an album of film score pieces and asked me if I'd ever thought of writing music for the screen. 'I have a few contacts in the business who might be able to help you get a leg in.'

I laughed 'A bit out of my league, I think.'

Pete gulped back some beer. 'If you can write songs you can write music. Leave it with me and I'll make some inquiries.'

I finished my beer. 'I'd better let you get to bed. It's getting late.'

Pete got to his feet, stumbling slightly while reaching for his guitar. 'Not till you sing us that song you promised. Vicky, hurry on! Johnny's going to sing one of his new songs.'

I took the guitar and tuned it as best I could in my tipsy condition. Vicky came back into the room, smiling. I took a deep breath, steadied myself and started plucking and singing.

Don Quixote

I'm Don Quixote, I'm on the road again;
My band's called Sancho, we're on the move again.
My horsepower now is in a transit van.
My lance has strings, I'm a music man.

For years I listened to the radio;
Each night I'd tune in to the music show,
I'd sing along with all the songs I knew;
They helped me bear the darkness as it grew.

My eyes were on the stars, though distant and far,
I followed in their course, searching for the source
Of energy and light to illuminate the night
And make my dreams bright.

Then the wild thought took a hold of me
That the bright dream was reality
And so begins the story
Of my quest for love through glory.

REEFER AND THE MODEL

In the night I had a dream, it felt so right I thought it real,
then I awoke and it was gone, but in its place I found the sun

After the Dream

After sitting around the waiting area with a group of extras for almost two hours, I was relieved when the film's director, Lelia Doolan, came and asked us in a friendly but forceful manner to file on to the set and take our positions at the dining tables as quickly and carefully as possible. 'Watch out for cables and wires; we don't want you tripping up and filing insurance claims. Shooting will commence in five or ten minutes. Hurry along now, time is money and we're fast running out of both commodities.'

While I was following a group dressed in smart evening wear, Lelia grabbed my arm and led me across the floodlit set, glancing at my tweed jacket. 'Not quite the thing for an upper crust evening out, but it'll do. You could be your addled lord of the manor who forgets to change after his afternoon ride with the hounds. Follow me. Joe wants to say a quick hello before I take you along to meet Eoghan Harris, our script editor. He wants a word with you about the score. Like yourself, he's doubling as an extra for the afternoon.'

We came to a floodlit dining table where Joe Comerford, the film's writer and producer, was engaged in an intense discussion with the two principal actors who were also being attended to by a make-up lady. Lelia prodded Joe's arm and smirked. 'Our maestro has arrived!'

Joe turned to me with a tense smile. 'Johnny! Sorry to have kept you waiting so long. We got bogged down in the last scene.' He sighed heavily and glanced towards the actors. 'You've already met Carol Scanlan and Ian McElhinney.' He scratched his ear. 'Carol tried that idea of yours of singing along with the theme song in the boat scene we filmed yesterday, and it worked really well. I'd like to show it to you later in the editing room.'

Carol smiled. 'It's a lovely wee song. That girl who sings it on the tape has a beautiful Connemara voice. I hope my Northern drawl is well disguised.'

Joe looked at me with concern. 'No sign of Pete? I hope he has that country and western singer organised for the next location?'

Before I had a chance to answer, a floor manager wearing headphones and carrying a script board came up to Joe and muttered a few harsh words. Lelia grabbed my arm and whisked me away. 'We'd better leave them to it. We're way behind. I need to get you to your place.'

Lelia led me to a nearby table and introduced me to a well-dressed man with a bushy mustache and a woman dressed in a pink evening gown. 'Mary actually owns this classy restaurant in real life and Eoghan is a well known broadcaster, journalist and bloody thorn in my side due to the amount of changes he keeps inserting in the script.'

I recognised Eoghan Harris, having seen him on TV a few times. I had spotted him earlier in the waiting area engaged in a heated political argument with one of the other extras. Up close he looked equally tense and charismatic. Lelia spoke to him for a moment and then glanced over her shoulder towards Joe Comerford. 'I have to get back and try to pacify the crew. Joe infuriated them by demanding countless retakes of the last scene. There were sparks flying. Now we're ruining way behind schedule.'

Eoghan rubbed his moustache. 'Tell Joe not to be so bloody precious about the takes. When he gets back to the editing room it'll be murder trying to decide which one to keep. The difference can often be so minuscule as not to matter a damn. Remind him that the film's a Connemara bank robbery, for Christ sake, and not one of your northern European introspective studies in existential angst.'

Lelia threw up her eyes. 'I'm dreading this next scene. It's the one where Reefer grabs the steak from the plate of an old lady and squeezes blood out of it while he's being turfed out of the restaurant.'

Mary shuddered. 'My God, that kind of thing would never happen in my establishment.'

Lelia smiled. 'Don't worry Mary, we won't be using your restaurant's name. But if you want the place restored to normal by six, I'd better get a move on. We have to get to the pub location for the scene with the country and western singer by seven o'clock.' She turned to me and frowned. 'That manager fella of yours, Peter whatshisname, was supposed to ring us about that this morning! Joe is furious.'

I shifted the fork at the side of my plate. 'I haven't seen Pete all day. But don't worry, the band are organised and the country and western singer has agreed to do it.'

Lelia started moving away. 'I'm looking forward to that. It should be a bit of light relief after this.'

As soon as Lelia was gone Eoghan turned to me with a solemn expression. 'So, you're the replacement for Donal Lunny? Joe was telling me he met you totally by chance?'

I hesitated, feeling slighted intimidated by the sharp tone of Eoghan's Cork accent 'I was under the impression that Donal was just one of a few people being considered for the job. But yeah, I met Joe in a friend's house, Peter Harkin, the fella Lelia mentioned. I had no idea who Joe was. While I was there I sang a song I'd just written, *After the Dream*, and Joe asked to use it in his film. After that Pete started pitching on my behalf for the full commission of the score. He passed on a couple of my albums to Joe and, on the strength of them, I got the job.'

Mary shook her head. 'The best things in life often come about like that. Fate or chance, who can say which it is. Do you find it difficult writing for the screen?'

I scratched my neck. 'To be honest, I wasn't sure I could do it at first. I read the script a half dozen times to get a feel for the characters. I didn't take to Reefer at all. He's pretty obnoxious. But I liked The Model. And I found the softening effect she has on Reefer's character one of the most interesting parts of the script. Very human.'

Eoghan's expression softened. 'Joe played me the theme song. Dolores Keane was a perfect choice to sing it. The disillusioned sentiment of the words captures the element of soured idealism of the cast of ex-IRA villains really well.'

I raised an eyebrow. 'The Model's Connemara roots and her vulnerability after her seedy London experiences were more what I had in mind. But I didn't write the song to order. The lyric comes from my own experience and is basically making the point that reality faced squarely can often be better that the stuff of dreams.'

Mary smiled. 'That's so true.'

Eoghan squeezed his chin. 'I notice in your written outline for the full score you intend using similar slow airs throughout the film?'

'I have a few uptempo pieces too, one for the car chase after the bank robbery and another for an upbeat scene on the boat.'

Eoghan rubbed his mouth. 'If you don't mind me saying, I think you need something fast and energetic for the opening scenes as well; something to put the audience on the edge of their seats from the word go. More Hollywood than European, if you know what I mean?'

'But the opening scene has no action. It's just a leisurely car ride in

Connemara. The music can only reflect what's on the screen.'

Eoghan began to object but was interrupted by the booming voice of the floor manager calling for silence: 'Please ladies and gentlemen, we're about to go for a take! Remember now, act naturally, as though you were out for a normal evening meal with your snooty friends.'

A man wearing a dicky bow at a table opposite us grunted. 'Waiter, waiter, my snooty friends and I know a cheap bottle of plonk when we taste one. Could you replace this vintage, please.'

Everyone in the room started laughing. The floor manager called for order. 'Now now Paddy, stop guzzling that Chardonnay; it's only there as a prop.' He turned to the rest of us. 'Calm down now, please, and remember, no looking towards the scene being filmed till I give the cue, then turn quickly as though you're shocked. And please, don't overdo the dramatics. Okay Joe, we're ready.'

'We'll go on three . . . one, two, and . . . Action!'

Like Eoghan and Mary opposite me, I pretended to be eating the cold meat and potatoes on my plate. Behind my back I could hear the actor waiter politely asking Reefer to leave the restaurant because his dining partner, the Model, wasn't a member of the club. Knowing the script by heart, I knew that Reefer was about to grab a steak knife from the table at this point and threaten the waiter. I felt an urge to glance over my shoulder but held back, waiting for the cue. Reefer's posh accent grew menacing behind me: 'If you don't take your hand away from my arm I'll cut your balls off!' The sound of chairs being moved abruptly could be heard, then heavy footsteps pounded across the floor followed by a loud female gasp. From the wings, the floor manager gave a sudden gesture and I, along with all the other extras in the room, turned suddenly towards the source of the commotion with a feigned expression of shock. In the glare of a floodlight, Reefer, with a sinister expression, was squeezing a large fillet steak above the plate of a lady who had a petrified look on her face. Joe shouted 'Cut!' The floor manager sighed loudly and ordered everyone in the room to remain in their places. 'We'll be going for another take in just a few minutes.'

After take seven Eoghan sighed heavily, looked at his watch and cursed. 'If Joe doesn't get it this time, he's going to be in trouble time-wise. It's almost half five and they still have to do the last scene where Reefer and the Model stalk out the door.'

At ten minutes past seven the last scene was canned and a mad rush ensued to get the equipment dismantled for the pub location in town.

I took a taxi ahead of everyone else to make sure that everything was up and running when the film crew arrived. When I got to the bar

I found the four-piece band practising on a small stage and a handful of extras drinking at the counter, but there was no sign of Pete or the country singer. The owner of the premises spotted me heading for the public phone and came towards me looking at his watch. 'You were meant to be here over an hour ago! The beer bill's mounting and the band are making noises about wanting to be paid overtime!'

I apologised and asked if Pete had been in. The bar owner shook his head. 'I haven't seen that lad since yesterday. Am I still up for that walk on part he promised me?'

I shrugged and rushed to the phone.

Pete's wife, Vicky, answered and told me that she hadn't seen Pete since morning. 'He got an early phone call and rushed from the house with a portfolio of photographs without saying where he was going.'

I went to the band and pacified them with promises of more money if the shoot ran overtime, then I started rehearsing the song with them. During our third or fourth run-through the film crew arrived without their cameramen or cameras. The sound engineer started setting up sound equipment at the front of the stage. Joe and Lelia drew me aside and told me that, due to the overrun at the Restaurant, they had decided that there was no time to film the bar scene. Joe sighed. 'It wasn't a very important part in the film anyway. I have another slot in mind for the song, so we'll just do the audio recording.'

Lelia glanced around the bar. 'Where's Peter, I want a word with him?'

I shook my head. 'He's not here, and neither is the country singer.'

Joe frowned. 'What are we going to do?'

I glanced at the band. 'I've been running over the song with the lads. I guess I'll have to sing it if he doesn't arrive in the next few minutes.'

Joe sighed. 'But I thought we were looking for the authentic country sound?'

I took a deep breath. 'I'll just have to try and feign a Nashville twang myself.'

Lelia laughed. 'This I have to hear.'

Twenty minutes later we went for a take and got it in one:

You come back into my life and expect me to love you again;
You know now I've got a wife and I know you've had other men;
And though you still look real good, you make me feel real bad.
When I do what I should, you're going to end up sad . . .

While the band and the engineer were packing away their equipment,

Lelia, Joe and I went to the bar and ordered a round of drinks. While we were joking about my Nashville performance, Pete arrived in the bar, flustered and full of apologies. 'Something really important came up, a life and death situation that I couldn't get out of. I'm desperately sorry.'

Lelia frowned. 'That's not good enough! Why didn't you let us know?'

Joe touched Lelia's elbow. 'It's all right, everything worked out okay in the end.'

Lelia cursed. 'It's not alright. This man gave us a commitment and he broke it!'

The bar owner approached Pete with a frown. 'I thought you said they were going to be filming in my bar and that I had a walk on part? I should never have listened to all that baloney you fed me about free publicity.'

Lelia looked askance at the bar owner. 'What walk on part?'

The bar owner glanced at Pete. 'He promised me a walk on part if I allowed you the use of the premises.'

Lelia glared at Pete. 'I never gave you authorisation to do that.'

Pete scratched his head.

Joe intervened. 'He told me about it, Lelia. It was just a small part.' He turned to the bar owner. 'Don't worry, we'll find some other part in another scene for you.'

The bar owner smiled. 'Fine. Now who's going to settle the beer bill with me? Because of the delay, the extras drank a lot more than was budgeted for.'

Lelia prodded the bar owner's arm. 'Listen mister, you gave me a flat rate for what the beer was to cost. You're not getting a penny more!'

After Lelia settled the bill, on her terms, Joe suggested going to the editing room to see the rushes featuring the theme song.

Joe, Lelia and Sé Merry (the editing engineer) went in Joe's car while I went with Pete in his old banger.

During the short journey to Dominick St, Pete started apologising for his day-long absence. 'Some very important people phoned me this morning with an offer to photograph a series of big houses in Scotland and England. Nothing's been finalised but if this comes off it could be really good for us.'

I gave a false laugh. 'Us! How the hell could that be good for me? Come off it, Pete. You really let me down badly today.'

Pete almost drove up a one-way street, swerving to get back on track. 'You have no idea of the pressures I'm under at the moment, Johnny. The building society are about to repossess our house, the ESB are going to leave us in the dark if I don't pay a bill of over six hundred quid by next week, and Telecom are going to cut off our phone if I don't pay them almost two grand by the end of the month, for the cock-up they made of not sending me a bill for over a year. I was banking on my twenty percent of the score commission to get my head above water, but the pittance they're paying you wouldn't pay my phone bill.' Pete paused, on the verge of tears. 'I'm thinking of flying to Holland on Friday to see if I can scrape up a bit of money over there. I have some contacts in Amsterdam who might be able to help me.'

At the editing room Joe and Sé were setting up the equipment to show the rushes. We sat around a small screen and Joe switched on the machine. Images of a boat at sea began to flicker before us and Dolores Keane's velvet voice began to sing in co-ordination with the rolling action, her pure crystal-clear tone tugging at the heart.

> In the night, I had a dream;
> it felt so right I thought it real,
> then I awoke and it was gone
> but in its place I found the sun.

ANTS

I once climbed the branches of our old pear tree
and found some hard fruit where none used be;
it tasted bitter, still we all ate . . .

Inviolate

I rose from the kitchen table and went to the back window. The darkening garden was a mass of dock leaves, burrs, nettles and thistles. Among the twilit weeds a black and white cat was sitting in front of our dilapidated shed at the bottom of the yard. On the rusted corrugated roof two other cats were crouched, staring at our back door. I glanced at my sister sipping tea at the table. 'Dad still feeds the neighbourhood cats, I see.'

Kay came to the window and looked out. 'Usually around this time when he gets back from his stroll to the river. He's a bit late this evening. Probably dropped into St Joseph's on his way home to say a prayer for Mam.'

I raised an eyebrow. 'Still keeping up that routine, is he?'

Kay nodded. 'A complete convert.'

I let my eyes drift around the shadowy garden. 'I notice the old pear tree is gone from the front of the shed.'

Kay laughed. 'That's been gone for years. Nothing ever grew on it.'

'Yes there did. One pear grew on it when I was eight or nine. Don't you remember; I offered you a bite, making a joke about my reverse role as Adam tempting Eve. You took a bite but spat it out, it was so sour and hard.'

Kay shook her head. 'I don't remember that.'

'Maybe it was Patti I gave it to, or Joan. I could have swore it was you.'

Kay shook her head decisively and looked back at the garden. 'Remember the pirate games you used to play out there, hanging hammocks made of bed-sheets from the tree and a nail in the wall. Mammy used to kill you when they tore.'

'Hard to believe we could have had such fun in such a bleak, confined space. It seemed much bigger then.'

Kay's eyes brightened. 'I used to love the summer picnics Mammy used to organise out there, right in front of the old lavatory beside the shed. A smelly old place it was. But on sunny afternoons, gorging on cheap lemonade, banana sandwiches and buttered Marietta biscuits, it was heaven.'

I glanced over my shoulder at the glass hatch to make sure my mother wasn't in the living room. 'Mam was okay most of the time back then, wasn't she?'

Kay flicked a strand of her long blonde hair over her shoulder. 'I think she only started going into St Joseph's on a regular basis when I was in first or second year at the Mount.'

I thought for a moment. 'Dad had just given up going to sea around that time, hadn't he?'

Kay looked at me. 'A bit before that, I think.'

I shook my head. 'Not much before. That might account for the tension between them. Suddenly, after years of him being away at sea, he settled down and Mam had to adjust her whole lifestyle to suit him.'

Kay backed away from me. 'What are you implying; that Dad was to blame?'

I hesitated. 'I've been reading a lot of books on psychology and psychiatry lately and they've set me thinking.'

Kay stared at me. 'A little knowledge!'

'Freud, Jung, Adler, Lang and whole hosts of others.'

Kay moved towards the kitchen table. 'Yeah, and they all have different theories.'

'Quite a few agree nowadays that it's not just the patients who need help . . .'

The kitchen door opened and my brother Eric (home on a flying visit from France) came into the room, rubbing his large stomach. While he was filling the kettle he glanced at Kay and me. 'What's up with you two? You look very serious.'

Kay looked towards the glass hatch. 'We were discussing Mammy.'

Eric turned to me. 'And?'

I hesitated. 'I've noticed over the years that any time she becomes even a little elated dad immediately assumes she's cracking up.'

Eric grinned. 'Would you classify getting up at four o'clock in the morning to go out looking for a newspaper – even though she never reads newspapers – as a *little* elated?'

I took a deep breath. 'I know she gets high; I'm not denying that. But maybe she goes that way out of a sense of frustration, to assert herself.'

Kay shook her head. 'You're wrong. But let's change the subject. I hate talking about this; it gets us nowhere.' She took some empty mugs from the table and brought them to the sink and started rinsing them. 'I'm going to have to go soon; I told my babysitter I'd be home before seven, and it's almost that now. I'll go upstairs first and see how Mam is. She must have nodded off. She didn't sleep a wink last night, Dad told me.'

After Kay left the room, Eric made himself a mug of tea and a sandwich and sat at the table opposite me. 'I thought you were heading back to Galway?'

I lit a cigarette. 'I'd planned to but I don't like leaving the way things are with Mam.'

Eric shrugged. 'She's been like this for over a week.'

'She probably just needs a change of medication. I've been trying to convince her to go for a check up, but she won't listen to me.'

Eric sipped his tea and chewed on his sandwich. 'How's the film music going?'

I took a pull at my cigarette. 'I managed to get Dolores Keane to sing the title song. The film's almost fully edited. It goes on general release later in the year. How about yourself – any news on the shop in Saint-Malo?'

Eric swallowed a mouthful. 'We have the premises; a lovely location in a secluded square opposite a small cathedral. I'm still sourcing the garments and other items we're going to sell. All top quality stuff. The French are hard to please.'

'You're okay with the language?'

'By this stage, I'm pretty fluent. My German's quite good too. And I have the bit of Italian and Spanish, not to mention Latin and Irish.'

I laughed. 'Your modesty's up to scratch too, I see. When do you move there permanently?'

Eric sipped his tea. 'I'm there permanently now. I'll be making trips home regularly like this, to purchase stock. You and Joan will have to come over on a visit.'

The front door could be heard opening. Eric glanced toward the kitchen door. 'Dad's home.'

My father came into the kitchen rubbing his hands. 'It's a cold night out there. We'll have frost again.' He took off his overcoat and placed it neatly on a hanger at the back of a door. Then he took a bowl of scraps from the side of the sink, poured milk in it and headed for the back door. 'I'd better feed the cats before it gets too dark. Is Kay gone?'

Eric got to his feet. 'She's upstairs with Mam. I'd better get a move on. I'm meeting a garment stockist for drinks down town at eight.'

I watched Eric leaving the room. 'You might help Kay and myself convince Mam tomorrow to go and see Dr O'Hara.'

Eric looked back and sighed. 'Fat chance she'll go, but we can try.'

My father came back from the garden and made himself a pot of tea and a meat sandwich. While he was putting mustard on the cold beef he glanced at me. 'You're staying after all?'

'I rang Joan and told her I won't be home till late tomorrow. Hopefully by then we'll have convinced Mam to go for the check up.'

My father bit into his sandwich. 'It's always excitement that triggers it. She's been on high doh ever since she heard about that film score of yours and the shop Eric's opening in France. She'll break my heart.'

I stared at my father, resentful at the way he was inadvertently blaming my situation for my mother's condition. 'Has it ever occurred to you, Dad, that you might be partly responsible for her breakdowns yourself?' The moment the words were out I bit my tongue. I looked at my father, waiting for him to explode.

'What do you mean?'

I hesitated. 'I just wonder sometimes if it ever crosses your mind that maybe, just maybe, you might be partly responsible for her general ongoing condition?'

My father put down his sandwich and drew a slow breath. For a moment I thought he was going to start defending himself, but he didn't. Instead his eyes grew soft and he sighed. 'Of course it's occurred to me, many times. And do you know what? I still don't know the answer.'

I froze in my chair, unable to think of anything to say. For a few moments I held my breath, then cleared my throat and leaned forward. 'I didn't mean to blame you.'

My father gave me a penetrating look and went back eating his sandwich.

While I was struggling to find something to say, the kitchen door opened and Kay came into the room.

'You're home, Dad. Mam's awake. I don't think she slept at all. I gave her two of them strong sleeping tablets at four o'clock and they had absolutely no effect. But shhh, I think she's coming.'

The sound of footsteps in the hall outside the kitchen made me stiffen in my chair. My mother came into the room patting her recently permed hair, wearing scarlet lipstick and fresh make-up. She was dressed in a neat navy suit with high-heeled shoes. Her shoulders were thrown back and her head was held high. In the plain domestic setting of our small kitchen, she looked totally out of place. She lit a cigarette and sat beside me, touching my shoulder. 'Kay was telling me, you're staying for another night. You can come out for a drink with us tonight. Can't he, John? All the girls will be there; Nancy, Marie and Rita. I've already told Nancy and Rita about your big film deal. You should have seen the look on their faces.'

I laughed and shook my head. 'Mam, it's only a low-budget film. '

An irritated look came over my mother's face. 'Yes yes, you said that already, but lots of low-budget films go on and win Oscars. Maybe now you'll be able to buy me that fur coat you used to promise me years ago. Remember?' She looked across the table at my father, who was shaking his head, finishing his sandwich. 'You remember how he was always promising me a fur coat when he was young, don't you, John?'

My father threw his eyes up to the ceiling. 'Give it a rest woman, will you!'

Kay started putting on her jacket. 'I remember it, Mam. But he has a wife and two kids to think of now, remember.'

My mother glared at Kay. 'I know perfectly well he has a wife. I'm forever asking him to bring her down for a weekend. But he never listens to me.'

Kay laughed. 'Where would they stay, Mam, in the guest suite?'

My mother tossed back her head and glanced at my father. 'We wouldn't mind giving them our room for the weekend. Wouldn't we, John?'

My father scowled. 'Don't be talking nonsense, woman. Where would we sleep? In the bunk beds in the boys' room with Barry in the single bed beside us!'

My mother shrugged and looked at me. 'Now do you see what I have to put up with in this house all the time! Is it any wonder I'm planning to get away for a long break next summer. By the way, did I tell you, Johnny, my cousins in Montreal have a swimming pool in their back garden and a full bar in their living-room. I'm really looking forward to another stay there.'

My father shook his head. 'Jesus Christ, don't start on about the holiday again. I told you a dozen times, you can't go on holidays on your own. Do you not remember the last one? It's out of the question!'

I looked at my father. 'Why don't you go with her, Dad?'

My father gave me an angry look. 'Who do you think I am, Rockefeller!'

My mother started laughing. 'Is it that man you're asking to take time off work to go on a foreign holiday! He can't even relax when we go on a day's outing to Kilkee. He's constantly looking at his watch, worrying in case we miss the last bus home. I couldn't suffer him to be with me. He'd drive me mad. It's away from him I need to get for a while.'

Masking a grin with the back of her hand, Kay took her handbag from the table and headed for the door. 'I'm away. I'll call again tomorrow. And Mam, don't forget, Johnny and Eric and I are taking you to see Dr O'Hara for that check up in the morning, whether you like it or not.'

My mother smirked. 'We'll see about that.'

Feeling awkward being alone with my parents, I made myself a sandwich and a mug of coffee just to be doing something. While I was eating at the table my mother lit another cigarette and watched me with an intense look on her face. 'Do you remember that time years ago, Johnny, when you were about to eat a cream slice that I bought in Frawley's shop up the street? Just before you bit into it you lifted the flaky pastry top and discovered ants crawling on the cream.'

'Jesus Mam, I'm trying to eat my sandwich!'

My mother took a pull from her cigarette. 'Sorry love, but do you remember?'

I glanced at my father and turned back to my mother. 'I remember it alright. But what put that into your head?'

My mother shrugged. 'I don't know what prompted you to lift the top of the pastry before taking the bite, but if you hadn't done it!' A look of horror came over her face.

I shuddered and glanced at my father. He shook his head and looked towards the ceiling.

> An old gash in a tree-trunk
> made me shiver as the scar
> of a flesh wound would.

> The same quiver ran through me once
> when I learned how my orphaned mother
> lost her reason when her first son died.

> The gaping scar in the wet bark:
> convulsed lips wailing
> after the axeblow.

THE CUP

Grasp your nettle tightly and it won't burn,
treat your failures lightly, your luck is bound to turn.

Don't Give Up Till It's Over

As the coach was pulling into Cork's bus terminal I was struck by a passage in the book I was reading, *Revelations of Divine Love* by Julian of Norwich. I underlined the sentence but didn't have time to reread it. I stuffed the paperback into the pouch of my guitar bag and got ready to change buses for the second leg of my long journey south.

With an hour to wait for my connecting bus, I decided to leave my guitar in the luggage department of the bus station and go in search of a sandwich bar rather than snack in the depot cafe, which I knew from experience wasn't up to much. While I was crossing the rain-drenched street I stepped on to an island to avoid being splashed by a passing truck and slipped headfirst on the wet tarmac. I managed to break my fall by placing my hands in front of me but cut both my palms on the gravelly ground in the process. Limping across to the pavement, I tottered on, cursing under my breath.

I was so distracted, I bypassed the shopping mall I intended snacking in and only realised my mistake when I was two blocks down the street. Rather than retrace my steps, I entered the first bar I came to and ordered a cheese sandwich and a mug of coffee. The sandwich that was brought to me was made of stale sliced pan and yellow processed cheese. After a couple of bites, I pushed the sandwich aside and sat brooding over the insipid coffee.

Since early morning – even before boarding the bus in Galway – I'd been out of sorts, mainly because the hundred and sixty mile journey I was making was a wild goose chase to a low-paying lounge gig in a remote southern town I'd never played in before. Originally I'd only taken the booking because it tied in with a show in an Arts Centre in a neighbouring town. When the main gig was cancelled a few days earlier due to low ticket sales, I tried to cancel the lounge gig as well but the owner added fifty pounds to my original guaranteed fee, and, fool that I am, I accepted the offer without doing my arithmetic. During the first leg of the journey, I calculated that my net profits for the show would be less than forty pounds. Measured against ten hours' rehearsal and eight hours' travelling, the figures didn't stack up.

I took a swig of coffee and looked at my hands. Both palms were caked in mud and blood. I went to the gents and washed, then left the bar without finishing the coffee.

As I still had some time before my bus was due to leave, I dropped into a chapel on my way back to the station to have a quick word with God about my situation. Half way through my prayer a wave of self-pity rose up inside me and I found myself in tears thinking back over the long haul of the failure of my career. I cursed God under my breath for having inflicting such bad luck on me. Then I rose from my knees and hurried out of the church without bothering to genuflect or dip my fingers in the holy water font.

The rain was coming down heavier than ever. By the time I arrived back at the station I was drenched to the skin. After a soggy five-minute wait in the dank terminal building, the bus arrived.

The second leg of the journey started ominously when the young bus driver tuned the piped radio to a pop station as he drove out of the depot. Outside the city, he yanked the volume up and started bobbing his head to the hammer-beat of a loud rap track. Knowing that I wouldn't be able to concentrate on reading with such a barrage of noise going on around me, I gritted my teeth and gazed out the window at the drizzling southern landscape.

It was almost dark when the bus finally pulled into the small town of Y. The driver dropped me on the narrow main street by a hardware shop displaying wellington boots and shovels in its front window. After a short walk up the street I located the venue. Situated beside a betting office, the facade of the bar didn't look very promising. A large hexagonal clock above the front door was stopped at ten to twelve and the letter L was missing from the name on the signboard.

Things didn't improve when I stepped inside the C_OCK TOWER. The bar was so narrow the customers sitting at the counter had the option of using the wall behind them as a backrest. To get by the line of stools I had to hold my guitar in front of me. The barman – a ginger haired young fella – spotted the guitar and smiled. 'You must be Johnny. I'd know you by your poster.' He glanced towards a glass-panelled door displaying one of my advertising posters. 'The place you'll be singing in is right through that door. The boss is uptown. He should be back any minute.'

Noticing that there was no cover charge printed on the poster, I glanced back at the barman but decided not to take the issue up with him. 'I'll go in and check the PA, if that's okay?'

'Fire away. I'll turn on the lights.'

The lounge turned out to be a large room with tacky furnishings. A rancid smell of stale tobacco, sour beer and urine was overpowering. Resting on a shaky foundation of plastic beer-crates, a small makeshift stage was positioned right beside the ladies' toilet. A single microphone in the centre of the stage was connected to a small amplifier with two of its three control knobs missing. At the front and sides of the stage, green plastic tables and chairs stood on a green and purple arabesque carpet, the busy design of which was threadbare and mottled with black bull's-eye burn holes. Old-fashioned wall-lights with pink frilly shades glowed at irregular intervals on three of the rust-coloured walls.

While I was trying to regulate the sound system the boss came into the lounge and introduced himself. 'I hope the PA's okay? It's a pretty basic amp but we have bands here all the time and they have no complaints.'

Dressed in a wrinkled suit with a pinched brown hat cocked slightly over one eye, the bar owner had the look of a sharp cattle dealer. After some small talk I went back to trying to readjust the bass control of the amplifier. With great effort I managed to twist the knobless holder up a notch but it had little effect on the trebly sound of the system. To compensate for the lack of bottom end, I turned the treble knob back a few notches. This made the sound slightly better but it was still lacking body and there was a loud buzzing sound coming through the speakers which I couldn't get rid of, probably due to the fact that the PA was unearthed. Realising that no amount of adjustment would improve things, I ran over a song and then joined the boss at the front of the stage. 'It should be okay; it's a small enough room.'

The boss squinted beneath the rim of his hat. 'We've had a fair bit of interest; we're hopin' for a big turnout.'

I took the bull by the horns. 'You have no cover charge, I notice?'

The boss shifted the hat further down over his eye. 'Punters around here are a bit shy of cover charges. I know you said you wanted one but I was afraid it might frighten them off. I don't mind payin' you from the till.'

'It's not that. Cover charges let people know it's not just background music they're coming to hear. It also keeps out troublemakers.'

The boss forced a laugh. 'Arah, you needn't worry about that. I have two strong bucks, Patsy and Jamsey, who take care of any rowdies we get in.'

Realising that it was pointless pursuing the matter, I headed off to a nearby B&B that was booked for me.

The room I was given had ugly floral wallpaper mottled with damp patches. Rather than sit there depressing myself, I walked around town for an hour, then had fish and chips in a roadside cafe. At eight o'clock I sauntered back to the venue with still a while to go before showtime.

Serving behind the counter, the boss gave me a wink while I was passing through to the lounge. 'Give it another fifteen minutes. The crowd hasn't started coming yet.'

I sat in a dark corner of the lounge sipping a glass of water, taking deep breaths in fearful anticipation of having to play to an empty house. As the minutes dragged by a few people came in and sat at tables furthest removed from the stage. The boss arrived looking depressed. 'You might as well start. The noise might bring a few more in from the bar.'

Reluctantly I got to my feet and started heading towards the stage. A loud commotion started up behind my back. As I turned to see what was up, the lounge door burst open and a crowd of thirty or forty came clamouring into the room with a fella waving a silver cup hoisted above their shoulders. One of the group spoke to the boss, then the cup was passed behind the bar where it was filled with a mixture of beer and spirits. I backed away from the stage and stood outside the ladies' toilet, watching the cup being passed around. After everyone in the group had taken a drink, the crowd jostled towards the stage and sat at the surrounding tables, laughing and joking. Trays of beer were quickly brought to them by the ginger-haired barman.

The boss came towards me, grinning. 'They won the county cup! No one was expecting it, but they did it, fair play to them. They won't be staying long. Their captain, Mikey, is a big fan of yours. He asked me to ask you to sing *The Voyage*. It's his favourite song. They played it at his wedding a few months back. Dedicate it to the team, will you.'

I gave a false laugh, glancing at the rowdy crowd. 'You want me to sing in front of them!'

The boss looked around the room. 'There's other punters here who have come a long way to see you. It'll be fine! I'll get up first and ask the lads to tone it down a bit.'

The boss's call for order fell on deaf ears. But then the team captain hopped up and roared for silence. The crowd immediately went quiet. I made my way to the microphone and congratulated the team on their big win. After a huge cheer, I dedicated my opening song to Mikey.

I am a sailor, you're my first mate.
We signed on together, coupled our fate.
Hauled up our anchor, determined not to fail;
For the heart's treasures together we set sail.
With no maps to guide us we steered our own course.
Weathered the storms when the winds were gale-force.
Sat out the doldrums with patience and hope,
Working together we learned how to cope.

The whole team joined in for the chorus:

Life is an ocean, love is a boat,
In troubled waters it keeps us afloat;
When we started the voyage there was just me and you,
Now look around us, we have our own crew.

At the end of the song, while the team members were clapping and shouting, Mikey brought the cup to the stage and offered me a drink. I looked at the frothy liquid swilling around in the silver goblet and took a sip. While I was heading back to the microphone a voice bellowed up a request for a Wolfe Tones number. I explained that I didn't know any Wolfe Tones songs and started to announce one of my own titles. Before I got through naming it, the Wolfe Tones fan jumped on stage and grabbed the microphone, asking me to back him on guitar. Before I had a chance to object he started singing. Though I didn't know the chord structure of the song, I tried to follow the singer as best I could. Midway through the first verse he dropped a couple of tones, wavered for a line or two, then went back up and wobbled in high C till the end of the song. Amazingly, the crowd gave the chancer a loud round of applause.

With the microphone back in my control, I decided that following my planned programme was out of the question, so I launched into *If I Were A Rich Man*. The crowd sang along in a variety of keys and enjoyed themselves so much I sang another few singalong standards. The downside of pandering to the mob was that the team remained in the lounge for a lot longer than they intended. Before they finally departed, Mikey requested *The Voyage* again, and, just to be rid of the team, I sang it a second time.

After a short break, I opened the second part of the show with

Just Another Town. At the end of the song a girl with purple spiky hair and a ring in her nose came to the front of the stage and requested *London Calling* by The Clash. I told her that I didn't know the words and announced another original song. The girl called me a 'dickhead' and went back to her table.

After seven or eight more songs, I announced that I was finishing with *Don't Give Up Till It's Over.* The small crowd joined in on the chorus and gave me a loud round of applause.

As I was stepping off the stage the boss came towards me with a rigid expression. 'It's only eleven o'clock, where're you going?'

'I've played for almost an hour and three quarters. My usual set's an hour and a half.'

The boss glanced at some people getting up to leave. 'If you want to get paid, get back up there for at least another half-hour. I don't want to lose the small crowd I have. I'm already losing money on you.'

I hesitated then reluctantly got back on stage, trying to think of what songs I might sing. A newcomer in the audience raised his glass and requested *The Voyage.* I explained that I'd played *The Voyage* twice already but the newcomer didn't care. 'Do it again!'

I drew a weary breath and sang *The Voyage* for the third time.

After I completed the extra half hour I picked up my fee and left the club without accepting a complementary drink that the boss offered me. When I reached the B&B, I went straight to bed.

I woke just after five the following morning feeling deeply depressed. After tossing and turning for an hour I switched on the light and glanced around the dingy room. A faded print of a purple mountain landscape on the damp wall facing my bed made me wince. 'So this is what it's come to!'

In an attempt to forget where I was, I decided to read in bed till it was time to go down for breakfast. I got my book from my guitar bag and, after getting back under the covers, located my page marker. Near the bottom of the left hand page the passage that I'd underlined the day before caught my attention.

"Our Lord was made a nobody for us, and we all stand with him, to be made nobodies in the same way, until we come into his glory."

While reflecting on these words, the trophy cup that the team captain, Mikey, had handed me the night before came into my head and, at the same time, I remembered a passage from Matthew's gospel where, after the mother of two of the apostles ask Jesus for a privileged place in heaven for her sons, Jesus rebukes her: "Can they drink the cup that I'm about to drink?"

MY GRAVITY

I sing for those driven insane
by the weight of the strain

My Gravity

While making up a batch of cassette copies of my *Just Another Town* album to send to friends and musical acquaintances for feedback, I found myself listening to the collection for the first time from a purely commercial standpoint. Though overall it was balanced with an equal number of fast and slow, happy and sad songs, a few of the melancholy titles were sadder than any I'd written in the past, and I was worried that the sombre tone might be a bit off-putting for the general public.

When the duplicates were ready I parcelled them up and headed off to post them in the general post office in the centre of Galway.

The bus dropped me in Eyre Square. It was a dazzling summer morning and the town centre was packed with hustling and bustling shoppers and tourists. When I turned into Eglington Street a car almost ran me down while I was crossing the road. I noticed a man in the middle of the street waving his fists and yelling at some passing cars. After what had just happened to me I almost felt in sympathy with him. Dressed in a dark suit and collar and tie, he looked normal enough but his antics clearly demonstrated that he was mentally disturbed. One of the drivers being yelled at rolled down his window and started hurling abuse at the man. Another driver began honking his horn. Soon everyone on the street was staring at the disturbed man, some with open hostility. I stopped by one of Moons' elegantly displayed windows and watched the bizarre scene unfold with a growing sense of unease. As the man passed me on the street I looked into his wild eyes and my mother came to mind. For a moment I thought of going after him to offer assistance, but I didn't. I resumed my walk towards the post office.

After I posted the parcels I hurried along Eglington Street, thinking about the people I was about to send the tapes to, wondering what their response would be. Again I started toying with the idea of maybe dropping one or two of the heavier songs from the collection. A studio in Dublin was already booked for the mastering sessions, but I still had a few days to come to a final decision about the song-count.

Approaching the Franciscan church, I decided to drop in to say a quick prayer for guidance. As I approached the grey building I noticed a wino slouched on the sun-lit portico steps with his back against one of the wide fluted pillars. Around him a group of schoolgirls in navy uniforms were giggling at his drunken behaviour. While passing the group, the thought occurred to me that I should tell the girls to stop laughing at the unfortunate man, but decided not to get involved.

In the church, after I made my pitch for divine guidance regarding my songs, I said a prayer for a recently deceased relative of mine, Uncle Jim, who had died at the relatively young age of forty five after years of alcoholism. As it happened, one of the songs from *Just Another Town* (*100 Miles*) was about him.

Rather than catch a bus home, I walked the two miles. When I arrived at the house I had a quick snack, then got my guitar and songbook and settled down to my day's work.

Over the past few years I had been working on a series of autobiographical songs roughly based on the book *Don Quixote*. Originally I tried to write the story in prose but the first draft was so incoherent I couldn't face a second. From the ashes of this failure a series of songs began to emerge. Some of the numbers were already completed, others were at various stages of development.

I opened my songbook now on a half written song called *Me And My Manager*. The lyric dealt with corruption in the music business, but the words were full of tired old rock'n'roll clichés. The only revealing quality about the song was the melody and one humorous line in the chorus:

I got the credit and he got the gold,
now I live on credit and he's rich, I'm told.

Clever, I thought, but not good enough to redeem an otherwise tired lyric. I turned another few pages and came to one of the pivotal songs of the collection, *There is a Time*.

There is a time in life, it seems,
for believing in dreams,
for me it's gone . . .

On the page the lyric looked nothing to write home about but when I picked up my guitar and started singing the words, it came alive like few other songs I'd written. While I was running through it I recalled the almost clairvoyant moment when I predicted that I would write the song. It was on the night my old girlfriend, Helen, came back into my life. Though I was flattered by her return, I told her that the only thing I saw emerging from her comeback was a good song. The cruelty of this prediction gave me a twinge of conscience now, but still I sang the song a second and then a third time for the shear pleasure of singing it.

When I moved on to other, half-baked songs from the collection the feeling of achievement quickly disappeared. I battled against the grain on a few stubborn lyrics for a couple of hours and then decided to go for a walk, to clear the cobwebs.

As I strolled down the Dyke Road my mind slipped naturally into song thoughts. Pondering on one of the lyrics from *Just Another Town*, it occurred to me that I rarely if ever felt completely satisfied with my work. No sooner was one album completed than another had to be tackled. Occasionally a real song came effortlessly, but this only occurred once in a blue moon. The rest of the time it was an uphill slog.

Passing the Waterworks, I noticed a man standing across from a shelter for the homeless. As I approached him I saw that his clothes were torn and tatty. At his feet a black and white mongrel was chewing a fly-infested bone. The man smiled and leaned forward. 'Excuse me, sir. Would you happen to know if it's free to stay in this hostel or do you have to pay?'

I glanced towards the shelter. 'I'd imagine it's free. The Simon Community run it.'

'Thanks. It's a grand day, isn't it?'

'Lovely.' I glanced down at the dog and walked on.

A few hundred yards down the road I turned on to the dirt track leading to the Corrib. Fifty or sixty feet ahead the river was gleaming in the sun. On my left a wide expanse of grassland dotted with dandelions, daises and buttercups spread all the way to the riverbank. I drank in the scenery for a few moments then automatically resumed thinking about my songs. I sighed heavily and said a silent prayer. 'Dear God, in the bible you often sent angels to people in distress. Please send me some kind of guidance now about the songs on *Just Another* . . .'

Interrupted by a dog barking behind me, I turned sharply. Two feet away, the man I'd spoken to earlier was talking to his dog, telling it to be quiet. Wondering if he'd overheard me talking to myself, I looked into his sunken eyes and started laughing to cover up my embarrassment. 'You gave me a fright there.'

'Sorry about that. I'm just going to the river to let Spot have a swim. He's tormented with the flies.'

We walked to the river together, the mongrel running ahead wagging its tail. Unlike other down-and-outs I'd come across in the vicinity of the Simon Shelter in the past, this man seemed completely at ease with himself. When we reached the riverside he picked up a stone and threw it out into the water. The mongrel leaped after it and swam through the spreading ripples. The man smiled. 'The fool. He'll stay out there now for ages wondering where it's gone.'

While we were watching the puzzled dog splashing around in the sun-lit water the tramp glanced downriver in the direction of town. 'I hate the city at this time of year. It's too packed with holidaymakers. I love walking in the country. We're just back from Menlo; it's lovely and peaceful out there.'

I put my hand in my pocket to see if I had any change but then it occurred to me that I might insult the man by offering him money. We went on talking till Spot finally realised the fool's errand he was on. When he emerged from the water shaking spray all over the grass, his master patted him on the head and glanced back in the direction of the Simon Shelter. 'I don't think I'll stay there after all. The place in town where I usually stop let me keep the dog in the room with me.'

While we were parting company I looked into the man's face and thought I recognised something familiar in his eyes.

When I reached home I made myself a mug of strong coffee and got back to work on my songs. I started singing *Me And My Manager* but stopped half way through the first verse, nauseated by the words. I went on humming the tune, trying to think of an alternative idea for a lyric. Events from the day gone by resurfaced in my mind. First I recalled the disturbed man on Eglington Street waving his fists at the passing traffic; then I thought of the old wino outside the church being laughed at by schoolgirls; and finally the old tramp and his dog by the river. While I was thinking about these unfortunate men, a few lines came into my head:

I sing for the lonely souls who haunt this world with unearthly goals,
in the streets of every town see them daily coming down,
see them daily coming down.

I sang the verse to the melody of *Me And My Manager* and it fitted it like a glove. I started singing it again, working on the melodic phrasing of each syllable. Halfway through the second line I began to see distinct parallels between the unfortunate men I'd run into earlier in the day and the characters from the three songs on *Just Another Town* that I was having reservations about – *Everything Will Be Alright* dealt with mental illness; *Let's Just Have Another Drink*, alcoholism; and *One Hundred Miles* was about a homeless man. The coincidence of the three matching subjects was so exact, I scratched my head.

Getting back to the new song, I started thinking about a second verse and my old flame Helen came into my head. I thought of the doomed passion of our teenage relationship and a few lines came to me without effort:

> I sing for the lovers, the drunks, whose high aim like that of monks
> is to rise above the weight of man's heavy earthly state
> of man's heavy earthly state.

For a moment I thought that the comparison between drunken lovers and holy monks was a bit daring, but I went with it.

A chorus line came to me and, again, I hesitated before writing it into my copybook:

> But most of all I sing to be free
> of a heavy heart in me, my gravity.

I hadn't a clue where this weighty line had come from but, after I gave it some thought, I realised that it was connected to my conviction that complete happiness is unattainable in our world, though we still need to strive for it.

For my next verse I thought of my mother:

> I sing for those driven insane by the weight of the strain
> of holding up beneath the press of a world under stress,
> of a world under stress.

I sang the song for an hour, working on the phrasing. Overall I was happy with the lyric but I kept thinking that there was something missing every time I concluded the second chorus.

Then it dawned on me that what it needed was simply to repeat the first verse at the end of the song and include myself as one of the lonely souls in the final line.

THE VOYAGE

I sing for the lonely souls who haunt this world with unearthly goals;
in the streets of every town see them daily coming down,
see *us* daily coming down

THE RED LION

A two faced clock in a distant tower
harshly struck an ungodly hour

Morning Star

A screech of brakes somewhere out in the Bronx woke me just after four thirty. Though there wasn't a stitch of bedclothes over me, I felt hot and sticky on the bed. I turned and looked towards the partly raised window, which had a wire mosquito screen blocking the opening. The first beams of daylight filtering through the steel mesh were silvering the edges of a drooping geranium plant on the sill. One of the few requests the nurse who was renting me the apartment had made before handing over the keys was that I water her plant on a daily basis while she was back in Ireland on holiday. Since I'd moved in almost three weeks before, I'd forgotten to do this three or four times. Taking mental note that the job had to be done as a priority when I got up, I tried to go back to sleep but couldn't manage it. Even at that early hour traffic noise out in the city was loud and constant, and, with no air-conditioning in the apartment, closing the window to block out the sound was out of the question.

I tossed and turned for more than an hour, then got up and sat in a hardback chair, preparing for my habitual twenty minutes' contemplation before facing the day.

Five minutes into the mental exercise my mind started wandering. Before I knew it, I was back at a music convention I'd attended with the head of my record company a couple of weeks earlier in a flashy hotel in central Manhattan. Every major and minor record company on the planet had stalls at the symposium, and each stall was pumping out the latest hits from their roster of top stars. The eclectic mix was so diverse and strident, I was forced to plug my ears while we searched for the Irish Stand. When we eventually located it I found two fellow Irish songwriters standing by the green stall, Noel Brazil and Jimmy

McCarthy. Noel greeted me with a tipsy smile. 'Welcome to the Tower of Babel, man.' Jimmy's welcome had a biblical overtone also: 'We've come to the mountain, Johnny!'

I came back to myself on the hard chair and concentrated on my mantra for a few minutes but then my mind broke loose again and travelled back to a couple of impromptu gigs I'd played with Noel and Jimmy on separate occasions in the week following the music fair. Both shows were in a small, noisy coffee house on the lower east side of Manhattan, a venue with a big reputation but a lousy PA system. The first time I played there, a weekend night, I found it difficult being heard about the rackety air-conditioning which had to be left on at all times because of the heat. Despite the awful sound, I managed to go down okay with the noisy crowd. Impressed by the reaction I got, Noel Brazil borrowed my guitar and played a manic set, flailing my instrument as though his life depended on making an impression. When he handed the guitar back to me I noticed blood spattered all over the wooden body and strings.

On a calmer midweek night, Jimmy and I played the same venue to a smaller crowd. During Jimmy's set a group of loud South Americans kept up a non-stop conversation in speedy Spanish, making it impossible for Jimmy's colourful Celtic-mystic lyrics to be heard. Jimmy lost his rag and called the group of Latinos a bunch of "shysters", an expression they luckily didn't understand. I didn't fare much better. Half way through my set a guy with spiky hair yelled up "pump up the action" while I was singing my ballad for down-and-outs, *One Hundred Miles*.

After my period of distracted contemplation, I read George Herbert's poetry till seven-thirty, then showered, dressed and headed out for early Mass.

Leaving the apartment building a few days earlier I had noticed an alarming new sign on the glass-panelled door of the lobby, which I glanced at again now:

Don't be kind to your neighbour in the way of leaving
this door open for them. They might just knife you in the back.

Outside in the street it was hot, even at that early hour. Traffic on the main road was brisk so I availed of the traffic lights to get across to St Michael's church. The congregation for early Mass was small and predominantly elderly. After the gospel reading the priest told a story about a twelfth century monk who despaired after years of confronting countless maimed and impoverished beggars that came seeking help to the monastery door: '"Why don't you do something to help these unfortunates," he cried out to God.' The priest hesitated before giving us God's response: "I am doing something: I'm telling you about them!"

I recalled the poor reception my ballad for the homeless had received in lower Manhattan a couple of weeks earlier and lowered my head.

After Mass I made my way to the post office to send a few postcards home to family and friends. Passing one of the many Irish bars with plastic shamrocks in the windows, I recalled going there on the night I arrived in New York to check out the prospect of getting a paying gig. Before approaching the bar owner, I discovered that one of my songs, *The Voyage*, was listed on the jukebox. Using this as a PR ploy, I made my pitch to a freckled-faced Kerryman who gave me a nod and a wink. "Sure you can play here, any night you like. And you might even make a buck or two, if you pass around a hat."

Back at the apartment I discovered that there was very little food in the cupboards. Rather than backtrack to the local store, I breakfasted on black tea and dry crackers while watching a grim item on the CNN news about a serial killer. After the news, a beaming weather reporter informed the state of New York that afternoon temperatures were set to maximise somewhere in the high nineties. 'Not as sticky as yesterday's one hundred and two but still hot enough to fry an egg on your bumper.'

I knocked off the set and took off my shirt, thinking back to the day before when I'd spent most of the afternoon shuffling in and out of the cold shower. In my vest, I got my guitar and song-copybook and settled down in the dank living room to work on an idea for a song on emigration that I'd jotted down a few days earlier.

> On my cross, a jumbo jet, I cried: 'Why have you forsaken me, Lord?'
> And something in me died; some last vestige of pride.
> I descended to the hell of New York (The Big Apple as Adam's curse?)
> blazing in a 100 degrees. I looked for work but found none.
> I felt humiliated. I grew humble.

I had a strong melody worked out but when I tried to refine the crude prose into a worthwhile lyric I came up against a brick wall. During my sixth attempt at a first verse, the phone rang. It was Tom Prendergast, an acquaintance from my hometown back in Ireland who ran a small independent pop record company in New Jersey. Tom had attended a low-paying gig I'd played a few nights earlier in a club in the Upper East Side. After the show, he invited me to stay overnight at his air-conditioned apartment in New Jersey. Before parting the next day he promised to look out for a few "worthwhile" gigs for me. Hearing his Limerick accent coming down the line now made my heart rise.

After some small talk about the heatwave, Tom told me that he'd managed to get me a gig for that very evening in a bar called The Red Lion. 'The fee's just a hundred and fifty bucks for three half-hour sets spread over a long night, but if you do well the boss'll book you back at a higher rate. What do you think?'

I laughed. 'You're a lifesaver, Tom. Where's the venue?'

After he gave me directions, Tom apologised because he wasn't going to be able to attend the gig himself, but he offered to put me up in his apartment in Hoboken again. 'It'll save you going all the way back to the Bronx after the gig.'

After I put down the phone I abandoned my emigration song and started rehearsing for the night's performance.

At five that evening I showered and put on my one remaining clean shirt and a pair of black wranglers. Though it was after six when I hit the streets with my guitar, the sun was still blazing in the clear sky above the high-rise buildings and the muggy air was sweltering. Before I reached the subway I was sweating like a pig.

I got off the train on Broadway and located a side-street music store where I bought a spare set of guitar strings, just in case. On my way back to Broadway I noticed a couple of Puerto Ricans waving their fists and shouting at one another in the middle of the street. Passing cars were honking their horns at them but the two antagonists paid them little heed. One of the two – a long-haired fellow in a purple shirt – pulled a knife from his pocket and started chasing the other guy in and out of the traffic. The line of pedestrians in front of me stopped to watch the altercation. The guy in the purple shirt caught up with the other man and stabbed him in the back several times. A loud gasp went up from the crowd around me. Close to the scene of the stabbing, a black man grabbed the guy in the purple shirt from behind and tried to take the knife from him. After a brief tussle the fellow in the purple shirt broke free and ran away. I thought of waiting to see how badly injured the victim was but the line of pedestrians before me started moving and I drifted along with them.

I arrived at The Red Lion more than fifty minutes before I was due on stage, feeling on edge because of the stabbing incident. The venue turned out to be larger than I'd imagined from Tom's description of the place. In the bar area I located the owner, a middle-aged man with a neat moustache and a Manhattan accent laced with middle-class Dublin undertones. He took me on a tour of the place, showing me a wall of framed photographs of celebrities who'd been his clientele over the years. Stopping in front of a black and white shot of The Clancy Brothers, he laughed. 'The lads were part of the furniture here at one time. Things are different now. I booked an Irish trad band last summer and they died a death.'

We moved into the main part of the bar, a large lounge area with an open restaurant at one side. The boss pointed to a small stage positioned between the restaurant and the lounge. 'Since we opened the restaurant it's been a bit awkward for our singers. Generally people who come to eat aren't that interested in entertainment, so don't be surprised if they pay you little attention.' He looked at his watch. 'Our resident singer, Billy, should be here soon. He'll be going on before you and then you'll be alternating half-hour sets till about one in the morning. I have to get back behind the bar now. We'll talk later.'

While I was checking out the PA system, Billy arrived with a battered guitar case covered in airport stickers. Dressed in faded denim jeans with designer holes at the knees, he gave me a sour look when he noticed me studying the PA amplifier. When I told him that I was sharing the bill with him he shrugged and started unpacking his guitar, muttering a few icy words of greeting in a rough Brooklyn accent. I went to the back of the lounge to watch his set.

Without introducing himself to the small crowd, Billy opened his performance with *Welcome To The Hotel California*, singing in the same west coast accent as The Eagles. The handful of people sitting around the lounge didn't pay him the slightest bit of attention. During the next half hour he played songs by Niall Young, Crosby, Still & Nash, John Denver and Cat Stevens, and for each cover his voice took on the exact intonation of the singer he was copying. The crowd increased, especially in the restaurant, but Billy continued to be ignored. At the end of his half hour set he left the stage to a limp round of applause without announcing that I was coming on next.

On stage I tried to break the ice with a bit of humour: 'This is my first performance in The Red Lion. My name's Johnny but I feel more like Daniel – that guy in the Bible who got chucked into the lions' den for saying his prayers.'

A couple of girls chuckled in the Restaurant but people in the lounge didn't appear to get the joke. I started singing *Just Another Town*. At the end of the song three black guys sitting at a table close to the stage broke into a strong round of applause and others joined in. Behind the bar the boss gave me the thumbs up. I raised my chin and started another original song. After my third number a burly guy in the restaurant beckoned to me with a steak knife: 'Hey buddy, how about *Sweet Caroline?'*

I explained that I only did originals and started *Let's Just Have Another Drink*, a song about an uncle of mine who ended his days on a barstool. In the middle of the second verse the fat guy burped loudly and raised his steak knife. 'Who cares about deadbeats. Sing us something we know.'

I ignored the taunt and finished the song. The black guys clapped but the rest of the audience remained silent. I tried to announce another original number but tubs interrupted me again. 'How about *Bridge Over Troubled Water?* Surely you know that one?'

I glared at him. 'I told you before, I only sing original songs.'

'Is that what you call them!'

I cursed into the microphone. 'Why don't you go back to stuffing your mouth, fats, and let me get on with my job.'

The black guys started chortling but the rest of the customers remained deadly silent. I started a song and glanced towards the bar. The boss was staring at me with daggers in his eyes.

I performed three more original songs and announced that I was taking a break.

As I was leaving the stage one of the black guys handed me an empty whiskey glass with a ten-dollar bill sticking out of it. 'You're a fine songwriter and a damn good singer. Stick with it, man.'

During the break the boss called me to the bar. 'You can play your other two sets and I'll pay you but you'll never work here again!'

Getting through the rest of the night was a strain. In stony silence, the boss paid me from the till at around one-thirty and I left the bar with a heavy heart. Outside, I ran into Billy, who seemed to be waiting for me. After the unfriendly way he'd treated me earlier I was surprised when he offered me a ride in his car to New Jersey. 'That was a brave thing you did earlier.'

'Stupid more like.'

'No no, you spoke up for yourself, man. That takes guts.'

Billy dropped me in Hoboken just before two in the morning. Half way down the dark, deserted street leading to Tom's apartment it suddenly dawned on me that I'd forgotten to water the geranium back in the Bronx. My heart sank. I sat on the edge of my guitar case clutching my head, wondering how I was going to tell Tom about the disastrous gig. Two loud chimes from a clock in a distant belfry interrupted my train of thought. Glancing in the direction of the two-faced clock, I recalled an Irish ballad that my daughter Niamh learned at school. The title eluded me but I remembered that there was a clock in it knelling the time before some patriot was hanged. Remembering the quiver that used to enter Niamh's little voice as she sang about the doomed man, I started to cry. For five or six minutes I wept my eyes out, thinking about how poor a provider I'd been to my wife and kids all my life. Glaring up at the heavens, I clenched my fist and cursed God for having dogged my heels at every step. The light from a bright star glittered in my wet eyes but I paid it little attention. The clock in the belfry chimed again. I got to my feet and walked on.

Tom came to his apartment door in his underwear, yawning. Luckily, he was too tired to chat, so I didn't have to give him a lengthy account of the gig. He directed me to the same air-conditioned bedroom I'd slept in during my previous visit and said we'd talk when he got in from his office the following afternoon.

In bed I tossed and turned for an hour before falling asleep. Next morning, Tom was gone when I got up. I showered, had some breakfast and headed out for a walk to clear my head.

On the main street of Hoboken I spotted a gold cross and chain in the window of a jeweller's shop that I thought would make a nice present for my daughter Niamh. Blowing most of the fee I'd received in the Red Lion the night before, I bought it. Further down the same street I came upon a second-hand bookstore I'd been in during my previous visit to Hoboken. I went in and took down the first book that came to hand, *Ascent of the Mountain, Flight of the Dove* by Michael Novak. By coincidence, it was the first book I'd browsed through during my previous visit to the shop. I smiled to myself recalling how I'd considered buying it simply because the title reminded me of the remark Jimmy McCarthy had made about the mountain at the music convention. I was about to put it back on the shelf again now when I noticed that the price tag on the cover had been reduced from $1.99 to $1.00. I smiled and opened the book. The first chapter was entitled The Voyage. I smiled again and dipped my hand in my pocket, searching for a dollar bill.

THE RIVER RETURNING

From the raft of his dying bed my father smiled at me
when I returned from the river and told him it looked heavenly

The River Returning

The rasping sound of my mother coughing in the room overhead woke me. By the luminous hands of my watch, I could just about make out that it was after five thirty. I raised my head and listened. My father's faint but even breathing came to me from his bed a few feet away from where I was lying in a sleeping bag on the floor. I lay back and tried to stretch my body to its full length but my feet were hampered by the steel legs of a mobile toilet. I turned on my right side and tried to return to sleep, but I couldn't manage it. A fragment of a dream came back to me. I was in a restaurant with my wife and our son and daughter and there was an empty baby chair beside our table which the kids kept pointing to. A few days earlier I'd left my wife in Galway soon after she'd arrived home from our GP with confirmation that she was pregnant. Minutes before, my sister Kay had phoned to let me know that my father was dying. At the time I was so disconcerted by the news of my father I hadn't given my wife's condition a lot of attention. Since then I kept thinking about the coincidence of learning about the impending death and future birth within minutes of one another.

My mother's coughing upstairs grew louder. My father groaned a couple of times and settled back to sleep. The coughing went on and on. Since she'd been released from St Joseph's a few days earlier my mother had been chain-smoking. At a quiet moment in the kitchen the day before I held her trembling hand and asked her how she was holding up. She let out a deep sigh. "I'm okay now but what'll become of me when he's gone?"

The headlights of a passing car moved slowly across the ceiling and the room grew dark again. A creaking sound from the stairway just outside the room made me raise my head. The door opened and the silhouette of my sister Joan's head appeared in the gap.

'Just getting a glass of water for Mam. Those cigarettes will kill her. How is he?'

I leaned forward. 'He had a quiet night.'

'He didn't need to use the toilet?'

'No, thank God. Tell Mam he's sleeping peacefully.'

The door closed. I lay back on the floor and started thinking about a family row that had broken out the evening before, a few hours after Joan had flown in from her home in the UK. While we were sitting around the kitchen table discussing the bedside roster for the following morning, Joan announced that she was prepared to sit by my father's bed all day, if necessary. My sister Patti didn't like the authoritative tone of this offer. She said that "dramatic sacrifices" weren't necessary and reminded Joan that Kay, Sue and herself had been looking after our father well enough since he'd been discharged from hospital the week before. My brother Michael and I tried to point out that Joan was merely trying to be helpful, but Kay and Sue rounded on us with a sharp reminder that we too were only recent arrivals.

I drifted back to sleep. An hour and a half later the groaning of my father woke me. I turned on the light and went to his bed. Stretching up from his pillow, he gazed at me with deep anxiety in his hollow eyes. He muttered something through his gums but I couldn't make out any of the slurred words. I brushed back a strand of dank hair from his wrinkled forehead and leaned towards his ear. 'What is it, Dad? Do you need to go to the toilet?'

A helpless look came over his face. I touched his cheek. 'It's okay; I'll help you. The mobile toilet's just over here. The nurse had it delivered yesterday. Do you not remember?'

I helped him out of the bed and supported him across the floor to the encased iron framed commode. Getting his pyjama-legs down and his nappy unfastened took ages. While I held his bony arm, he sat gripping the toilet seat with a strained look on his face. He began to tremble on the unstable seat. The purple arteries near his wrist, gnarled and scarred from years of dialyses, started bulging and throbbing from his exertions. For almost five minutes he tried desperately to relieve himself, then groaned loudly and leaned to get up. 'It's no good, it's no good, I can't do it.'

'Don't worry, Dad, the nurse is due early this morning. She'll have something to relieve you.' I helped him back to bed and tucked the covers up around his stubbled chin. He thanked me and turned towards the wall. Moments later he was asleep.

Back in the sleeping bag I started thinking of my arrival at the house three days earlier. After the solemn way my sister Kay had told me over the phone that my father had "only days to go", I was surprised to find him sitting with my mother on the small settee with a rug tucked around him. His eyes lit up when he spotted me coming through the parlour door and he almost sang out my name, "Look who's here, Chris, Johneeeee." Not being used to such warm greetings from him, I was taken aback. I went over and touched his arm. From his compliant, almost child-like expression I gauged that he was aware that his condition was imminently terminal. I glanced at my mother and smiled. 'I wasn't expecting this; two love birds sitting in the evening sun.' My mother tried to laugh and nodded towards my father. 'Give him a kiss.'

I hesitated then leaned down and put my lips to my father's hollow cheek. He raised his free hand and touched my neck. Again, the unusualness of this intimate gesture surprised me. I pulled a chair up beside him and started talking about his grandchildren. 'Ronan told me to be sure to tell you that his school team have made it through to the county semi-finals.' My father's eyes brightened. My disinterest in sport had been a missing link between us all our lives, so this reconnection through his grandson was as important to me as it was to my father.

I glanced at the familiar framed photograph of my grandfather on the wall behind the settee and smiled. 'By the way, I have some good news. A new addition to the Duhan clan is on its way. We got confirmation earlier today.' My father smiled and squeezed my mother's hand.

The sound of my mother's coughing upstairs broke my reverie. It was after half- seven. I got up and dressed and went upstairs to let my brother Michael know that I was leaving the house. In the small bedroom we once shared with two other brothers, Michael went to get up when I woke him. I put my hand on his shoulder. 'No need to go down straight away. He's sleeping peacefully now. Just listen out for him. I've left his room door open.'

Michael lay back on his pillow, yawning. 'Where are you off to so early?'

I hesitated. "Mass, and a walk to the river."

Michael held back a sneer.

I backed towards the door. 'By the way, I didn't get a chance to tell you how impressed I was by the photos of those new bronze sculptures you sent me a few weeks back. Terrific.'

Michael put his fingers through his long fringe. 'You should see the one I'm working on now, life-size.'

I backed further out of the room. 'We must get out for a drink and a chat tonight, if Dad stays okay. Don't forget to keep an ear out for him.'

I arrived at the Redemptorist's as eight o'clock Mass was beginning. I took a seat near the back of the church in a pew I'd sat in regularly as a kid. There was just a handful of old people in attendance. Behind the front altar (a simple candlelit slab of dressed marble) an elderly priest said the opening prayers at a snail's pace. I glanced around the high-ceilinged building, noting the familiar alcoves and side altars on either side of the dark chapel. The place seemed smaller than I remembered, but the ornate main altar behind the priest's back still looked as impressive as ever, with its elaborate angular candelabra structures pointing upwards towards the curved mosaic ceiling. While a chapter from St Paul's letter to the Corinthians was being read by one of the congregation, I recalled a Christmas Eve Mass I'd attended in the church with my mother and sisters many years before when the whole altar was lit up with a thousand candles. I was so impressed by the spectacle I told my father about it when we got home, but he just laughed at my wonderment and told me that he didn't go in for church pomp and ceremony.

The old priest started mumbling the Gospel reading which dealt with the journey the risen Christ made to Emmaus in the company of two of his unsuspecting disciples. While the story was being related, one of my father's bizarre expressions of unbelief in an afterlife came back to me from my youth: "When I die just stuff me in a dustbin and chuck me in the Shannon; I don't believe in any of that fairytale lark about life after death."

After mass I headed for the docks. When I arrived at the waterfront the sun was well up, though a faint full moon was also visible in the hazy blue sky above the river. After my disturbed night's sleep I felt muzzy and light-headed. I stood on the quay by an embankment of granite boulders near the dock area and gazed out over the misty Shannon. A group of swans and gulls near the centre of the river caught my attention. One of the swans broke away from the gaggle and started paddling towards the quay where I was standing. As it approached, it stopped moving and looked up at me, then slowly began to float downstream, drawing my gaze with it towards the docks. Noticing a lone ship moored in the port enclosure, I recalled a time when the place used to be jam-packed with freighters from every quarter of the globe. A coloured photograph of a ship my father worked on floated into my mind. He and a sailor friend were on deck standing beside a heap of thick mooring ropes with their exposed arms around one another's shoulders. My father was a handsome nineteen- or twenty-year-old. Though it was years since I'd seen the snap, I could still recall every detail of it, from my father's disheveled quiff and muscular bare arms to the bright red bandana his friend was wearing around his solid neck. The bandana impressed me so much I started borrowing my mother's coloured headscarves and tying them around my throat.

Moving down the sunlit quayside, I came to a wharf set out a little from the chained-off walkway. A familiar iron bollard near the edge of a grassy embankment brought a smile to my face. I sat on it and instantly was back more than a quarter of a century with my father standing beside me, hand on my shoulder, pointing towards a long narrow rowing boat straining against the current.

A low-flying gull flashed in the sun above Cleeves' Bank across the river and brought me back to myself. I started humming a tune that had come to me out of the blue while I was sitting by my father's bed the day before. Automatically I found myself analysing the sequence of notes at the time for song potential but stopped when I realised what I was doing. The same thing happened again now. I started thinking about the rhythm, wondering what lyrical subject might suit it. But then the thought of my father lying in his fusty old bed waiting to die came into my head. I stopped humming and looked out over the river. Sunlight sparkling on the water held my gaze. The thought struck me how unfair it was that the whole riverside area that my father loved was so vibrant and alive while he himself was fading away. I glanced down river and thought of the wide uninhabited expanse of the Atlantic ocean. I thought of its unfathomable depths and then I thought of the gulf that lay between my father's dying and his living presence in my memory. I lowered my head and muttered a prayer.

Back at the house I dropped in to see my father before going to breakfast. He was alone, propped up on his pillows with his eyes open. I stood at the end of his bed and told him about my walk to the river, outlining some of the sunny details. He smiled and his eyes livened and then blazed in his head.

While I was having breakfast the nurse arrived and spent some time alone with my father. Before leaving, she left some suppositories, telling us that they were only to be used if my father's constipation persisted into the afternoon.

During the next couple of hours my father's bladder as well as his bowels began to seize up. My brother Michael and I helped him to the mobile toilet on two occasions but each time he couldn't go. At midday my sister Joan gave him a suppository and twenty minutes later he soiled his nappy without managing to urinate. After we cleaned him he was less anxious but still worried about not being able to 'make his water'. We phoned for a doctor and one arrived in the early afternoon while my sister Joan was out visiting a friend. On entering my father's room the doctor – an elderly man with a dour expression – glared at the mobile toilet and turned to my mother. 'Have you no bathroom?'

My mother nervously explained that the nurse had suggested the mobile toilet because our bathroom was at the back of the house, far removed from my father's room. 'She thought it would save him the exertion of the long trip.'

The doctor made a dismissive gesture. 'The man's not used to these contraptions; that's why he's having trouble going to the toilet. Let's get him up and we'll see how capable he is of making his way to the bathroom. Come on, John, try and get to your feet. Your son here will help you.'

I felt like objecting but instead helped my father from the bed. Out on the floor he groaned heavily while I clasped his shoulders and gripped him under one arm. My mother bent down and fumbled trying to put his slippers on. A look of impatience came over the doctor's face. 'Come on now, John, you're a strong man still. You'll be able for this, won't you?'

My father drew a deep breath and sighed.

My mother opened the room door and I helped my father out into the hall. Going before us, my mother opened the kitchen door. Halfway down the hall my father gave another load groan. I turned my head towards the doctor. 'I'm not sure if this is a good idea; he seems to be in great pain.'

The doctor flicked his hand forward. 'He'll be okay. Where's the bathroom?'

'At the back of the house.'

'Well, keep going; you're doing fine.'

Half way through the kitchen my father stopped suddenly and his bony body went rigid in my clasp. A look of panic came into his eyes and he groaned heavily. His hand came up and gripped my elbow. For a moment I thought he was going to die in my arms. Instead he let out a loud cry and his body went limp. A few seconds later he had the runs all over the floor. Standing in a widening pool of diarrhea and piss, he started shaking and sobbing. To insure that he didn't slip in the mess I got in behind him and propped him up, holding him firmly under his arms. In panic, I called out to my brother Michael upstairs, but he didn't hear me. My mother surprisingly remained perfectly calm. She went to the sink and got a basin of water and a towel and then spoke consoling words to my father, telling him that everything was going to be alright. Removing the bottom part of his soiled pyjamas, she started to clean his mired legs and flaccid buttocks. While she was doing this the doctor remained detached, not offering any help or assistance. I felt like cursing him but held my tongue.

Slumped in my arms with his hands outstretched, my father glanced back at me and started mumbling some slurred words of apology. Positioned behind him, I could only see into the corner of his left eye. I lowered my mouth towards his ear and told him that he had no need to apologise or feel ashamed. 'I'm your son.'

He rested his head on my shoulder and went silent. Time seemed to stand still. I looked down at my mother. She was wiping shit from my father's feet. But she was doing it with such love and devotion, the act seemed somehow pure and holy. As she worked the towel gently between the crevices of my father's soiled toes she kept muttering 'Sacred heart of Jesus we place all our trust in thee.'

> Supporting my dying father too weak to stand;
> his sharp backbone in my ribcage, his listless arms
> extended for my supporting hands. If I was a cross
> behind him, then he drooping in my arms was a mired Christ
> in the reverse role of a father depending on his son.

THE FALL

*The tree that fell in the storm created a lacuna in the wood's crown
that enlightens the fall*

The Fallen Tree

Ronan turned from the window with a pained expression and groaned.
'Where are we now, Dad?'

'A few miles further on from when you last asked me.'

'What time did you say we get in?'

'Six-thirtyish.'

'What time's it now?'

'Five minutes after the last time you asked.' I patted him on the
head. 'There's still a long way to go, Ronan. Be patient. I warned you
that it was going to be a long trip. I won't take you to any more gigs if
you keep moaning.'

Ronan lapsed into silence and I went back to reading my book.

As the bus neared Waterford city I got out my address book and
checked the name of the street the venue was on. A twinge of pre-gig
worry I'd been feeling all day intensified. It had been almost two years
since I'd last played Waterford, so I had no idea what the night held
in store. Though my previous performance in the town had been well
attended, I attributed this to the fact that Christy Moore's version of
my song *The Voyage* and my own *Family Album* were receiving a lot of
airplay on national radio at the time. No such media focus was on me
now, even though I'd recently released my album *Just Another Town*.

Ronan's spirits rose dramatically when the bus pulled into the
Waterford depot. While we were making our way across Redmond
Bridge, he jumped in the air to get a better view of the twilit city above
the iron girders of the bridge. 'Is Waterford bigger than Galway, Dad?'

'No.'

'It looks kinda bigger. Is it just a town?'

'No, it's a city.'

'A small city?'

'Yeah, a small city.'

'If it's a city then there should be a McDonalds here. When're we going to eat, I'm starving?'

I looked at my watch. 'As far as I remember, there's a pretty good, cheap restaurant a few blocks down the river where we'll get a decent meal. But we're going to have to be quick; it's pushing on. I need to get to the venue to do a soundcheck and find out where we're staying.'

'I'd prefer McDonalds.'

'I wouldn't and I'm the boss.'

While we were making our way to the restaurant, I scrutinised a number of billboards and shop windows but didn't spot any of the advertising posters I'd sent to the manager of the venue a month before. After our meal, I dropped into a newsagent's and browsed through the entertainment page of the local broadsheet to see if it was carrying any mention of my gig, but it wasn't. While I was putting the paper back on the rack I noticed copies of the latest edition of *Hot Press* music magazine on a shelf below the newspapers. Knowing that my album *Just Another Town* was scheduled for review in the issue, I grabbed a copy and located the page *Let 'Em Roll – The Dice Decides*. Spotting the title of my album mid page, I totted up the score of the twin dice cubes at the bottom of the review and was disappointed that they added up to a mere seven out of twelve The review itself was scathing:

Johnny Duhan makes heavy records. So heavy, in fact,
that you could give yourself a hernia listening to them.
Just Another Town is quintessential Duhan. It's bleak,
grey and mournful . . . weighty and intensely personal . . .

Gutted, I read on and was informed that my melodies were often formless and that the album was full of 'grinding contradictions'. I skipped to the end of the onslaught and was puzzled to find this contradictory summation:

Casual listeners are probably not Johnny Duhan's target
audience. This is a complex and intense album freighted with
a starkly compelling honesty that many will find difficult to face.
Not for the faint-hearted.

Noticing a pop album review by the same writer on the same page, I browsed through the glowing opening lines and realised that the reviewer's chosen niche was bubbly pop. I cursed the editor for misdirecting my album to the wrong critical quarter and tossed the magazine back on the shelf.

'Put down that comic Ronan and let's get a move on. We're running late.'

Ronan gave me a puzzled look. 'What wrong, Dad, you look angry.'

Before leaving the newsagents I took directions from the girl behind the counter and, after a ten-minute walk, found JB's bar and club at the end of a narrow back street. The bar at the front of the venue was small and grubby but the club itself turned out to be impressively decked out like a French Cafe with round tables topped with wine-bottle candle-holders. A young man sorting glasses behind the bar counter told me that the manager never arrived before opening time at nine. He gave me a phone number and directed me to a public phone in the hall beside the men's toilet.

After just one ring the manager came on the line full of chat. Cutting into his small talk, I questioned him about the lack of posters around town and the absence of PR in the local press. 'It doesn't augur well for the gig!'

The manager stuttered. 'What do you mean? I sent out press releases and photos to two different papers and I personally put up posters in all the key locations in the town centre. It's not my fault that you're a good looking guy and all the birds want to take you home to pin you to their walls.'

Brushing aside the plámás, I lunged at the receiver: 'People can't take posters from behind shop windows! Are you expecting a good crowd?'

The manager hesitated. 'The club's not going that long, but we're getting there. Thom Moore had a smallish crowd last week but there's been a great buzz around town about your gig. I believe you had a full house in The Deck the last time you were in Waterford?'

'That was almost two years ago, and the manager of the place did plenty of spade work before the gig, as that was the time local radio stopped including Irish music in their playlists.' I was tempted to inquire how small the 'smallish' crowd had been for Thom Moore but was too frightened to ask. I took the address of my pre-booked B&B and told the manager I'd see him at nine.

After a quick sound check, Ronan and I walked to the nearby B&B. The place turned out to be a cut above the average and the landlady was very facilitating when she saw that Ronan was with me. At no extra charge, she gave us a room with twin beds and a TV. The moment we stepped through the door Ronan jumped on the bed nearest the TV set and grabbed the remote control from the locker. 'This place is as good as a hotel, isn't it?'

I looked around the small, poorly furnished room and smiled. 'I don't know about that, but it's a lot better that the kip we stayed in in Cork a few weeks back. Do you remember that place?'

Ronan attention was so taken up with the TV remote control he didn't hear me. 'This zapper's a lot different than our one at home. I wonder what these blue buttons are for?'

I threw my bag on the free bed and went to have a wash at the sink. While I was drying my face Ronan let out a cheer. 'Look, I got it working!'

I glanced at the lit-up screen. 'Well done. Now you've got exactly ten minutes to watch it before we head back to the club.'

While Ronan was watching a quiz show I changed my shirt and then paced the room worrying about the night ahead.

During the five-minute walk back to the club a premonition came over me that I was heading towards a fall, but this was a common sensation before gigs. As we approached the side entrance to the venue – avoiding the main pub door – there wasn't a sign of life anywhere. A shiver of apprehension ran through me. I said a silent prayer as we entered the neon-lit hallway. A blonde-haired girl sitting at a ticket desk gave me a feeble smile as we approached. While passing, I glanced into a metal cashbox on the desktop and noticed that it was almost empty. Another fit of the jitters ran through me. I pushed open the inner door and let Ronan go ahead. One glance around the club confirmed my worst fears. Except for some bar staff and two couples sitting at candle-lit tables furthest removed from the stage, the place was empty. Ronan turned to me in bewilderment. 'There's nobody here!'

In stunned silence, I stood rooted to the spot. Given the ups and downs of my career, I was well seasoned to small audiences, but none as small as this. I glanced towards the bar and noticed a fellow in a red shirt with a yellow tie. I went over to him. 'Paul?'

'That's me. Johnny? You're different than your posters.'

I glanced over my shoulder. 'Things aren't looking great?'

Paul scratched his head. 'I can't figure it out.'

I studied his yellow tie knot which was slightly askew, then looked at my watch. 'At this stage I wouldn't say it's going to improve much. What do you want to do?'

Paul glanced towards the entrance and cursed. 'It's up to you. If you want to call off the gig, that'll be fine with me. I'll still pay you your guarantee, so you needn't worry about that.'

I glanced back at the people sitting with candle-lit faces at the two occupied table at the rear of the club and conjured up a false smile. 'I'll go on.'

Paul gave me a quizzical look. 'Are you sure?'

I paused. 'No, but I'll do it anyway.'

I moved back from the counter and asked Ronan to go and sit at a table near the side of the stage. 'I'm just going to the toilet, then I'm going on.'

Ronan gaped at me. 'But the man said you don't have to. It's ridiculous playing to just four people.'

'I have to do it. It's like you and your horse: if you have a bad fall you have to get back up and ride or else you lose your nerve. Anyway, it wouldn't be fair on the four people if I pulled out.'

Ronan lowered his head and looked away.

While I was in the toilet I remembered another failed gig I'd taken Ronan to a few years before in Donegal. Only a dozen or so people showed up but Ronan was so young at the time he didn't notice my humiliation. For the duration of the gig he sat at the side of the stage watching my performance and, when the small crowd gave me a standing ovation at the end of the night, he looked as proud as punch.

While washing my hands at the toilet sink, I started crying. The door opened behind me and a fellow came in. Lowering my face, I waited till he was positioned in the cubicle then wiped my eyes with the towel and started to leave. Behind me the fellow mentioned my name. 'Sorry about the crowd but there was very little publicity. My wife only heard about the gig by chance this morning. I have all your albums. *Just Another Town*'s your best. I got it when it came out a few week's back and I haven't stopped playing it since. I suppose you'll be calling off the gig?'

'No, I'm going on right now.'

'Great. Sing a few songs from *Just Another Town*, will you?'

'Sure. What's your name?'

'Joe, Joe McFadden. My friend Gerry loves you too. He couldn't come but he thinks *Just Another Town*'s a masterpiece; the best album ever made by an Irish songwriter.'

I thought of the *Hot Press* review and smiled.

As I was mounting the stage I spotted Ronan in a shadowy corner at one of the few tables without a lighted candle. When he saw me looking his way he turned to hide his embarrassment.

While I was strapping on my guitar I noticed the fellow I'd met in the toilet settling himself back in his chair. I glanced around at the other empty candlelit tables and stepped up to the microphone. 'I've played to more people than this at parties at home but I've travelled a long way, so here goes. I'll kick off with the opening song from my new album, *Just*

Another Town. And I'll dedicate it to Joe, one of the handsomest men in the club.'

Outside the sun has announced another morning,
It's red and warming, I feel it in my bed.
Down in the street I can hear people walking, I hear them talking,
They mumble in my head.
The Sun is shining down in the city; the sky is clear and blue,
Young girls going to school will look pretty, it's time I was up too . . .

While singing, I glanced at Ronan but he looked away. In the middle of the song the club door opened and a fellow came in and sat on a stool at the bar. No one else showed up during the next two hours, but I played my full set and ended the night with the final song from *Just Another Town*, which I dedicated to Ronan:

A Winter's Night

Winter was the season in the chilly street
When a young boy among children, unsteady on his feet,
Looked above the rooftops where in the sky
A million stars like hoarfrost twinkled in his eye

And the moon like an angel spread its opal wing
Above those chosen children and threw light on everything,
Threw light on everything.

So like an angel whose opal wing above the children
Threw light on everything.

Warm was the feeling in the young boy's soul
While the other children shivered in the cold
Till the young boy told them of the wondrous sight
Then all together they looked up into the night

Where the moon like an angel spread its opal wing
Above those chosen children and threw light on everything
Threw light on everything.

So like an angel whose opal wing above the children
Threw light on everything.

FLAME

*The countless discarded briars of my rose song
have become my crown of thorns*

Song Journal

I was surrounded by crumpled pages of discarded lyrics when the phone
rang. It was Joe Comerford, the producer of *Reefer and the Model*. For a
moment my heart rose, thinking he was calling with a new commission.
Speaking in his hesitant tone, Joe asked me if I'd read *The Irish Times'*
arts page. When I told him I hadn't, he suggested that I get a copy
straight away. 'Some critic has done a hatchet job on you. Vicious stuff.
It's in a review of your new album, *Don Quixote*, but it's more an attack
on your character than on your songs. The reason I'm telling you this is
that someone wrote a similar piece on me a while back and I complained
to the editor, which resulted in Fintan O'Toole writing a more balanced
article a week later.'

After I put the phone down, I weighed the situation up and decided
to go on working on my song rather than rush off to depress myself.
Back at my desk I picked up my guitar and sang the second last verse
of the lyric to lay the groundwork for the inspiration for a final verse:

And fire won't glow if wind doesn't blow on the hearth;
The yellow blaze smoulders and fades,
And you're left to cope with the cinders and smoke that remain;
But without air you will despair of the flame . . .

I played a brief guitar interlude while trying to conjure up an idea
for the final verse, but nothing came. I picked up a few failed verses from
the floor to see if any of them might stimulate something but found
nothing concrete to work from. Thinking back on the hundreds of other
failed final verses I'd written in the past, I threw the crumpled sheets

back on the floor and tried to remember how long I'd been working on the song. I couldn't recall. I looked up my song journal and, after trawling back to an entry made more than three years before, I came upon the first verse:

March 1992
A rose won't grow if the soil below goes dry.
It withers and droops and dies at the root,
And it's red petals drop like blood that won't stop from a wound,
And then the flower without any power lies ruined.

Below these lines I found a note:

This metaphor for the absence of love formed itself like a tendril
around an old melody I've had for a few years. But where to go with it?
Trying to figure that out has caused me a splitting headache.

I shook my head in disbelief that I'd written the verse so long ago. Skipping through other entries made during the following years, I charted the lyric's snail-paced development, reliving again some of the mental torture I'd put myself through in pursuit of the song's illusive completion:

17 April '92
The countless discarded briars of my rose song have become
my crown of thorns.

25 March '93
The very threads of my reason are coming undone because of a verse.

18 Nov. '94
The rose song has caused me more struggle than any other song
I've written . . .

The phone started ringing. I put the journal to one side and answered it. An unfamiliar female voice came over the line. 'Is this Johnny Duhan? You don't know me, my name's Mary. I've been an admirer of your songs for years. I'm just ringing to let you know that I totally disagree with everything written about you in *The Irish Times* this morning. That's all I wanted to say. Keep up the good work.' Before I had a chance to thank her, she hung up.

I scratched my head. 'I'd better get a copy of this paper and see what all the fuss is about.'

On my way back from our local shop I scanned *The Irish Times* and located my *Don Quixote* title half way down the arts' page as part of a review of three new Irish albums. The piece was written by a music critic I was acquainted with. After attacking the family values and small town mentality of my previous work, several lines from the lyrics from *Don Quixote* were taken out of context and misquoted, and one of the misquotes was attributed to the wrong song. While I was reading the review I recalled a row I'd had with the reviewer at the launch of another of my albums some years before. It started when I half-jokingly taunted the man for being over precious about 'rock history'. I was pretty tipsy at the time, so I couldn't remember details of the argument but it ended with the reviewer glaring at me from the opposite end of the bar at the end of the night.

When I got back to the house I re-read the review and the misquotes really began to irk me. It was obvious that the reviewer had only given my album a cursory listen before sharpening his pen. I phoned a close friend, Paddy Houlahan, for advice on what I should do. After I read the review over the phone, Paddy drew a long breath. 'Sounds pretty nasty alright, but I'd like to read it myself. I'll get a copy of the paper and maybe we can meet up at the Bridge Mills around lunch time and discuss it.'

When I arrived at the basement restaurant a couple of hours later I found Paddy drinking herbal tea by the large oval window overlooking the millstream, with a copy of *The Irish Times* open on the table in front of him. While I was settling into a seat, he glanced at the newspaper and laughed. 'He really has a go at you alright. And I always thought he was okay as a reviewer.'

I glanced at the bright silver zips of Paddy's black leather jacket and smirked. 'That's because you and he are birds of a feather.'

'What do you mean?'

'Rockers who still believe in the dream. *Don Quixote*'s the opposite of that.'

I ordered a coffee from a passing waitress and proceeded to tell Paddy about the row I'd had with the reviewer several years before. Paddy sipped his tea. 'You should never rub journalists up the wrong way; they're prickly creatures.'

'Pricks more like.' I pulled a two page letter from my inside pocket and handed it to Paddy. 'I'm sending this to his editor. Joe Comerford suggested that I write it.'

Paddy put on a pair of reading glasses and read the letter slowly, running his free hand through his grey hair as he read. 'I wouldn't go into such detail about the row, if I were you. Hone it back to the key issue of the misquotes. That was very unprofessional of him. You have him there.'

'What about all the stuff about my character? He obviously has something against the fact that I'm Catholic and sing about family matters.'

'Keep the focus on the misquotes. They show that he didn't give the album a fair listen. The object of the exercise is to get a fairer review.'

When I got home I spent a couple of hours refining the letter, paring it back to just a few lines.

Dear Sir,
In a review of my latest album, *Don Quixote*, in the arts page of
this morning's issue of your newspaper there are no less than three
misquotations of my song-lyrics and one of the misquotes is attributed
to the wrong song. These gross inaccuracies completely distort the
meaning of my work and give a false impression of the overall album.
It's one thing for your reviewer to misuse his forum in your newspaper
to ply a scurrilous vendetta against me over a row we had years ago,
but it's another thing entirely when he uses the lowest form of shoddy
journalistic malpractice to achieve his spiteful aim.
Given the extent of the mistakes, I must ask for a written apology by
the reviewer in next Friday's edition of the newspaper. And I would also
hope that you might consider commissioning a more balanced and
less prejudiced review of my album in the same issue.

While I was reading over the letter a car pulled up outside the house. It was Joan and the kids home from school. Glancing at my watch, I couldn't believe it was so late. I hopped up from my desk and went to the kitchen to start dinner. Moments later, my nine year old daughter Niamh came running into the room ahead of the rest of the gang. 'He hasn't started cooking dinner yet, Mammy!'

Joan arrived shaking her head and smirking. 'We'll have to sack him. This won't do at all.'

A ball came rolling into the kitchen followed by our sons Ronan and Kevin. When they realised that dinner wasn't ready Ronan started carping. 'What are we having anyway. I hope it's not that stupid brown rice again.'

Kevin looked at me. 'Can I have saussies and chips?'

I tapped him on the head. 'I told you before, chips are banned in this house. Why don't you and Ronan go into the living room and do your homework. And you, Niamh, practice your violin upstairs. Dinner won't be ready for at least an hour.'

Ronan kicked the ball into the hall. 'Let's go outside and play, Kev. We'll do our homework later.'

After the kids left the house I gave Joan a detailed explanation for why dinner wasn't ready. I showed her the newspaper review and handed her the letter I'd just finished editing. While she was reading the review, I started preparing dinner, cutting up mushrooms and peppers and opening tins of tomatoes.

When she finished the review, Joan threw the newspaper on the table and shrugged. 'It's just one man's opinion. I wouldn't let it worry you. It's not the first bad review you've had. And you got a great review in *Hot Press*.'

'No no, you don't get it. Read my letter and you'll see what I'm narked about.'

After she read the letter Joan shook her head. 'If I were you I wouldn't send that.'

'Why not? Every word of it is true!'

'I still wouldn't give him the satisfaction of showing how upset you are.'

'What about the misquotes?'

Joan hesitated. 'If he'd given the album a good review would you have been as upset about the few mistakes?'

'Few?! One of the misquotes is taken from the wrong song, for Christ sake!'

Joan glanced at the frying pan. 'I think something's beginning to burn.'

After dinner I helped with the kids' homework then went for my usual evening walk to the Corrib. On the way I automatically found myself trying to come up with an opening line for the final verse of the song I was working on, but nothing came of it. When I reached the river I started thinking about the letter addressed to the editor of *The Irish Times*. A quirky thought came into my head and I started bargaining with God: 'Send me the final verse and I'll tear up the letter and put the whole thing behind me.' Realising that I was trying to bribe the Higher Powers, I lowered my head.

When I got back to the house I helped Joan get the kids to bed, then I got the letter and threw it in the living room fire. Joan watched me from the couch. 'You decided not to send it after all?'

I sat beside her. 'You're right; if it had been a good review I wouldn't have written it.'

Joan put her foot on my lap. 'There's an old film staring Jimmy Stewart starting after the news.'

'Great. I need to lose myself for a while.'

From the rooms above our heads the sound of our kids' talking and laughing came to us. During the news, they began to quieten down.

Halfway through the film I started massaging Joan's leg. She was wearing a denim mini-skirt. Before the end of the film we knocked off the set and lay on the rug in front of the mounting flames.

The following morning, shortly after Joan and the kids left for school, I got my guitar and went to my desk with the beginnings of an idea for a new final verse stirring in my head.

Flame

A rose won't grow if the soil below goes dry,
It withers and droops and dies at the root,
And it's red petals drop like blood that won't stop from a wound,
Then the flower without any power lies ruined.

The heart is the same, the stream in the vein gives it life;
Cut off the flow and it won't go,
For blood is the source of all that force in the beat,
Body and soul need it to roll for heat.

And fire won't glow if wind doesn't blow on the hearth;
The yellow blaze smoulders and fades,
And you're left to poke at the cinders and smoke that remain,
For without air you would despair of the flame.

When my first flame died and you became my love,
Your fresh breath of air made sparks appear,
And my heart like coal lit up and my soul took fire,
While out in your bed you grew blushing red my flower.

THE LODGER

A warming flame heated my blood when You came

All at Once

I was singing my new song *Flame* at the kitchen table when a tapping on the window behind my back interrupted me. I glanced over my shoulder but couldn't see anyone in the dark outside. I resumed singing but almost immediately the tapping recommenced. I turned quickly just in time to see the top of a head ducking below the outer window ledge. I put down the guitar and went over and banged on the glass. As I was expecting, Joan's eighteen-year-old nephew, Davy, raised his head and grinned through the frosty pane. I gave him a sour look and went back to the table and took up singing where I'd left off.

After he deposited his bicycle in the shed Davy came into the kitchen through the back door rubbing his hands and complaining about the cold. 'The boss made me work overtime at the plant again. You don't know how lucky you are, Johnpon, sitting here all day in the heat with nothing to do but sing your songs and count your royalties. Any cheques come today?'

I ignored the taunt and went on singing.

Davy took off his heavy jacket and snooped around the cooker, peeping into pots. He came over and looked over my shoulder at the lyrics I was singing. I stopped in the middle of the second last verse and slammed my copybook shut. 'What do you think you're doing?!'

Davy backed away. 'Just taking a peep at the words. What's it about?'

'Nothing that would interest you.'

Davy grinned. 'It has an awful lot of words. It's nice, though. Very catchy. I'd say you'll earn a good few royalties from that when it comes out.'

I looked at Davy. He was a nice enough young fellow, but there was an almost constant beam of mischief in his eye that irked me to distraction. 'Why don't you go into the living room. Joan's finished the kid's homework. They're all in there watching TV.'

Davy walked back to the cooker and raised a saucepan lid. 'What about din-dins?'

'We've eaten. Joan put yours is in the microwave. Heat it up and eat inside.'

Davy grinned. 'But you're always telling Niamh and Ronan that they can't eat in front of the telly. They might get jealous if they see me getting special treatment.'

I sighed. 'Heat up the food and get the fuck out of here, fast! I have a recording session coming up and I have to practice these songs.'

Davy grinned. 'Now now, Johnpon; I thought cursing was banned in this house.'

I gritted my teeth and moved on to another song.

With Davy out of the way I worked on until twenty-to-nine. Then I put my guitar away and went to get Kevin to put him to bed. The first thing I noticed on entering the living room was that Davy was sitting in my armchair in front of the TV with the remote control clasped firmly in his hand. At the far side of the open fire, Joan was reading a magazine. Our three kids were sprawled out on the settee glued to the box. I tapped Kevin on the head and told him that it was time for bed. He made his usual groan of protest but got to his feet straight away. Davy watched him sympathetically, then turned to me. 'Why don't you let poor Kev stay up for another few minutes. There's a great bit coming up soon. I've seen this episode already on Sky.'

I glared at Davy. 'How many times have I told you not to interfere in things that don't concern you!'

Davy muttered a curse under his breath.

I took a step towards him. 'What did you say?!'

'Nothing, nothing.'

Joan looked up from her magazine. 'He's just concerned for Kevin, that's all. He didn't mean anything by it.'

I stared at Joan. For three months she'd been defending her nephew every time I tried to correct him. I drew a deep breath and started to leave the room. Before closing the door I turned back and stared at Davy. 'When I come back I want you out of my chair. I'm watching the news and there's a political programme on after it that I want to see also.'

Davy looked at Ronan and Niamh, then glanced at me. 'We were planing to watch a Bond film on BBC1, weren't we lads?'

'Yeah.'

'Please Dad, it's supposed to be one of the best.'

'Tough!'

I closed the door and followed my seven year old upstairs. After he brushed his teeth and got into bed I read him *The Good Samaritan* from *The Children's Bible*, then tested his memory by asking who was the goodie in the story. Kevin gave me a crooked smile. 'The Samaritan, daw.'

I kissed his forehead. 'Good boy. Now off to sleep. The others will be up soon.'

As I was leaving Kevin called to me: 'Dad, how come you don't like Davy?'

I stood by the door. 'I do like him. He just annoys me sometimes, that's all.'

'Is that why you're always giving out to him?'

'Am I always giving out to him?'

Kevin smiled. 'You know you are.'

I shrugged. 'I guess I'll have to try and be nicer to him, won't I?'

Kevin nodded. 'Like the Good Samaritan.'

I laughed. 'Yeah, like the Good Samaritan. Now, go to sleep.'

Downstairs I went to the kitchen to make some tea. Joan was there, by the microwave with a tin of hot chocolate open on the counter before her. I plugged in the kettle and leaned to get a tea bag. 'Making Davy hot chocolate again, are we?'

Joan frowned. 'What of it?'

'Nothing, nothing. If you want to act as his personal maid that's fine with me. How long more's he staying? He's beginning to grind me down.'

'Poor ladeen, he doesn't mean it. He's just a jokey kind of boy, that's all.'

'Jokey? Infuriating more like.'

The microwave bell rang. Joan retrieved the hot milk and scooped three spoons of chocolate powder into a cup and stirred it, then left the kitchen. I followed her a few moments later with my mug of steaming tea.

Re-entering the living room I was relieved to find that my chair was vacant and that the TV channel had been switched to the Nine O'Clock News. Ronan and Niamh gave me stony looks from the settee but kept their mouths shut. Sitting between them, Davy glanced at the remote control in his hand and grinned. I bit my tongue, sipped my tea and turned my attention to the TV.

Halfway through the news Ronan groaned loudly in the middle of an agricultural item on milk quotas and begged me to switch over to the Bond film. Niamh added her voice to the plea. I sighed: 'Okay, okay. You can watch it till ten o'clock, then I'm switching back to *Today Tonight*. It'll be your bedtime then anyway.'

Davy zapped the remote control and Sean Connery appeared on the screen skiing down a snowy mountain slope with a half dozen military skiers in white boiler suits coming after him with rattling machine guns. Ronan laughed. 'This is more like it!'

At ten o'clock I asked Davy to change channels and told Ronan and Niamh that it was time for them to go to bed. Niamh reluctantly started rising from the settee but Ronan gave me a defiant look. 'I can't see why I have to go at the same time as her; I'm more than a year older than she is. Can I stay up for just ten more minutes, please dad?'

'No.'

'Till this bit's over then?'

'No I said.'

'I just want to see does Bond kill this guy.'

'Don't make me go over to you, Ronan!'

'Aw Dad, just one more minute.'

I let a roar at Ronan, telling him to get upstairs immediately. Ronan glanced at Davy. Davy smirked. The Bond film was still blaring away at high volume. I leaned down and tried to grab the remote control from Davy but he pulled away and started laughing. I went to the TV and switched off the set manually. Davy grinned. I glanced at Joan. 'If you don't get that bastard out of my hair I swear I'll kill him!'

Joan stood up, 'Stop grinning, David. And you two, get up to bed this instant and do what your father tells you!'

Ronan and Niamh left the room and went upstairs. I followed them a few moments later to make sure they were in bed. After I turned out their lights I decided to go to bed myself rather than return down stairs and risk losing my temper with Davy again. Twenty minutes after I got under the covers Joan arrived up and got in beside me, apologising for her nephew's behaviour. 'I had a word with him and he promised he won't do anything like that again.'

I grunted and turned on my pillow and nodded off.

At four-thirty I woke and couldn't go back to sleep, thinking about the turmoil of the night before. I recalled some of the harsh words I'd said about Davy and felt guilty. I knew that a lot of his clowning stemmed from insecurities he carried from his past. I'd been making allowances for this ever since he'd come to live with us, but somehow I just couldn't overcome the irritation I felt every time I came in contact with him.

I turned on my pillow and a line from *The Imitation of Christ* came into my head: 'To be able to live at peace with obstinate and undisciplined people is a great grace.'

I got out of bed and sat on a hard-backed chair, trying to clear my thoughts for a period of contemplation. It was still pitch dark and bitterly cold. After three or four minutes of shivering I got back into bed and tried to contemplate in a semi-prone position propped up on my pillows. Two or three minutes into the exercise I started nodding off. I shook myself awake and got back out on the chair. Hugging my body for warmth, I started an *Our Father*. Halfway through the prayer the words began to merge into a single groan that went on and on like the drone of an uilleann pipe. I began to sway backward and forward in time with the slow rhythm in my head. The icy air pressed hard against my face and shoulders. I shook and shivered, feeling utterly miserable from head to toe. The intonation of the drone changed into the single syllable Godddddddd. For five or six minutes I bombarded the heavens with this long drawn-out moan. Just as I was beginning to grow tired I heard a loud booming noise like thunder in my head. In an instant everything went silent and still. The silence and stillness spread through my mind and body in warm waves. A tremendous sense of calm came over me. My eyes were closed but somehow I felt bathed in bright light. The warm sensation radiating through my mind and body began to carry me away into a state of complete tranquility. How long I remained like this, I have no idea, but when I came back to myself there was light filtering through a gap in the curtains. It was still quite dark but I could make out Joan's sleeping body heaving gently to the slow rhythm of her even breathing in the bed. For a moment I thought of waking her to tell her of the experience I'd just had, but I realised that it would be impossible to describe what I'd been through.

Sounds of movement downstairs came to me. It was just after eight by the clock on the chest of drawers at Joan's side of the bed. I dressed and went down to the kitchen. Davy was at the table eating cereal. When he spotted me, his head jerked. 'Johnpon! You're late this morning! Not like you.'

I rubbed my eyes. 'How did you get the night?'

Davy looked at me, slightly askance. 'I always sleep like a baby.'

I smiled. 'Sign of a pure conscience, they say. Did Joan make the sandwiches for your lunch before she went to bed?'

'They're in my *póca*.' Davy tapped a bulge in his jacket pocket and gaped at me. 'Are you alright?'

'Never better.' I filled a bowl of cereal and ate it standing by the window, looking out at a pink skyline. 'It's going to be another fine day by the looks of it.'

Davy swallowed a last spoon of cornflakes and got to his feet. 'Very cold, though. Look at the ice on the glass. I'll have to be careful on me bike.'

I looked at the frosty window. Sunlight was glittering in crystal angular formations in the four corners of the pane. The pink, blue and silver reflections held my attention so keenly I didn't notice Davy leaving the room till he passed the window outside on his way to get his bike in the shed. As well as his heavy jacket, he was wearing a pair of knitted gloves. While he was passing back to the front of the house he smiled through the window. Noticing a strain in his expression that I hadn't noticed before, I waved at him, thinking of the mundane dead-end job he was heading to in the factory. A deep sense of sympathy welled up inside me. I recalled some of the harsh things I'd said to him the night before and felt a sharp pang of regret. Tears welled up in my eyes. The back door opened and Davy's grinning face appeared around the jam.

'Any chance of borrowing your furry hat with the ear muffs, Johnpon?'

I laughed and shook my head. 'Not a chance in hell. But I have a nice woolly cap you can have. Wait here and I'll get it for you.

NASHVILLE

In the night I had a dream,
it felt so right I thought it real

After the Dream

After the anticlimax of our poorly attended showcase at the Bluebird Café the night before and the run of meetings, parties and other engagements that preceded it, I was longing for an evening alone with *St Teresa of Avila* rather than another social outing, so when reception rang and told me that Ryan O'Grady, manager of a local radio station, was waiting for me in the lobby, I sighed, took a deep breath and went to meet him.

Bespectacled and dressed in a white shirt and tie (no jacket), Ryan greeted me with a limp handshake and asked me how I'd been getting on. 'Sell any songs on Music Row?'

I smiled. 'No, but I got talking to someone at Emmylou Harris's manager's place who gave me a code number to print on a CD package for dropping off at their office, which will get full attention from management, if not the lady herself.'

Ryan smiled. 'Not bad for a guy on a five-day visit to town. My car's just outside.'

As we drove up Broadway and on to 14th Avenue North, Ryan brought up the subject of the failed gig I'd played the evening before with Paul Brady, Donagh Long and Celine Carroll. 'Talking about Emmylou, I found out at the station this morning that the reason for the low attendance at your Bluebird show was that Ms Harris gave an impromptu free gig in Cumberland Park last evening, down by the river. A huge crowd showed up. I'm sure a few of them would have gone to see you otherwise.'

'Just our luck.'

Ryan pulled up at a set of red traffic lights. 'Luck's what Nashville's all about. Sometimes things just go against you and there ain't a darn thing you can do about it, 'cept wait till the lights turn green. There are literally thousands of songwriters scouting Nashville at any given time, all aiming for the same prize.'

I looked at Ryan. 'But how many of them have real talent?'

The lights turned green. Ryan drove on. 'Quite a few, I should think.'

I rubbed my neck. 'I wouldn't be so sure about that. I remember a documentary I saw on a Nashville songwriter who spent most of the programme on a barstool bemoaning the fact that he had never got a break in five years of living here. Then very subtly the producer inserted a brief interview with Kris Kristofferson who offered the opinion that most songwriters of genuine worth rise to the top, if they're dedicated enough and don't get swamped in the bottle. I haven't had a lot of commercial success myself, but I believe that's true.'

Ryan gave me a bemused smile. 'I read your CV in the Bluebird. Your songs have been covered by lots of top artists. What about *The Voyage*? Wasn't that on a million seller album here in the States not so long ago. Friends of ours had the song played recently for their 25th wedding anniversary and they were telling us that the song's become hugely popular at such celebrations all over the States.'

'So I believe.'

The driver of a passing truck threw Ryan a sour look for being in the wrong lane, but Ryan ignored him and turned to me. 'If you don't mind me asking, who's got the publishing rights on *The Voyage*?'

I hesitated, wondering if this was the reason for the dinner invite. 'I retain the full copyright to all my songs and lease them to anyone who wants to cover them.'

Ryan laughed. 'Wise as well as diligent.'

We took a slip road into a leafy neighbourhood of big houses with wide wooden verandas and eventually arrived at a detached bungalow with a large garden. Even before we got out of the car the strident sound of a house-alarm could be heard coming from a neighbouring property. As we entered the house Ryan cursed. 'Looks like we're going to have to put up with that damn noise for another night. I thought one of the neighbours might have complained to the authorities.'

Inside the house the alarm wasn't so loud but it could still be heard whining in the background like a trapped animal. Ryan led me into a large living room and went straight to a hi-fi system. 'I'll put on some music and it'll block out the alarm. My wife'll be home soon. She works in an attorney's office in town. She'll rustle us up some fried chicken.

We intended a barbecue but with that racket going on out there, that's out of the question now. Take a seat and I'll get us a couple of beers.'

A country song started playing with a brash spiritual message that was hammered home with the first line of the chorus: "It's in God's hands now; He's got all the answers . . ."

Ryan returned with two cans and handed me one. 'There's a huge PR campaign behind this single right now. It's playlisted all over the southern states. This copy only came in to the station this afternoon.'

We sat listening to the song in silence, Ryan tapping his foot on the wooden floor. When the track came to an end Ryan looked to me for a response. I sipped my beer and cleared my throat. 'It's a big sound.'

Ryan gave me a puzzled look and replaced the single with an Emmylou Harris album, probably for my benefit because of the inroads I'd made at her manager's office. 'A lotta new blood has taken over this town since Emmylou's heyday but she's still one of the queens of country, though Reba McEntire's way outpacing her and Dolly in the charts these days.'

I took a swig of beer. 'I was down at Reba's building the other day – that massive place on Music Row with the helicopter pad on the roof. I managed to get talking to one of her execs who informed me that Reba has her own *stable* of songwriters and never accepts unsolicited material, even when it comes in the form of an album gift.'

Ryan nodded. 'That's understandable. Down at the station I hear stories all the time about copyright lawsuits.'

Knowing little or nothing about the radio station that Ryan worked for, I broached the subject. 'How long've you been working in radio?'

Ryan took a swig of beer and rubbed his jaw. 'Twelve or thirteen years, but it feels like twenty. It's not one of the top stations but the pressure's still intense. I'm thinking of branching into publishing. I've made a lotta contacts over the years. I might be able to help you in some way.'

I waited for Ryan to elaborate but he took a swig of beer and changed the subject. 'How's Ralph Murphy from ASCAP treating you guys – open any doors for any of you yet?'

I hesitated. 'He's been generous with his time, driving us around and introducing us to people in the business. He organised some songwriting collaborations between a few Nashville based songwriters and members of our team. I didn't go myself, as I'm not into collaboration.'

'Why not?'

'I couldn't see anything real coming out of a couple of hours spent in an office with a stranger. I explained to Ralph that a few of the songs on my latest album took me years to write. I gave him a copy. He was puzzled that there're no choruses in most of the songs. He asked me to name one hit record that didn't have a catchy chorus in either country or pop over the past twenty years. Off the top of my head, I gave him two – *Ode to Billy Joe* and *The Boxer*. It stumped him, but he claimed that the repeat line of the ode – 'the day that Billy Joe McAllister jumped off the Tallahatchie Bridge', and the 'Li li li' section of *The Boxer* – could be construed as choruses. Something I begged to disagree with.'

Ryan scratched his neck. 'I think I'd weigh in behind Ralph on that one. Catchy choruses are the hallmark of modern country.'

'I'm not disputing that. My point was that there's exceptions to every rule. Quite a lot of great folk songs don't have choruses. And in opera most of the top arias don't have choruses. Choruses in opera are separate entities.'

Ryan shook his empty can and got to his feet. 'You have me there, buddie. I know nothin' about opera. You want another beer?'

Soon after Ryan came back with the cans his wife arrived laden with grocery bags. She came into the living room glaring at her husband. 'I thought you were going to do something about that alarm!'

Ryan stood up, flummoxed. 'What do you mean?'

His wife shook her head. 'Call the authorities, like I asked you to do at breakfast.'

Ryan sighed heavily. 'I thought we agreed that that would be a bad idea. You know how much they charge for coming out. I didn't want to be the one to impose that on Mike and Connie. I was hoping one of the other neighbours might do it.'

'Well they haven't, and now we're going to have to put up with it for another night.'

Ryan glanced at me and turned back to his wife, smiling. 'Can we deal with this later, honey. This is Johnny Duhan, composer of *The Voyage*. This is May, my bundle of joy.'

May gave her husband a sour look and nodded in my direction, glancing down at the bags in her arms to indicate that she didn't have a free hand for shaking. I stood up and tried to smile. May went off to the kitchen and returned a few minutes later more composed, asking me if I liked fried chicken. 'We were going to cook and eat outside, but it'll have to be indoors now.' She threw her husband a crooked look and left us.

Ryan gulped back his beer fairly fast and went to the kitchen to get another couple of cans. He returned moments later with just one can, which he handed to me explaining that his wife had reminded him that he had to drive me back to the hotel after the meal. A few minutes later the lady of the house came and announced that dinner was ready.

For such a large house, the dining room turned out to be fairly cramped. The table was so small the three of us were in one another's faces from the moment we sat down. At one end, Ryan was able to remain seated while filling our glasses with Chardonnay. When it came to pouring some for himself, May kept a sharp eye on him till he stopped well before his glass was half full.

During the main course of fried chicken, mashed potatoes and corn cakes, May asked me for my impressions of Nashville. 'I know you've only been here a few days but what do you make of us Tennesseans?'

I hesitated. 'Most of the people I've met in the music business seem friendly enough, but they're very protective of their turf. People are like that everywhere, but it somehow seems more pronounced here. But maybe that's just the circles I've been moving in.'

May poured me a second glass of Chardonnay. 'No no, I think you're right. I hate going to showbiz gatherings in town. Whenever Ryan drags me along to an event I generally come away with a bad impression of the people I meet.'

I smiled. 'There was one nice lady I met at a luncheon in the CMA Building, a big exec I think she was. I can't remember her name . . .'

May interrupted. 'You should make it your business to remember people's names. Bad memory is nothing but laziness.'

I smiled at May's frankness and went on with my story. 'Anyway, lots of top executives from the country music industry were at this lunch, including someone from Garth Brooks' management. The main topic of conversation was the phenomenal success that the latest crop of country singers are enjoying worldwide. In the middle of this self-congratulatory spiel by the Nashville contingent this lady sitting opposite me asked for my impressions of Nashville. I told her of a visit I'd paid to a Hank Williams' museum and asked her what Hank would make of modern developments in country music. The woman put down her knife and fork and started talking about Hank in glowing terms, as though he were a saint. She admitted that his record sales paled in comparison to some of the top sellers now, but she questioned whether the integrity that Hank had brought to country still existed in Nashville. This sparked off a heated debate on whether contemporary country music had sold its soul over recent years. Some at the table thought so, others made the point that some of the better country songwriters of our time were far more sophisticated in their writing approach than anything that had been produced in Hank's day. I agreed with this assessment, naming a string of fine modern country songwriters like Guy Clark, Towns Van Zandt, and even Bob McDill, who operates the more commercial end of the market.'

May smiled. 'You know your country, Johnny.'

During dessert I studied a framed picture on the wall behind May's back that had grabbed my attention when I first sat down. It was a portrait of a frail young woman sitting awkwardly in a brown field, leaning on her hands and looking forlornly towards a wooden house on the horizon. 'I really like that picture. Is it an original?'

Ryan glanced at the painting and nodded. 'Yeah, I got it in a gallery in New York during a visit there to see our daughter when she was in college years ago.'

May gave her husband a crooked look. 'That's a darn lie!' She turned to me. 'Don't mind him; that's just a print of a famous painting by Andrew Wyeth called *Christina's World*. We got it in New York alright, but it cost less than forty dollars, with the frame.'

While Ryan squirmed in his chair, I looked back at the picture. 'There's something very mysterious about it. I really like it.'

Ryan gave a false laugh and lowered his eyes. 'I'm mixing it up with another painting we got upstairs.'

May gave her husband a doubtful look and shook her head, then she glanced back at the print. 'The model for the portrait was said to be a neighbour of the Wyeths. The reason she's sitting kind of awkward is that she was a cripple.'

I looked at the woman in the print. 'I see that now, the way she's slumped. It's a powerful image, the way she's staring at the house. My mother's name was Christian, and she had dark hair just like her.'

After dinner we sat chatting for a while about Ireland. Noticing me stifling a yawn, May suggested that I might be in need of an early night. I didn't contradict her. After thanking her and Ryan for the meal, Ryan went off and got his car keys. May surprisingly gave me a kiss on the cheek while saying goodbye.

During the journey back to Nashville, Ryan started telling me again about the many musical contacts he'd made at the radio station over the years, but I was too tired to take in all he was saying. When we reached the hotel, he insisted on accompanying me into the lobby, though I told him there was no need. In the reception area I thanked him again for the meal and told him that I'd enjoyed his wife's company. He looked at me like he didn't believe me and handed me a card with his contact details. 'I really meant it when I said I can help you get your songs placed with some big selling acts, so stay in touch.'

'Sure.'

I said a quick goodbye and went to get my key at reception.

In my room I kicked off my shoes and lay on my bed. As it was just after ten, I decided to do a bit of reading before lights out. I went to my guitar bag to get Teresa of Avila's autobiography from the pouch. Though it was the only book I'd brought along on the trip I hadn't had a chance to read it since dipping into it during the flight over from Dublin five days earlier. I unzipped the pocket but there was no book in the pouch. I rummaged in my clothes bag, but it wasn't there either. I cursed, realising that I must have left it on the plane.

THE VINNIES

The peace we gain when we forget ourselves
in thoughts of others

In Thoughts of Others

As we turned into the small council estate Mary changed down to first gear on account of the icy conditions. A group of children skating on a patch of polished ice in the middle of the road moved aside to let us pass. Recognising Mary's car, several of the kids followed us to the first house on our list, Mrs Brady's. While we were taking bags of toys and books from the boot, one of the young onlookers – the daughter of another of our clients – nudged one of her friends. 'The Vinnies have stuff for us too. I'm going home to tell my Da.'

Mrs Brady's scrap of front garden, normally an eyesore of weeds and rubble, was glittering under a blanket of sunlit hoarfrost. As usual, Mrs Brady took ages to answer her front door. Surrounded by a brood of kids with tight crew cuts and bulging eyes, she rubbed her hands down the front of her soiled green cardigan and stared at us with a blank expression. 'I'm just washing out a few socks.' She glanced at her kids. 'You'd never be finished slaving for this lot.'

Mary bent down and touched the youngest boy's nose, glancing at his mother. 'How come you got them such tight haircuts in such cold weather?'

Mrs Brady looked away. 'On account of the scratchies; they've come back again. I had to get stuff at the chemist to rub all over them. It burned their skin. I had to put it on as well. And I had to wash out all the sheets. It's a right nuisance, so it is.'

Mary handed her a bag of toys and a white envelope. 'We've marked down the age group on the parcels, and there's a couple of dolls for the younger ones. This year we're giving food vouchers instead of food. That way you can get what you like at the supermarket. There's seventy pounds worth in the envelope, but, remember, that's for two weeks.' She glanced at me. 'We have some books for the kids as well.'

I handed a carrier bag to Mrs Brady's eldest daughter, glancing at Mrs Brady. 'I hope you're still putting on the light for them at night so that they can read? If they get into the habit of reading, it will help them at school. It's not good for them to be always in the dark anyway.'

Mrs Brady's face grew stiff. 'They're never completely in the dark; we always keep the telly on.'

Mary frowned. 'Having the telly on constantly isn't good for them either, Mrs Brady. I thought you agreed with that?'

Mrs Brady took a step back into the hall. 'The bulbs keep blowing out and they're very expensive to buy. My husband's going to get a set of Christmas lights and a Christmas tree today up at Dunnes.'

I glanced at Mary then turned to Mrs Brady. 'You're husband's home, is he?'

Mrs Brady nodded. 'He got out yesterday but he has to go back for two months after Christmas. Then they'll be lettin' him out for good behaviour, in a few months' time.' She took a step back into her hallway and began to close the door. 'Thank's very much for everything.'

'Happy Christmas, Mrs Brady.'

As we made our way down the slippery path a robin scrutinised us from the frosty lid of a dustbin lying in the dazzling grass. In the white setting, its red breast glowed like an ember. Spotting me staring at it, the bird darted upwards in a sequence of rhythmic flight manoeuvres and perched on a bush in a neighbouring garden.

Out on the street the neighbourhood kids were sliding on the ice, white plumes of frosty breath billowing from their mouths.

We got back into the car and Mary started the engine. I took a couple of envelopes from a pile on the dashboard and looked at the names. 'Lily's next, then the Ferrets.'

Mary drove round the corner and parked beside a lamp-post scrawled with graffiti. Before getting out of the car, she took a brolly from the back seat. 'Just in case that wild mongrel's on the prowl near Lily's.'

I took a bag of toys from the boot and suggested doing separate runs, to save time. 'As you're afraid of the dog, I'll call on Lily and you can do the Ferrets.'

Mary grinned and took the bag of toys from me. 'No thanks, I'll take my chances at Lily's. You get on better with Mr Ferret.'

The Ferret's doorbell was broken so I rattled the letterbox. Mr Ferret, a man of indeterminate age, opened the door almost immediately and squinted through the thick lens of his glasses. As usual, he had a pained expression on his pinched, grey face. 'Good day, sir.' He glanced up at the clear blue sky. 'Isn't it lovely? If only it wasn't so cold. I suffer from chilblains, and the cold also affects my kidneys. I was up half the night last night, going to the lav. My chest pain has cleared up, though, thank God. Dr Burke says it was only a minor infection. He gave me a prescription and the pills worked wonders. I have to go back to him again next Thursday for a more thorough check-up. He's worried about my heart. I might have to go to the hospital for an x-ray, he says. Might have to get stents in. He'll know next week when he examines me.'

'And how is Mrs Ferret? She's home from hospital, I believe?'

Mr Ferret groaned. 'She is, but I think they might have let her out too soon. A fallen womb, she had. And she still has those awful back pains. She didn't get a wink of sleep either last night. I think we're going to have to get her one of those orthopaedic beds. They're very expensive, but the social services people said they might help us out on account of us being on disability.'

In the narrow hallway behind Mr Ferret I spotted Mrs Ferret emerging from a room. She came towards us, stooped and groaning, dressed in a pink padded nightgown. Her husband moved to one side to let her through. 'Good day, sir. 'Aren't you very good calling on us on such a cold morning. And you're all alone, I see?'

'Mary's at another house. We have a lot of calls, so we're operating separately. Glad to see you're out of hospital for the Christmas.'

Mrs Ferret smiled but then pulled a long face. 'If only my ingrown toenail would give me a bit of peace. Mrs O'Gorman, my chiropodist, says I have one of the most acute conditions she's ever seen. I hardly slept last night because of it.'

Mr Ferret squinted at his wife. 'I thought it was your back that kept you awake?'

Mrs Ferret sighed. 'My back was at me too, but my toe was worse, so it was.'

I held back a smile and handed Mr Ferret the white envelope. 'There's seventy pounds in vouchers there. That's what we're giving in lieu of the hamper this year. We've also arranged for the extra bag of coal you asked for. It should be delivered on Monday morning.' I took a step away from the door. 'I'd better get a move on. We have a good few calls to make. Good day to you both. And happy Christmas.'

When I got back to the car I found Mary going through the remaining envelopes. 'Lily's place is looking lovely; the living room's decorated with tinsel and ivy, and she has a small Christmas tree with coloured lights. She's managed to get a temporary job in a supermarket for the Christmas. The remedial place in Oranmore is looking after Sheila and her brother's looking after the other kids. She still hasn't heard a word from her husband since he ran off with that young one a few months back, but she seems to be coping better. It's probably the job that's got her out of herself. I have great admiration for her. She's a great woman.'

'Who's next on the list?'

Mary held up two envelopes. 'Mrs Barrett and Martin. I think the two of us should call on Martin, and we may as well do the Barretts together as they're right beside him.'

Martin greeted us with his usual smile, taking a thin roll-up cigarette from his mouth. Beside him, his nine-year-old daughter, Kathleen – the girl who had run home from the street when she spotted us taking the bags of toys from the boot – was sucking her thumb, staring at the bag in Mary's hands. Martin invited us into the house but we declined, explaining that we had too many other calls to make. I gave him the envelope and explained its contents while Mary handed the bag of toys to Kathleen, warning her that she wasn't to open it till Christmas morning. Kathleen disappeared back into the house with her cache of toys. Martin thanked us and took a long pull from his cigarette, glancing across the street towards a house where his recently absconded wife was now living with another man. 'She came over last night to give Kathleen money for clothes for Christmas. I wasn't going to let her in, but then I thought it wouldn't be fair on Kathleen.' He coughed. 'She told me they'll be moving out of the estate soon. Your man, it seems, has a managerial job lined up in a bar on the other side of town. They're planning to rent a house in an uppity estate near Merlin. She always wanted to live in a nice neighbourhood. She hates living here.'

Mary shook her head. 'What about Kathleen? Is she going to take her with her?'

Martin lowered his eyes. 'Weekends. She says your man would feel awkward with her around on a permanent basis.' He took a hard drag from his cigarette and his face grew tense. 'I ran into him the other day up at the shop. The bastard said hello to me. Would you believe it? I felt like lashing into him.'

Mary touched Martin's arm. 'What ever you do, don't resort to violence; it'll do you no good. Think of Kathleen. She's your main concern now.'

Martin's eyes grew moist. 'I found her crying in bed last night. But she's grand again today. I put up the Christmas tree this morning and that took her mind off things.' He drew a wheezy breath and sighed.

'We're just going to have to get used to the fact that her mother won't be coming home.' He paused. 'I didn't tell you, he has her pregnant.'

Mary sighed and touched Martin's arm.

Martin started sobbing.

I turned away. Mary took a step back from the door. 'We'll say a prayer for you, Martin. Try and keep your chin up, for Kathleen's sake.'

Martin pulled himself together and wiped his eyes with the back of his hand. 'Don't worry, I'm not going to let myself go under.'

Mary touched his arm again. 'That's the spirit! We'll see you after the New Year.'

I was about to wish him a happy Christmas but bit my tongue.

Walking away, I glanced towards the house where Martin's wife was now living. 'Jesus, I don't know how I'd handle a situation like that. It's really tough on him, isn't it?'

Mary sighed. 'It's tougher on Kathleen. I can't understand how a mother could abandon a child. A father, maybe, but a mother! It's not natural. But we're not supposed to judge.'

We came to the next house. Mr Barrett answered the front door in his vest. After wishing us a happy Christmas he went upstairs. A few moments later Mrs Barrett arrived down looking distracted. 'Me youngest, Finbar, has the flu. We've all had it but his dose is worst of all, vomiting and diarrhoea. The poor lad's drained to nothing. But, please God, he'll be better be Christmas.'

Mary handed her a large bag of toys. 'You should have enough there for the seven of them.'

Mrs Barrett sniggered. 'It's only six now, Mam. Me eldest, Sheila, got married a few months back. Didn't ye give me the extra bit of help at the time?'

Mary smiled. 'I have a memory like a sieve. Sheila is the tall girl who looks like yourself? I didn't think she was old enough to marry?'

'She'll be seventeen in March.'

Mary pointed to the bag of toys in Mrs Barrett's hand. 'You can give the extra toy to one of your other daughters.'

'Thanks very much. I'll include you in our rosary tonight. You've been very good to us. Happy Christmas.'

After four other solo runs the envelopes and toys were all distributed. On our way back to the car we decided to call on a client who was no longer on our books, just to wish her and her kids a happy Christmas.

Though I gave the letterbox a good rattle, there was a long delay before the door opened. A young woman with sunken eyes and hollow cheeks appeared before us, totally transformed from the last time we'd visited her. For a moment she didn't know who we were, then a flicker of recognition came into her dull eyes. 'I'm just out of bed.' She glanced at a passer-by and started fumbling with the buttons of her disheveled blouse. 'Come in, come in.'

Though we hadn't intended going into the house, we followed her to the living room, which was freezing cold. Two of her boys were hugging themselves beneath a blanket on a grubby settee watching TV. There was no fire in the grate and not a sign of a Christmas decoration anywhere. Mary glanced at the soiled carpet and shook her head. 'Jesus, Helen, what's going on? This isn't at all like you. I thought things were going well for you?'

Helen glanced at the two boys. 'Conor, Jimmy, turn off the telly and go upstairs. I want to talk to these people. Bring the blanket with you and check and see are Mary and Paul okay. Make sure Mary's covered up well. And no fighting, hear!'

The two boys reluctantly got up from the settee and left the room, complaining about the interruption. Once they were out of earshot their mother apologised for the mess, lowering her gaze to avoid eye contact. 'I've been meaning to tidy the place up but I just can't seem to get round to it. Everything's been piling up on me for the past few weeks.'

I looked at the dark shadows under her eyes. 'You're not back taking stuff, are you?'

She shrugged. 'A bit of hash, when I can afford it, which isn't often.'

I noted her sunken cheeks. 'Are you sure you're not on anything stronger? You look fairly caved in.'

She gave me a sour look and folded her arms. 'I'm positive. Jack was doing coke alright, but he's gone now, the bastard. I kicked him out. I caught him stealing the children's allowance money from my bag. That was it! I've put up with enough from him. It was bad enough when he was drinking but the coke made him devious and aggressive. I don't need that kind of agro in my life. I'm fucked up enough as it is.' She clenched her teeth. 'Mick, my last partner, often gave me a beating after a feed of drink but he never stooped so low as to steal the kids' money.'

I glanced towards the empty grate. 'It's freezing in here. Have you no coal?'

Helen shook her head and lowered her eyes. 'I was doing fine for a while but Jack really messed my head up. He's living with another one now in Shantalla. She's only seventeen or eighteen, the poor bitch.'

A child started roaring upstairs. Mary and I moved towards the door. As we backed into the narrow hallway a high-pitched voice came down the stairs: 'Are the Vinnies gone yet, Mammy? You'd better come up. Conor's murdering Tommy.'

Helen let a roar: 'If I go up to you, Conor, I'll put you in hospital.'

At the front door Mary touched Helen's arm. 'We don't have any vouchers with us but we'll contact our president, Nonie, and she'll get you some before the day is out. We'll also get you some decorations and toys.'

Helen smiled. 'I have a few decorations myself; I just didn't have the heart to put them up.'

I stepped outside. 'We'll get you some coal delivered, straight away.'

Mary smiled at Helen. 'Try and cheer up for the children's sake. And don't be worrying, we'll help you tackle the bigger problems after the New Year.'

Helen started crying. 'I'm sorry about this, I really am. After all the help you gave me in the past I couldn't get up the courage to go to you again.'

The roaring upstairs intensified. I backed away from the door. 'You'd better go up to them or they'll kill one another. Happy Christmas.'

On stormy nights on muddy route to visitations –
rain-soaked and wind-lashed –
I've often wondered why we do it.
At worst we're duped by those we help,
at best we do them little good. But there's also the almost selfish reason
that informs the heart even in the hardest weather
of the peace we gain when we forget ourselves
in thoughts of others.

JERRY & GERRY

A man was shot down in cold blood,
out in the street, love, when you appeared

When You Appeared

Ken and I arrived in Dingle at five in the evening, a few hours before our publisher's anniversary concert was due to begin. The driver who had been sent to pick us up at the bus depot in Tralee an hour earlier dropped us at Heatons' Guest House on the seafront, arranging to collect us again half an hour later for a dinner appointment at our publisher's house a few miles out of town. As time was pushing on, Ken and I were eager to get to our rooms to tidy up but the owner of the guesthouse detained us when she realised who I was.

'Johnny Duhan! I've been looking forward to meeting you all week. I'm an old friend of your sister, Joan, from Limerick. We worked together in a hairdressing salon in Cecil Street as teenagers. I used to call to your house regularly. Nuala McCabe, remember?'

I studied her face. 'McCabe? The name's familiar.'

'It's my maiden name.'

I shook my head. 'I have a poor memory, I'm afraid.'

'It was a long time ago. I think your sister Patti's husband knew my brother, Jerry.'

From the Limerick association, I immediately connected her brother's name to a guard who had been shot dead by the IRA some time before in a bank stakeout. I looked into the woman's face and knew by her expression that she was the murdered man's sister. Stuck for words, I lowered my eyes to let her know I knew who she was. A newspaper photograph I'd seen of her brother at the time of his murder came into my head – the image of a man in the prime of life with a healthy smile on his face. At the time of seeing it I remembered feeling sickened that anyone should be gunned down so mercilessly, leaving a family without a husband and father.

I glanced at Ken. He looked away.

Nuala went behind a desk and came back with two keys. 'Your rooms are just through this door on the left. Only one of them has a view of the sea, I'm afraid, so it's only fair that I let you pick the keys without telling you which it is.' She smiled at Ken. 'You must be Ken Bruen, the crime writer? I read about you in the paper. Are you expecting a big crowd tonight?'

Ken glanced at me. 'This fella's songs are very popular and with Gerry Adams topping the bill I'm sure it will be well attended. What I'm not so sure about is how big crime fiction is in The Kingdom. Are you going yourself?'

Nuala lowered her eyes. 'My husband and I rarely have time for any kind of social life running this place .'

We came to a room and Nuala offered us a pick of the keys. Though Ken allowed me first choice he ended up with the sea view. Nuala pointed to another door down the hall. 'I'll put you in there Johnny, it's one of our most comfortable rooms. Breakfast's from nine till eleven on Sunday mornings. We might get a chance to have a chat then. I'll call you when the car comes to pick you up.'

In the room I sat on the edge of the bed thinking about Nuala and her brother. I recalled a debate I'd heard on the radio some weeks before in which a leading Sinn Féin politician defended the right of Jerry McCabe's murderers to be released from prison under the terms of the Good Friday Agreement. Though he put forward a persuasive argument – stating that similar hard cases had been met from the Loyalist side where a number of their long-term prisoners had come in for early release – I remembered being swayed against his position by a police spokesman who reminded the listeners that the bank robbery and murder had taken place in our free state and not in any "occupied zone". He also reminded us that Sinn Féin originally denied that the IRA had anything to do with the murder.

Instead of having a shower I got out my guitar and started to run over a song I'd originally planned to include in my programme but changed my mind because I thought the lyric too sensitive for the occasion:

All the stars were shining, the moon was climbing,
    when you appeared.
Your mother and I were smiling, the doctor was smiling,
    when you appeared.
But a man was shot down in cold blood, out in the street, love,
    when you appeared . . .

During the drive to our publisher's house a few miles out of town Ken let me know that he had twigged who Nuala was earlier. 'That was quite a chilling moment when she mentioned her brother's name. It took the wind out of me. I looked away because I couldn't think of anything to say.'

'I wasn't sure you realised.'

'I'm a crime writer for Christ sake. I felt bloody awkward mentioning Adams when she brought up the concert. But I have great admiration for what the man's trying to do in the peace process.'

'So have I.'

The car dropped us at the end of a grassy laneway leading to an old farmhouse. Our publisher, Steve McDonough, came to the front door to greet us with a carving knife in his hand. 'I'm still preparing dinner, a little behind schedule. Great to see you both.'

Ken looked at the knife and laughed. 'For a moment there I thought I was meeting one of the characters from my books.'

Steve chuckled and pointed to a door. 'Go ahead Johnny, straight through. Gerry's just arrived. He's looking forward to meeting you.'

On entering the room I spotted Adams standing by a glass bookcase with a number of people chatting in an open kitchen area in the background. Noticing me, he came forward with a hand extended. 'Johnny Duhan? Good to meet you. I know your songs.'

As I stepped towards him I remembered something a close friend, Paddy Houlahan, had said to me when I told him I was scheduled to have dinner with the Sinn Féin boss: "If I was ever introduced to Adams I'd feel obliged to tell him how much I abhor the IRA, and I wouldn't shake his hand."

While I was shaking Adams' hand, Ken came up beside me with his arms extended. 'Gerry, my mother told me to give you a hug for your great efforts in the peace process. I hope you're not embarrassed by this?'

Gerry did appear embarrassed but he returned Ken's embrace with a strained smile. 'Have you not read the papers lately; I'm big into hugging.'

Steve laughed. 'I thought that was just trees, Gerry?'

'Awk, you're a prude Steve, like Martin McGuinness. One time in London after a successful series of negotiations with a particularly hard-necked bunch of conservative politicians we all started embracing but Martin backed off saying, "I draw the line at that kind of thing."'

We moved into the room and Steve introduced us to his sister, Mary, and some other guests, including Galwegian poet, Mary O'Malley, and

Frank Lewis, a local radio presenter who was booked to interview Adams on stage at the concert. Glasses of wine were handed around and Steve went back to the kitchen. A few minutes later his sister Mary asked us to take our places at a long wooden table.

During soup, Frank Lewis brought up the subject of the forthcoming national elections and predicted that Martin Ferris was set to walk away with the local seat and that Fianna Fáil was going to end up in coalition with the PDs. Gerry Adams stroked his beard and smiled. 'You wouldn't need to be a genius to figure that out Frank.'

I looked towards Steve at the head of the table, then glanced at Adams sitting opposite me. 'The Fianna Fáil machine is certainly up and running in Limerick. While our bus was passing through there this morning I noticed Willie O'Dea's moustache on every telegraph poll we passed.'

Everyone laughed.

Mary O'Malley threw back her head and smirked. 'In the Party's interest, you'd think Bertie would make him shave that ridiculous thing off.'

Gerry Adams smiled. 'Aha but would it be in the party's interest? What if the poor man has something to cover up?'

Mary laughed. 'All politicians have something to cover up. What are you implying, Gerry, a cleft lip?'

Gerry laughed. 'I'm not implying anything, but you never know what people keep hidden behind their image.'

More laughter.

Frank Lewis tried again to inject some gravitas into the conversation by asking Gerry what he thought of the recent racist remarks made about asylum seekers by the brother of the local independent politician Jackie Healy-Rae. 'Some people are suggesting that Jackie should be expelled from the Dáil until he condemns his brother's comments.'

Gerry put his spoon down. 'I'd agree, with the addendum that he shouldn't be allowed back until he gets rid of that ridiculous plaid cap of his.'

More laughter.

During the main course of salmon and salad, Frank Lewis tried for the third time to get a serious political debate going but Gerry pulled him up. 'No disrespect Frank but our interview doesn't start for another hour. And let me remind you, I'm down here to discuss my books, and not just the political side of them.'

The atmosphere grew a little tense but Steve defused the situation by telling an amusing story about an article he once wrote for a French pornographic magazine during his student years.

I sipped my second glass of wine and glanced across the table at Adams. 'How do you manage keeping up a writing routine with your political life?'

Gerry shifted his glasses. 'I've only written the one book that I could really call my own – my short stories. Steve cobbled the others together from notes I scribbled on trains, cars and planes during my travels. A major regret I have is that I don't have more spare time for writing. How about yourself? How long did it take you to write your autobiography?'

I swallowed a sliver of salmon. 'Three or four years, on and off. It's a lot different than songwriting. It can take me four or five years to come up with a full album of songs, but the daily commitment isn't as intense. I also miss being guided by melodic structure when I'm writing prose. It's a totally different form.'

Gerry nodded. 'Have you ever performed up north?'

'I did the Belfast Festival at Queens once.'

'You should play our Féile. Jimmy McCarthy did it last year. I'll give you a contact name, if you like?'

While I was jotting down the contact details I overheard Steve McDonough asking Ken Bruen at the end of the table if the guesthouse he'd booked us into was to our liking. Ken glanced in my direction. 'It's as good as a four star hotel – isn't it Johnny? – and we're getting special treatment because the woman who runs the place – a lovely lady – is an old friend of one of Johnny's sisters.'

Steve looked in my direction. For a moment I thought I should mention the Jerry McCabe connection, but I glanced at Adams and lowered my eyes. 'Yeah, my sister worked with her when they were young. She's from Limerick.'

I didn't speak for the rest of the meal.

While Steve was serving desert, the car that had brought Ken and myself to the house returned to take me to the venue earlier than the others, for a guitar soundcheck. As I was leaving I almost said 'break a leg' to Adams while wishing him well at the concert. I told this to the cab driver when I got into the car and he cracked a wry joke: 'Yeah, break a leg, Gerry, but not mine.' Though I smiled along with the driver, I felt a pang of guilt at having initiated such a below-the-belt comment without thinking.

By the time I reached the hotel the hall where the concert was due to take place was three quarters full, so there was no opportunity for a sound check. After I deposited my guitar by the stage backdrop (a poster display of book covers, my own included) I went and chatted to one of Brandon's administrators at a bookstand near the entrance. A few minutes before the concert was due to begin, Adams arrived, surrounded by a group of autograph hunters. Dozens of Gerry's books were sold and signed within a matter of minutes, then a photo opportunity for the press was organised. Gerry had shots taken with a number of supporters and fans, then one with Steve and another with Ken. Anticipating that I might be called on to join him next, I backed away from the group and went and sat near the stage at the opposite side of the hall.

The concert was late getting started. After a long speech by Steve and a highly entertaining opening reading by Ken, Frank Lewis introduced Gerry Adams to a rapturous round of applause. Because the debate was being recorded for a future broadcast on Radio Kerry, the opening part of the discussion was quite stilted. Even when things settled down the questions and answers seemed choreographed and artificial. Despite Adam's rebuke to Frank earlier at the dinner table for trying to engage him in political banter, Gerry himself now steered the discussion into well-tested political waters, using his familiar artillery of pat, anti-British slogans to hammer home his Sinn Féin propaganda. In the middle of his performance I lost interest in the rhetoric and started thinking about how I was going to manoeuvre my way onto the stage when it was my turn to go on. While I was pondering this question, Frank asked Gerry to read a passage from one of his short stories about a man he once shared a cell with in the Maze Prison. Recalling what he'd said earlier about his short stories, I refocused on Gerry as he leaned to get his book.

Though overtly political, the story dealt with a long-term prisoner's harrowing account of the break-up of his marriage due to the strain of long separation. In a few deft lines Gerry managed to bring out all the human emotion and pain that the man suffered after receiving the defining letter from his wife.

At the end of his performance Adams received a standing ovation that went on for five or six minutes. While this was going on I made my way towards the stage, thinking that I was about to be called on next. As I neared the steps at the left hand side of the platform I noticed Steve McDonough descending the steps at the other side behind Adams and Frank Lewis. At the same time a group of local traditional musicians came on stage and started setting up their instruments in front of the microphones. In confusion, I made my way across the hall and reminded Steve that I had yet to do my performance. For a moment Steve didn't appear to know what I was talking about but then realised his mistake. Off the top of his head, he suggested letting the trad group play for twenty minute before my spot. 'It will give the audience a bit of a breathing space after the intensity of Gerry's interview.'

I knew this was a mistake but I was powerless to do anything about it. In the middle of the trad band's opening set of jigs and reels, hotel staff started moving the audience and clearing away the concert seating. Because of this disruption, many people left the hall while others gravitated towards the bar area. By the time Steve remounted the stage and announced my name the place was half empty.

Because I hadn't done a soundcheck, my guitar sounded very ropey for my opening number, *Just Another Town*. Half way through the song a drunk in the bar started making catcalls, but this worked to my advantage. A loud voice called for order, and after that you could hear a pin drop.

In the middle of my set I glanced towards the entrance and noticed Ken, Steve, Frank and Mary standing near the bookstand, partly hidden in shadow. I tried to locate Adams in the group but couldn't see beyond a certain point. Still, I leaned towards the microphone and introduced the song I'd practised earlier in my room: 'I wrote the lyric of this song soon after our first son Ronan was born. Though the birth was the highlight of my life up to that point, the occasion was marred by a news item I heard on the radio soon after I left the hospital.'

> All the stars were shining, the moon was climbing,
>> when you appeared.
> Your mother and I were smiling, the doctor was smiling,
>> when you appeared.
> But a man was shot down in cold blood, out in the street, love,
>> when you appeared.
>
> The lights were bright in the theatre, spotlighting your mother,
>> when you appeared.
> Your mother was laughing and crying, crying and laughing,
>> when you appeared.
> But a man was shot down in cold blood, out in the street, love,
>> when you appeared.

IN THE CLOUDS

They've taken all I had but you, love,
but you love are all I need.

All I Need

The bus dropped me near a misty byroad in a remote part of Co Donegal and I started walking towards Neem, a coastal village three or four miles from the main road. After the six-hour coach journey north, I was tired and hungry but I'd been told by my promoter that I would have no bother hitchhiking the few miles to the B&B that was booked for me in the village.

Guitar in hand, I walked for twenty minutes without a single vehicle passing me, in either direction. The rugged landscape was nice to walk through but my stomach kept rumbling and the palms of my hands were smarting from the rough handle of my guitar bag. Just as I was beginning to resign myself to the full four-mile trek, a car pulled up beside me and a musical acquaintance from Dublin, Conor Byrne, rolled down the passenger window. 'Johnny Duhan! You look like you could use a lift. Hop in. I think we're going to the same place. You know Mattie, my bouzouki player?'

I nodded to the driver as I got into a back seat and turned to Conor, a traditional flautist who'd played support to me a few times in Dublin folk clubs over the years. 'So it's you I'll be playing with for the next few days? The promoter mentioned a Dublin duo but didn't say your names. I'm glad you showed up. The first gig's at four this afternoon.'

Conor looked back at me as the car took off. 'In Glenveigh Heritage Centre and the one this evening's in Dunlewey beside Mt Errigal, a spectacular place. Mattie and I've played up here many times.'

The B&B we arrived at was situated in a secluded coastal inlet. After we booked into our rooms I had a quick look around the area – climbing a steep rocky hill at the back of the B&B to get a look at the coastline and the Atlantic. The view from up there was breathtaking but there was no time to explore the place on account of the afternoon gig.

Cancelling a car that had been arranged to pick me up, I went along with Conor and Mattie. We arrived at the centre with just a quarter of an hour to show time. While making our way through the lobby I noticed a poster advertising the three gigs of the mini tour on a wall beside the ticket office. Conor's and Mattie's names were written in bold print at the top of the A2 sheet with my name in much smaller font at the bottom. In confusion, I located the manager of the centre and told him that I had been booked as the top of the bill and not as a support act. The manager listened sympathetically to my objection but told me that he had nothing to do with the billing. 'You need to talk to your promoter. He's the one who had the posters made up. You can try phoning him from my office, if you like.'

With only fifteen minutes to go, I tried to phone the promoter in Donegal town but his answering machine came on. I barked an angry few words into the receiver and rushed to the dressing room. Conor and Mattie were seated in front of a wide mirror, running over a tune. They stopped playing when they spotted me and Conor stood up. 'What way do you want to arrange the show?'

I started unpacking my guitar, trying to hide my annoyance. 'I'm not sure if you noticed but there's been a mix-up in the billing. I wasn't booked as a support act.'

Conor glanced at Mattie and turned back to me. 'You have a bigger national profile than us. We'll go on first.'

Taken aback by the ease of their compliance, I stuttered. 'How about we both do two sets. You go on first for twenty minutes, then I'll do twenty, then you twenty, and I'll finish.'

Mattie looked at Conor. Conor nodded. 'That's fine. We'd better go on so. They're real sticklers for timekeeping in this place.'

During the boys' opening set of jigs and reels I peeped out into the small auditorium and noticed that the place was more than half empty. After the fuss I'd created, I felt silly. By the time I took to the stage another few people had arrived, but I found it hard settling into my stride for my first twenty minute set. During the boys' second spot Conor played a haunting Irish air that deservedly received a huge round of applause. Towards the end of my final section the lights went up in the hall in the middle of my last song, ruining the atmosphere and spoiling my chance of receiving an encore. The lighting man later apologised but said he had no alternative as he was working to strict time guidelines.

Because of the rumpus I'd created over the billing, I felt

uncomfortable making the journey to the next venue with the two boys, though they treated me no differently. The drive took us over a range of cloudy hills and misty shrubland. After a half an hour of winding roads Conor pointed towards a huge mountain peak in the distance. 'Errigal!'

As we approached the precipice I looked up at the grey, rocky incline jutting into the overcast sky and gasped. 'Pity the top's covered in cloud.'

Conor looked up. 'The last time we were here it was the same. It's almost always cloudy up here.'

The venue in Dunlewey – a lounge bar decked out like a Swiss chalet – was situated at the bottom of a narrow boreen close to the base of the mountain and overlooking a wide lake surrounded by cloud-topped hills. After we had a meal and tried out the PA system, I went for a walk by the lake and met a man standing near a moored rowing boat. A sign with the words 'Boat For Hire' was propped up in its stern but there were no potential customers around. In passing, I asked the man how business was doing. He doffed his cap and scowled at the cloudy hills on the far side of the lake. 'The weather's ruining the season on me.'

When I returned to the lounge there was a small crowd of locals seated at the front of the stage. The first half of the night was pretty low key but during Conor's and Mattie's second set a bus load of American tourists arrived and things picked up. The boys ended their spot with a lively set of jigs and reels that had a few local couples up dancing. For my final spot I had a bit of a battle trying to restore order for my slower ballads. Towards the end of my set an American yelled up a request for *Danny Boy*. I pretended I didn't hear it and started to sing *The Voyage*. The Yank tried to object but several people – a few of his own US compatriots included – shouted him down and asked for quiet. At the end of the song, I received a huge round of applause and decided to use this as a cue for announcing my final number. 'In honour of Mt Errigal, I'd like to end with a song about a mountain climb I made with my wife and kids some years back. There's quite a few verses in this one, so I'd appreciate a little quiet.'

> When we saw the white beacon near the top of the hill,
> The children stopped their fighting and went suddenly still,
> And before we brought the engine to a stop
> They said, "Please let's climb the mountain to the top."

Just as I was about to start the second verse a drunken customer started an argument with one of the bar staff and the noise caused me to lose concentration. Though I eventually picked up the thread of the narrative after a few duff lines, the audiences were no longer with me. By the time I completed the song I had lost the attention of most of the crowd. A few people called for more as I was leaving the stage but the applause wasn't loud enough to warrant an encore. Instead of singing another song I called on Conor and Mattie to play a finale of jigs and reels, which went down a treat with the Americans. After they came off stage, Conor and Mattie had a few celebratory drinks while I nursed a sour beer till it was time to head back to the guesthouse.

When we got to the B&B, I went straight to bed and immediately fell asleep. A couple of hours later I woke in a disturbed frame of mind. After tossing and turning for half an hour or more I got out of bed and sat in the dark trying to calm myself with a bout of contemplation. While I was struggling to focus on a single syllable I noticed the tangy scent of the sea coming through the open window and could hear the faint sound of breakers out in the dark ocean. The uneven heave of the waves was soothing but I found it impossible to go deep into contemplation. After ten or fifteen minutes of failed mental effort I gave up and turned on the light. Knowing that I still wouldn't be able to sleep, I got a book from my guitar bag – *Mere Christianity* by C.S. Lewis – and opened it at random on a chapter called 'The Great Sin'. In the middle of the first paragraph I came upon a passage that stopped me in my tracks:

> There is no fault which makes a man more unpopular, and no fault which we are more unconscious of in ourselves. And the more we have it in ourselves, the more we dislike it in others. The vice I am talking of is Pride or Self-Conceit: and the virtue opposite it, in Christian morals, is called humility.

My behaviour of the day gone by came back to me, with a sting. I underlined the passage and got into bed and fell asleep almost immediately.

After a quick breakfast the following morning I headed out to explore the coastline. During an hour-long trek on headland above the shore I did some soul searching and decided that I owed Conor and Mattie an apology. When I returned to the B&B I found the two boys packing their instruments in their car, getting ready to drive to Glencolmcille for the final gig of the mini tour. Though I hadn't arranged to travel with them, Conor insisted on me coming along. During the roundabout, scenic route that Mattie took, I tried to pluck up the courage to offer my apology but couldn't find the words.

After stopping for a meal en route, we arrived in Glencolmcille at seven thirty and went straight to the Arts Centre, Foras Cultuir Uladh, where the show was due for an eight o'clock start. On our way to the dressing room I spotted the poster with my name at the bottom of the sheet, and I smiled. At five to eight, the manager of the centre came to the dressing room and told us that it was time to begin the show. 'Brostaigh ort, más é do thoil é.'

Conor and Mattie went to pick up their instruments but I stopped them. 'I'll go on first tonight, lads; it's only fair; you've done it for two shows running.'

Conor looked at me, askance. 'Are you sure?'

I glanced at Mattie and could tell by his expression that he relished the idea of topping the bill. 'Yeah, I'm positive. And I'll play just one forty-five-minute set.'

Conor objected. 'There's no need to do that. We can play two sets each like yesterday. That would be fairer.'

I grabbed my guitar. 'No, I'd prefer to do it this way. It'll save a lot of chopping and changing.'

The venue, I was surprised to find, was full to capacity, mainly with American and European tourists. After the manager of the centre gave me a brief introduction in both Irish and English, I stepped into the limelight and sat with my guitar on my lap. The audience was clearly visible, especially those in the front row, as twilight coming through windows at the sides and back of the hall added light to the stage lighting. In deference to the location, I opened with a cupla focal and a gag. 'I'm just a humble folk singer so I'll start with my opus on pride, *Daredevil*.'

> I'm up here where the night is stare freckled,
> The moon on my head is a lily petal,
> And a thousand eyes are looking up at me,
> Will I stay alive that's what they're waiting to see.
> I'm employed in a carnival, I climb high to dare the devil;
> Aflame in the sky, like a bird I fly,
> And when I dive they sigh, 'Will he die?'

While singing, I could tell that the entire audience was absorbed in every word of the lyric. At the end of the song there was a long round of applause. As the clapping was dying away, a voice called up a request in a strong American accent for *The Voyage*. Not having the song scheduled for the early part of my programme, I hesitated while trying to think of a polite excuse for doing a different song but the Yank appealed again:

'Come on fella, we've come all the way from Wisconsin just to hear you sing it.'

I laughed 'How could I refuse such dedication.'

I sang the song and, by doing so, won the approval of the entire crowd. Not only did I receive a huge round of applause at the end of *The Voyage* but every other song in my set received the same positive reception and, at the end of my performance, I was called on for an encore. I sang a flawless version of *The Beacon* and left the stage in a glow of glory. And that wasn't the end of it. At the close of Conor's and Mattie's equally successful set, Conor called me back to the spotlight to sing the finale. I chose the only sing-along song in my repertoire and the entire audience joined in on the chorus:

Don't give up till it's over; don't quit, if you can;
the weight upon your shoulder will make you a stronger man.

THE PROCESSION

Pure as a lily flower closed in its petalled tower
you opened to the power of love

The Burning Word

The long cavalcade of wheelchairs moved out of the shaded porch of the hotel and made its way slowly into the evening sunlit street, holding up traffic as the procession crossed to the other side of the road. Directing the group, our CEO, Michael Duignan, beckoned to the wheelchair attendants to hurry them on while at the same time signalling to the drivers of held-up cars to assure them that we wouldn't be long. When the full line of invalids and elderly pilgrims was safely across the street and had formed into a fairly neat phalanx, Michael called out to the two standard-bearers at the head of the cortege to raise the group's insignia (a fringed and tasseled stretch of green velvet with the embroidered name *The Notre Dame Invalid Trust* emblazoned between two poles) and then ordered the group to start moving. 'Keep in line and keep an even pace. As this is our final event, I would like to remind those of you who wish to take home Lourdes' water that this will be your final opportunity to get some at the taps after the Rosary procession.'

At the rear of the group, I pulled the peak of my sun cap down over my eyes, glad that I wasn't hampered with my guitar bag for a change, and kept in step with Tommy, my roommate for the past ten days. Switching his carrier bag of empty plastic bottles from one hand to the other, Tommy waved to five or six solemn faced tourists who had stopped to observe our group from the far pavement. I glanced at them too and smiled. 'You'd think they'd be used to processions like ours, wouldn't you?'

Tommy nodded. 'I suppose they stop out of respect, in the same way that we stop back home for funerals.'

Tommy's reluctance to fall in with my mild cynicism was

characterlstic. Over the past ten days I had come to realise that there wasn't a bad thought in his head. He was one of life's goodies, genuine and charitable to the core. A recent widower, he had shown me a photograph of his recently deceased wife on our first day lodging together and told me that the main reason he was making the pilgrimage was because he and his wife had made the trip the year before she'd died and he wanted to return in a spirit of gratitude for the blessing of the final year they'd had together.

As the procession turned into the busy commercial district (lines and lines of shops and kiosks selling holy ware) our group was held up by traffic in a narrow street outside an open-fronted store bedecked with Marian statues, framed Marian pictures, crucifixes and strings and strings of rosary beads, scapulars and miraculous medals. Pressing his carrier bag of empty bottles into my hands, Tommy rushed off to make a last-minute purchase. 'Mind those. I won't be a tick; just want to get something for a niece I forgot to include in my shopping list earlier.'

When he rejoined me minutes later he showed me an almond-shaped silver medal of Our Lady of Lourdes in a small square red box inlaid with blue velvet. He also produced a postcard of Padre Pio whose facial expression changed to a different portrait when the card was tilted slightly. 'That's for you, a small token of my appreciation of your good company over the past ten days. I know you don't go in for holy knick-knacks but I thought you might like this after that story you told me the other night about the dream you had of Pio when your mother was ill.'

The dream Tommy was alluding to had come to me some years before while my mother was in a coma in the intensive care unit of the Regional Hospital in Limerick. When she was at her lowest ebb, I dreamt of Padre Pio, even though I'd never given him much thought till this time. In the dream he asked me to lick what looked like a medallion of white soap. When I awoke the thought occurred to me that the soap must have been a Communion host. Soon after this my mother recovered and I returned home to Galway. A day later my sister Kay, whom I'd told about the dream, phoned to tell me that she had just found a faded newspaper cutting of Padre Pio in an old wallet belonging to our deceased father. The amazing thing about this was that my father had never been known to talk about Padre Pio, or any other saint for that matter, during the course of his life.

I thanked Tommy for the gift but reminded him that I viewed the incident as an inexplicable coincidence rather than a divine happening.

Before we reached the grotto enclosure, our group stopped off at a candle stall where we purchased long-stemmed candles encased in wind-protective cardboard containers for the rosary procession, prior to entering the sacred compound which was cut off from the commercial activity of the rest of the town.

While bypassing the underground Basilica of Pius X a dramatic moment from a service we'd attended there some days before came back to me. While the officiating priest was raising the monstrance for Benediction a young Spanish woman sprang to her feet in front of me and held a large framed photograph of a beautiful looking teenage girl above her head – her daughter, I imagined, who had probably been too ill to make the pilgrimage to Lourdes with her mother. In a faltering voice the lady cried out a few words in Spanish (a prayer no doubt) and then sank back on her chair, dabbing her eyes with a black lace handkerchief.

As there was plenty of time before the procession was due to commence, Michael led our group down to the grotto where Our Lady was said to have appeared to Bernadette, for one last prayer. On the way we were held up by a French pilgrim group who were having technical difficulties with one of their wheelchairs. When we eventually arrived at the grotto our group dispersed to different vantage points. Some of the attendants positioned their patients' wheelchairs just inside the barrier rails – where some invalids were happy enough to ply their beads at a distance from the cave mouth – while others followed Michael to a queue ranged at the stoneface so that they could touch the rock below the elevated statue where the sacred presence was said to have taken place. On the first evening of our arrival in Lourdes, Michael had taken me on a tour of this area and had shown me some of the key features of the site, including the altar at the front of the grotto where daily masses were said by different pilgrim groups who booked the services in advance. Originally, Michael had booked the altar for a mass for our group, but a few days before we set out on the trip the booking was cancelled to facilitate an Italian delegation led by an archbishop. I was disappointed by this turn of events as I had been looking forward to singing a new song I'd written for Our Lady called *The Burning Word* at the grotto.

By the time we arrived at the Basilica of the Immaculate Conception and took up our position for the Rosary Procession, Tommy and I had become separated by several rows of wheelchairs. I now found myself standing beside a middle-aged woman on crutches. Having noticed her sitting alone at quite a few of the services I'd sung at during the course of the past ten days, I asked her how she was getting on. She raised one of her crutches and pointed it towards one of the wheelchairs in front of us. 'I'm grateful not to be in one of them yokes. You're our singer?'

I nodded. 'One of them. Michael's wife, Margaret, invited me to come along after I sang at a memorial service in a little chapel in University Hospital back in Galway.'

The woman smiled and introduced herself as Deirdre. 'What do you make of this place?'

The question took me by surprise. I hesitated. 'It's been a great experience; I'm glad I came.'

She gave me a penetrating look and glanced back towards the grotto. 'But you're sceptical, I can sense.'

I smiled. 'I suppose I am, it's my nature, but I'm respectful too, I hope.'

The procession started moving very slowly. People began to light their candles around us. I lit mine and helped Deirdre light hers. In the growing twilight the line of flickering flames ahead of us gave the proceedings a fairytale quality. Leaning on her crutches, Deirdre inched along beside me, struggling to keep her candle aloft while at the same time maintaining a hold on the handles of her crutches. 'This is my sixth trip; my second on crutches. I was in one of those before that.' She raised her right crutch and pointed it at a wheelchair. 'The first time I came in a wheelchair was humiliating. I was paralysed from head to toe after a massive stroke. I couldn't do anything for myself. The stroke came out of the blue while I was having my tea one evening after a long day at the Post Office where I worked. I was forty-five at the time. I'm fifty-one now.'

The thought of telling her that she looked younger than her years passed through my mind, but I didn't lie. 'Had you no family support?'

'Both my parents died the year before it happened. Maybe that contributed to it. I never married. I have a sister in Canada. She came home for a month and was a great support but she had to return to her family then. She has six children.'

'How did you manage to get back on your feet?'

'Dogged determination. Relearning how to talk properly was one of the hardest challenges.'

'Your speech seems perfect now.'

'Almost.' She drew a long breath. 'I suppose I keep coming back here out of a sense of gratitude. Or maybe it's fear that the bloody thing might happen again.'

'You're a brave woman.'

Deirdre smiled. 'That song you keep singing for us, *Don't Give up till It's Over,* hits the nail on the head. It was terrific the other day at that retreat centre up in the Pyrenees when the whole group joined in on the chorus. I'll never forget that.'

I thought back to the moment Deirdre was alluding to, a moment that would live long in my memory also. After an outdoor Mass I sang the song as a request for a man suffering from autism and the whole group of invalids on crutches and in wheelchairs spontaneously joined my fellow musicians, Charley and Anne, in singing the chorus with tremendous spirit: "Don't give up till it's over, don't quit, if you can; the weight upon your shoulder will make you a stronger man."

From an intercom now, a high-pitched voice started reciting a decade of the rosary in French and then moved on to Spanish, Italian and English, with the candlelit congregation responding in the various languages.

Deirdre fell behind and started chatting to a frail young woman in a white blouse called Ann. Though I hadn't spoken to Ann during the course of the pilgrimage, I was struck by how thin she was the first time I saw her on the bus to the airport. Later, on a number of occasions in the hotel restaurant, I noticed that she only drank fluids at meal times. Michael's wife and fellow organiser, Margaret, a retired matron nurse, told me at breakfast one morning that Ann suffered from Anorexia. Margaret explained that Michael and herself would never have accepted Ann for the pilgrimage had they known of her condition at the outset. Though the group included a team of voluntary medical practitioners, included a fully qualified GP and five or six nurses, they weren't equipped to deal with a psychological problem as serious as anorexia under the constraints of a pilgrimage situation. Already the woman had fainted during a Mass and there were growing fears for her permanent health because she hadn't eaten any solids in the previous ten days.

As the sun began to set, the procession, winding the path skirting the long rectangular green in front of the Basilica, took on a magical look, lit up as it was by myriad handheld candles. The slight barrier created by the rosary being said in different languages was broken by the communal singing of such internationally popular hymns as *Ave Maria* and *Hail Queen of Heaven*.

Darkness deepened and the stream of pilgrims took on the aspect of a river of light. Camaraderie between the different nationality groups spread and the atmosphere grew almost carnival-like.

When the procession finally made it's way into the square in front of the lit-up Basilica, the invalids in wheelchairs and their carers were segregated to a privileged place at the front of the church while the rest of us were conducted to standing areas at the back of the square. By this stage an almost full moon was glowing like a halo above the church's steeple and clusters of pinpoint stars in a navy sky seemed like reflections of the sea of lit candles in the hands of the vast congregation.

More prayers were recited and more hymns sung and then the proceedings were brought to a close with the crowd of thousands joining together for one final chorus of *Ave Maria*.

As the crowds dispersed, I made my way to the Lourdes' water taps thinking that I might meet up with Tommy, who I knew had many bottles to fill. Even at that late hour there were queues lined up for the holy water, but there was no sign of Tommy. After filling one small bottle that I'd brought along in my pocket, I made my way back to the hotel and found my room mate packing his bags in our room in preparation for our early departure the following morning. On the table by the open window his carrier bag was standing with the tops of six large bottles showing.

'I see you got your Lourdes' water.' I took the small bottle from my pocket. 'I got some myself. My wife's mother will appreciate it.'

Tommy looked at my little bottle and laughed. 'If I went home with something like that I'd be shot. A number of my neighbours asked me to get bottles as well as members of our extended family. It's precious stuff in our quarters. More valuable than whiskey. Which reminds me, as soon as I have this case packed we'll go down and join the others and I'll buy you a final drink.'

I smiled. 'It's my round. And maybe you'll break your habit and have two or three as it's our last night.'

Downstairs, we found the lobby and lounge teeming with pilgrims, not only from our group but from several other delegations as well. After some searching we managed to find a table close to a sliding door leading to a patio. While crushing my way towards the bar to get drinks I was stopped several times by members of our group, invalids and attendants, who thanked me for my singing services during the ten days. One of the people to stop me was the mother of a young boy called Joey, who had come to Lourdes covered in bandages, suffering from a chronic form of eczema which the doctors back home were unable to cure. The evening before, while Tommy and I were having a nightcap on the patio before going up to our room, Joey came running over to our table bandage-free and jumped up on my lap – calling me the "song man" – telling us that he had been cured at the baths earlier that day. His mother came over and apologised for her son's behaviour, though she too was highly animated, believing that a miracle had occurred. Though more restrained tonight, she still believed that her son had been fully cured, telling me that even the group's doctor and head nurse couldn't account for the clearance of his skin. 'Maybe it won't last but I can't tell you how wonderful it is to see him so happy for a change.'

Making my way back to Tommy with our drinks, I ran into Deirdre, the lady on crutches I'd befriended during the procession. While we were swapping small talk, the anorexic, Ann, came towards us, supported by one of the nurses. A few words passed between us and then the nurse and her ward moved on. When they were out of earshot Deirdre told me that Ann had almost fainted towards the end of the procession back at the Basilica. 'A few stewards had to help her find somewhere to sit. I went with her. While we were sitting back from the crowd a funny thing happened. Little Joey came along with his mother and started showing us his arms and legs, telling us about his cure. Ann perked up and asked him if he was "the miracle boy that everyone was talking about?" Joey nodded and threw another question back at Ann, asking her if she was "the lady who doesn't eat that everyone is worried about?"' Deirdre laughed. '"Food for thought for Ann", I said to the nurse later.'

When I finally got back to our table with our drinks I found Tommy in conversation with our organiser, Michael. After some chitchat, Michael told me that a large number of our group had asked him to ask me if I would sing for them one last time before going to bed. I took a sip from my beer and went upstairs to get my guitar.

The Burning Word

And angel came to you
out of the mystic blue
while you were praying to God above.

Pure as a lily flower
closed in it's petalled tower,
you opened to the power of love.

Though pain would ensue
from the flame that burned in you,
still you embraced the burning Word.

The angel flew away
after he had his say
on that most sacred day for love.

Gabriel came to you
out of the mystic blue
while you were praying to God above.

MY FIRST SONG

And another clear day begins,
it makes me happy, it makes me sad

Ballybunion Blues

Sunlight seeping through a gap in the curtains of my hotel room woke me just after seven. I got out of bed and drew back the drapes. The river Sieve glittered before me, with Listowel racecourse in the background. An elderly man walking a dog on the narrow pathway by the riverside brought John B Keane to mind. It was said that Listowel's most famous writer had walked this path every day of his adult life. During my performance in St John's Arts Centre the night before, I had drawn on a wry remark made by John B on *The Late Late Show* a few years before he died as an opening joke before singing *The Voyage*, the title song of my show: "Marriage is an ongoing war in which there are occasional outbreaks of peace." The quotation drew the expected laugh from the small crowd and paved the way for the night's artistic success, which compensated somewhat for its commercial failure.

After dressing, I totted up my earnings for the night before – seventy five euro in CD and book sales and two hundred representing slightly more than seventy percent of the door, which the manager of the centre, Joe, was generous enough to give me. After deducting my various expenses, I calculated that my profit for the night was roughly one hundred and twenty euro. Measured against two days' travelling plus practice time, the sum amounted to mild depression.

During breakfast in the near empty dining-room downstairs, I recalled a burning sensation that had come over me just before I went on stage the night before, after I learned that less than twenty people had shown up to see me. I had experienced the feeling many times in the past in similar circumstances, but never with such intensity. Thinking back on it now – as I swallowed some hardboiled egg – brought to

151

miiid a passage from Dante's *Purgatory* where the poet is forced to step through fire to purify himself before entering Eden to meet Beatrice. The spotlight I had stepped into the previous night more than singed my pride but, once I made eye contact with the small audience and cracked John B's marriage gag, I gained courage to put my heart and soul into singing *The Voyage* with more spirit than I'd ever sang it in the past. And I went on from there to give one of the most intense shows of my career, singing the many songs I'd written over the years on family relationships and family history, including *Inviolate*, which I'd never sang on stage before because of personal family revelations exposed in the raw lyric. The loud round of applause it received took me by surprise, and, after the show, I was deeply affected when an elderly lady who had attended my performance took the trouble of coming to my hotel just to let me know how moved she'd been by the song. I recalled her sunken eyes on the verge of tears as she complimented me, and I guessed that the song's lyric – written for a deceased brother of mine who died before I was born – had resurrected some similar tragedy from her past. Reflecting on this now, as I munched toast and sipped coffee, gave me a feeling of elation, far beyond any feeling of success money might bring.

After I checked out of the hotel, the notion came over me to drive twenty miles south to the coastal town of Ballybunion for a walk on the long beach before heading north to the midlands for my next show. Ballybunion held a special place in my memory, as I had visited the resort regularly as a kid on family summer outings, and it was also the place where Joan and I spent a glorious week camping during our first summer going out together back in the early '70s. Glowing recollections of the place attracted us back to the town five years later for our honeymoon – with disastrous consequences. The hotel we ended up staying in had a resident band that kept us awake till all hours during our three night stay and our daytime outings to the beach and cliffs were spoilt by constant drizzle and rain. Now, however, almost thirty years on, the sky was aqua blue and a warm autumn sun was so bright on the windscreen of my car I was forced to wear sunglasses as I drove towards my Shangri-La.

Approaching the seaside resort, I noticed a couple of dark clouds above the town. Driving down the main street at ten o'clock on a Friday morning in mid-October turned out to be a pretty bleak experience. The place was almost deserted and most of the shops were boarded up and bolted for the coming winter. Passing a familiar bar where Joan and I had been regular customers in the summer of thirty-odd years before, I recalled the interior 's granite walls bedecked with fishing nets, oars and lobster pots. I remembered a dark corner where Joan and I used to sit sipping drinks while chatting the night away after long days spent on the beach, swimming and sunbathing. Now, at the side of the bar's front door, I noticed a black and white mongrel pissing against a flowerpot with a wilted shrub hanging over the rim.

I drove past the locked Amusement Arcade and parked on the side of a sloping road leading to the strand. The town's main dancehall was still there, perched on headland above the roadway. I recalled nights spent busking outside the ballroom with Joan, cap in hand and blushing to the gills, collecting coins from casual listeners who stopped to hear me sing on their way into the dance. One fellow who watched me briefly turned out to be an old boyfriend of Joan's from Galway. He threw a single penny into the hat while congratulating Joan on having "come up in the world".

I set off walking along the deserted beach now, enjoying the tangy smell of brine and the slapping sound of the breakers on the strand. The tide was on its way in. I picked up a flat stone and went to the water's edge and took a low throw to try and skip it on the sea's surface. It hopped twice and then a breaking wave engulfed it. Out at sea, more clouds were massing on the horizon but it didn't look like it was going to rain in the immediate future.

I walked for about a mile and sat on a boulder with my back to some sand dunes and gazed out to sea, cursing the encroaching clouds that were threatening to spoil my trip down memory lane. I picked up a small dun-coloured shell and studied the even pattern of whorls perfectly entwining the sun-baked cone. I thought of the little sea creature that had once inhabited the shell and pictured it in my mind's eye scuttling along the sea bed with its home on its back. The little object's design was so intricate and perfect, it seemed a shame that its function no longer existed. I threw it back in the sand and started making my way back towards the cliffs.

The idea came to me to contact Joan to let her know where I was. I got out my mobile phone and scrolled down to her number. Her voice came to me bright and clear with the muffled sound of her class in the background. 'Good morning. How did the show go?'

I hesitated. 'Small crowd but great reaction.'

'The story of your life. Did you sell any CDs and books?'

'A few. But that's not why I'm calling. You'll never guess where I am?'

'Limerick?'

'Ballybunion, our old camping ground.'

Joan laughed. 'What brought you down there?'

I hesitated, 'It was a lovely morning in Listowel, but it's gone cloudy now. I guess I just wanted to revisit our past.'

Joan spoke but the sound of kids' screaming drowned out her words. She started remonstrating with her class, then apologised. 'I'll have to go; they're acting up. You can fill me in later. I'll call you this evening when I get home.'

I put the phone back in my pocket, a little disappointed that my call hadn't awoken any nostalgic feelings in Joan.

When I got back to the main beach I felt a drop or two of rain, but it held off. Beyond the seaweed baths, I trudged up a steep hill and reached the narrow track of the official cliff walk. Passing a deserted caravan site, I noted how desolate the place looked without its summer residents.

Following the dirt walkway close to the cliff's edge, I eventually came to the field where Joan and I had set up camp all those years ago, close to an abandoned convent that was empty even at the time we visited the area. The field I was standing in was eerily silent with nothing but a few barren rocks poking their lichen covered heads above the stubbly grass.

I located the actual spot near a boulder wall where we'd pitched our tent for shelter and stood looking down at the rubbery grass, trying to recover some tracings that might connect me to the past. A snail on a rock overshadowed by some dock leaves took my attention. I recalled how Joan used to cling to me whenever we found large insects or spiders in the tent at night, and how I used to take advantage of her vulnerability at such moments to deepen our intimacy. A whole series of recollections rose up in my mind. One centred on an incident I'd completely forgotten about. While I was sitting outside the tent one sunny afternoon singing a new song I'd written about my mother's mental illness, a feeling of weariness came over me, like a premonition that my future career as a songwriter was going to be a long hard struggle due to the subject matter I was intent on writing about. As the presentiment took hold, I remember thinking about Joan snoozing in the tent close by, wondering if I had the right to be with her given the uncertainty of my profession. Recalling this now made me realise that the same nagging insecurity had disturbed me during most of my working life, even up to the commercial failure of the night before.

I made my way to the edge of the cliff – right out onto the flinty precipice – and gazed down at the secluded inlet of Nuns' Cove. Nuns from the nearby convent once swam here, away from the public gaze. I recalled spying on a group of them back in the early '60s with my brothers Eric, Michael and Barry. Without their coifs and wimples, the novice nuns seemed just like any other young nubile females, though their ample black swimsuits weren't nearly as alluring as the colourful bikinis that were on open display back on the main beach.

A giant escarpment of rock dominating the middle of the inlet took my attention. Teams of squealing gulls – descendants no doubt of the very birds that had scoured the rock for perching ground when I was a boy – were navigating the winds around the scarp of jagged limestone while below, foaming waves were being driven through a huge cavity in the rock by the force of the incoming tide.

A vivid memory of a morning I had taken Joan down to the rocky beach to try and teach her to swim came to me. Because of her fear of heights, I had a tough job coaxing her down the hairline track that zigzagged the steep descent. And I had an even tougher job cajoling her out into the lively brine. When we were in above our waists, Joan clung to me, trembling. I tried to coax her to dip below the surface, but she resisted in squeals of frightened laughter. Jokingly, I reminded her of a warning I had given her when we first met that she was getting in over her head by associating with me. She smiled. I enfolded her in my arms and drew her down into the sudsy water. She clung to my shoulders, begging me not to let her go, laughing in fear and excitement. Her laughter mingled with the sound of breaking waves and gull-cries. I kissed her and tasted purifying salt in her mouth.

The squeal of a gull directly over my head broke my reverie. It hovered above me on outstretched wings for a few moments then rode the wind out over the concave of grey water and perched on a shelf of the giant rock. The sky above the limestone was a darker grey than the slate-grey of the sea. The grey of the rock and the grey of the sky and sea drained me of the desire to go on plumbing my memory for recollections to feed my heart. The past was a mere scarp with room enough for the mind to perch on only for brief durations.

I made my way back to the dirt track and retraced my steps to the main beach.

While crossing the wide strand I noticed the remains of Ballybunion Castle on its high crag overlooking the sea. I had never taken much interest in this landmark building in the past but now the crumbled structure drew me to the steep tier of steps leading up to it. At the top, I walked around the one remaining wall and read a brief history of the building on a plaque that informed me that the castle had been built by the Geraldines in the fourteenth Century and passed to the Bonyons who had the distinction of having Ballybunion named after them. I looked up at the dilapidated wall and thought of the empty shell I'd cast aside earlier on the beach. Dead things with the life gone out of them.

Rather than retrace my steps down to the strand I took the promontory route back to my car. On the way, I came upon a natural alcove overlooking the main beach and remembered sitting there on the first night that Joan and I had arrived in Ballybunion. While hitch-hiking to the resort we had been involved in a near fatal car accident with a couple of US tourists who had given us a lift, and I suffered a bout of delayed shock that drove me to walk alone to this spot in the dark. Sitting here gripped in inexplicable anxiety, I began to think that I was having a nervous breakdown. A rotating lighthouse beam across on the Clare coast caught my attention and brought the memory of a childhood night-game I used to play with my sisters when our mother was in hospital back to me. In the game we used to count car lights on a bedroom ceiling to distract us from our fear of the dark and the uncertainty of our home situation. The recollection of this long forgotten incident calmed me down, and the following day it gave me the inspiration to write the song dealing with my mother's mental disorder, *Everything will be Alright*. In an essential way, *Everything will be Alright* was related to the song that the old lady had complemented me on the night before – *Inviolate* – and it was also connected to all the other family songs that formed my collection *The Voyage*, which I was now touring. Thinking back on the trauma I'd experienced in this spot all those years ago, it occurred to me now that the pain I'd gone through back then was nothing more than the birth pangs of my first real song.

While I was reflecting on this, the heavens opened.

Sister we're alone in the middle of the night,
counting car lights on the ceiling, everything will be alright.
Mother had a breakdown, 'cause she was sad.
Let's just count the car lights, no mother isn't mad.

SONG OF THE BIRD

I know when you die, though we'll sit and cry,
you'll be at peace, you're pain will cease
and your spirit will begin to fly

When You Go

Joan and I had spent most of the night up nursing our kids and grandkids, three of whom had come down with a tummy bug after eating in the hotel restaurant the evening before, so when my mobile phone started ringing at twenty past seven I found it painful opening my eyes. I put the device to my ear and my sister Kay's voice came on the line, quivering. 'Johnny, is that you? Mam is dead. She died during the night in the Regional Hospital. Patti and myself are on our way out there now.'

Jolted, I took a deep breath and sighed. 'My God, I was planning on visiting her today.'

Kay's voice shook. 'When we left her last night she was fine; I'm not sure what happened. We'll find out when we get to the hospital.'

I took another deep breath and explained that Joan and I were on a two-night break with the family in a hotel in Ennis. I gave her a quick account of the bout of sickness that had kept us awake half the night and told her that I'd be in Limerick within the hour. 'I'll see you at the hospital.'

While dressing, I woke Joan and told her about my mother. We had a quick confab and decided that the best thing to do under the circumstances was for her and the kids to cut short their stay in the hotel and drive home to Galway (luckily we'd come in two cars).

On the new motorway, it took me just twenty minutes to reach the outskirts of Limerick but another hour to negotiate rush-hour traffic through the city. I arrived at the hospital just before nine and found out at reception what ward my mother was in.

A young nurse on the second floor told me that I had just missed my sisters, who had left minutes before. 'They told me to tell you that they'll see you down town in the Grove Restaurant later. Would you like to sit with your mother for a while?'

'Please.'

The nurse conducted me to a small public ward and led me to a bed screened off from three other patients. Gesturing towards a chair at the side of the bed in which my mother's body was lying, she gave me a sympathetic look. 'If you need anything, I'll be just down the corridor.'

As the nurse was leaving, the thought occurred to me that I should ask for details of when and how my mother had died but I couldn't get the words out. I went to the side of the bed and looked down at my mother's face. It was ash-grey and her pouting lips were a peculiar purple colour. In my addled state, the thought occurred to me that my sisters had put purple lipstick on her mouth and I began to wonder why they hadn't used the red shade she usually wore. Then it dawned on me that rigor mortis was responsible for the livid tone.

I touched her forehead. It was stone cold, which meant she had been dead for some time. The expression on her face was striking; her chin was pointing upwards and her nose appeared to be protruding from her face like the beak of a bird. Her whole facial expression was like an eagle straining skyward at the moment of taking flight. Somehow, I felt consoled by this, imagining that the upward thrust of her face meant that she was leaning up towards some benevolent force at the moment of death.

I sat by the bed and started whispering some prayers. First I thanked God for having taken my mother in the middle of the night in what appeared to be a peaceful passing. For years I had been praying that she die peacefully in her sleep, so now, mingled with grief, I felt relief.

After a silent decade of the rosary, I sat back in the iron chair and tried to settle into a period of contemplation, concentrating on the word God. The other patients in the ward must have thought I had left, for in the middle of my spiritual exercise one of them started talking. 'Do you think she'd mind if I turned on the telly?'

While I was wondering if the 'she' meant the nurse or my mother, another voice made things clear: 'I don't think so; she was a lovely woman, God rest her.'

'It's just that there's a repeat of one of my favourite soaps coming up at ten o clock and I missed half of it the other night because of visitors.'

I smiled at my dead mother and tears started streaming from my eyes. I didn't try to stop them.

After I had a good cry I got to my feet, kissed my mother's icy forehead and started to leave.

As I emerged from behind the screen the two patients who had been talking about my mother looked at me in surprise. I smiled and one of them came forward and put her arms around me. 'You must be her son? She was a lovely woman. She was only with us a couple of days but you could tell in that time that she was a real lady. Couldn't you, Margaret?'

Margaret gave an embarrassed smile and nodded. 'A real lady.'

After I left the hospital I drove to a nearby chapel and was lucky to find that Mass was just commencing as I entered a side door. During the service I remembered a visit I'd made to my mother in the hospital I'd just come from three or four months before while she was recuperating after a bout of pneumonia. Though she was barely conscious for most of the twenty minutes I was with her, she perked up at one stage and told me in a faltering voice that she was "going to be crowned in heaven". She pleaded with me to look out for my brothers and sisters when she was gone, "especially Barry".

After mass I drove to our old family home on Wolfe Tone Street to call on my brother Barry, who had been living alone in the house for several years since he'd returned from a spell of working at odd jobs in America. As I approached the house I noticed that the roof was sinking and the gutters sagging from the weight of not having being cleaned in years. The whole front of the terraced building was mottled with ugly mortar holes and patches of paint erosion. Barry came to the door looking gaunt and tired. On a previous visit I had offered to help him tidy the house up but he dismissed the offer as unnecessary, asking me not to interfere in his concerns.

On this occasion he didn't invite me in, but greeted me with a sympathetic smile, putting his arm around me. 'Kay dropped by and broke the news. Poor Mam.'

We spoke for a few minutes at the door and I persuaded him to accompany me down town to meet our sister Kay at her daughter's health-food restaurant in Cecil Street.

Kay was behind the counter when we got there laying out trays of salad and brown rice in a perspex display compartment. Her daughter, Suzy, was at the ovens tending to the cooked food. When Kay spotted Barry and myself, she came from behind the counter and gave both of us a hug, then she poured us mugs of coffee and joined us at one of the tables. 'I know it's not right for me to be working but I just don't know what to do with myself. Poor Mam; she just slipped away unnoticed.'

We sat talking about my mother until the restaurant started filling up with lunchtime customers. I arranged to phone Kay later that evening from Galway to discuss funeral details. Then I walked Barry back to Wolfe

Tone Street and picked up my car and drove to Galway.

During the journey home I noticed for the first time that the day was brilliantly clear and sunny. I slipped an album of Bach's piano concertos in the CD player and kept skipping to the slow pieces.

As I drove into the outskirts of Galway I phoned home and discovered that Joan was in bed, having picked up the bug herself. I filled her in on my visit to the hospital and told her that I was going for a walk in Salthill before going home.

I parked in Blackrock and walked the narrow pathway by the golf links, close to the rocky seashore. The tide was almost fully in. I found a spot among some rocks and sat on a boulder gazing out over Galway Bay. The Atlantic was as calm and still as I'd ever seen it. Little wavelets were curling onto the shingle in front of me, making gentle hissing sounds like breathing, followed by long silent pauses. A recollection from the distant past came to me of a morning after an excruciatingly painful visit to my mother in St Joseph's mental hospital. As I awoke I cursed God for the turmoil and suffering he kept inflicting on her, and at that moment a gentle voice whispered in my head: "I do this for the soul", which completely put me at ease. The same feeling of tranquility came over me now and I began to imagine that the stillness of the day was somehow connected to the fact that my mother was now finally at peace after her long turbulent life.

The squeal of a low-flying gull pierced the silence. I turned and watched the bird hovering above some barnacle-covered rocks at the water's edge. Another gull flew in and fluttered above the first bird, then both birds wheeled about and flew off together just above the still surface of the steel-blue water.

The bird-like look on my mother's face in her hospital bed came back to me, and again I imagined that the upward thrust of her features somehow augured well.

My gaze drifted across to the rolling hills of the Burren on the far side of the bay. The day was so clear green fields were visible among the grey rocky stretches of the hilly coastline. I recalled gazing over the same terrain on a dull day a week or so earlier when the same hills were black and dark purple. The variation of shades that the Burren was capable of taking on never ceased to amaze me. And the clarity and brightness of the landscape today somehow lessened the intensity of my sorrow.

I bent and picked up a stone and threw it far out into the sea. A neat round ripple spread from the splash and arched towards me in a slow bulging movement. As I watched it grow into a perfect circle, a recent dream I'd had of my mother came into my head. In it Jesus was lying on a darkened bed and my mother told me to go and whisper a petition in his ear. "Tell him of the many trials you've been through In the music business and ask him for a little success. He'll give it to you." When I awoke I laughed, thinking of my mother's forwardness with her Saviour. And I smiled to myself thinking of it again now.

I made my way back over the stones to the narrow path and started retracing my steps to Blackrock. As I walked along, glancing at a golfer about to take a putt on the green to my left, a couple of small birds flew over my head and perched on the top of the wire fence dividing the path from the golf course. One of the birds started whistling and the other started flapping its little wings. I stood and watched the golfer take his shot. The little birds in front of me didn't fly away but went on whistling and bobbing to their hearts' content. I looked straight at them and still they remained where they were. Another memory from the distant past came back to me. In it I arrived home with a bird with a broken wing when I was nine or ten and my mother allowed me to keep it in our garden shed, where we nursed it back to health. A smile stretched my face and a sense of joy welled up inside me.

Song of The Bird *(in memory John Griffin)*

She let him nurse the frail bird with the broken wing;
She gave him bread for the bird and the bird began to sing.
She came alive in the boy who now hungers for the word
To tell the world of the joy of the song of the bird;
And so I sing to the world of what was heard
In the song of the bird.

She lost her mother as a child and as an orphan bride,
She lost a son; she lost her mind and her spirit all but died.
But she came alive in the boy who now hungers for the word
To tell the world of the joy of the song of the bird.
And so I sing to the world of what was heard
In the song of the bird.

She gave him faith in the sun, he gave her hope in the light.
And now he prays, as a son, for her song to take flight.

THE SETTLEMENT MEETING

They've taken all I had but you, love,
but you love are all I need

All I Need

As the bus journeyed towards Dublin I read over some material related to the infringement case of my song *The Voyage*, even though I knew most of the documents inside out. I focused particularly on a copy of a *Sunday Times* article on The Irish Tenors dated December 2000 that specified that US sales for the trio's first album were one and a half million. As my legal team had lost a motion for discovery of documentation related to American sales of the album, this figure was my only means of assessing what I was owed, though I was aware that it couldn't be used as hard evidence in a court of law. Allowing for the possibility that the figure had been inflated for promotional purposes, I was still satisfied that a sum close to a million tallied with sales information I had gleaned from other off-the-record sources since the infringement of my copyright had taken place. Going on this calculation, I'd concluded that the sum of seventy thousand euro that I'd fixed on as a baseline settlement figure was reasonable.

As almost seven years had elapsed since I'd read the full Irish Tenors article in my hands, I skimmed through the story of their meteoric rise to popularity in the US after the PBS TV network had broadcast their video all over the States on St Patrick's Day 1999, and I gritted my teeth because of the stress and strain that they had inadvertently caused me over the past eight years due to loss of royalties and other infringements. Though the journalist who had written the piece was deferential towards the trio's huge success, almost every sentence of his article spoke of his disdain for the type of Oirish schmaltz that had given the tenors their overnight leg up to fame and fortune in the new country. The fact that a song of mine had been an atom in the equation of that success had mellowed my attitude towards the enterprise until I found out about the hatchet job that had been done to the lyric of my song in a CD booklet, on top of my loss of royalties.

The bus arrived in O'Connell St a few minutes late, but, as I still had plenty of time before my meeting at the Four Courts, I dropped into a chapel on the quays to say a prayer for a successful outcome. In the middle of an *Our Father* the figure of seventy thousand euro raised its head and I asked myself if I was being greedy in aiming so high. I reflected back to the time when I was planning to buy a new car for my wife with my first US royalty cheque from the successful album, a present I felt Joan deserved for her unwavering support over my long unprofitable career. Instead of the arrival of dollars, all I got was a receiver's official letter informing me that one of the companies involved with the Irish Tenors had gone into receivership and I was advised not to expect any US royalties for album sales for the crucial twelve-month period after the show was broadcast. I recalled the feeling of almost suffocation that overcame me when I took in the full import of what the letter meant and I also remembered the guarded relief I felt when I discovered that I had a legitimate case to go after the companies who originally produced the video because they had failed to obtain my copyright clearance.

I finished my prayer by mentally rubberstamping the seventy thousand settlement figure and left the church with a determined step.

As I approached the Four Courts, I looked up at the huge copper dome of the main granite building with a feeling of gratitude towards the institution of law that made it possible for an individual like me to pursue justice against a corporate group of companies that had trampled on my artistic integrity and failed to protect my interests.

Seeking directions from a gatekeeper at a side entrances to the complex of grey buildings, I entered the Law Library section of the Four Courts hesitantly, a flutter of butterflies slowing me down. A young woman in a smart grey trouser suit carrying a bulging satchel bypassed me. I caught up with her and asked for directions to the restaurant. She looked me up and down and pointed to a stairwell leading downwards. 'I suppose you mean the coffee shop in the basement. The canteen upstairs is off limits to the general public.'

The coffee shop was cavernous, made up of a number of dim nooks and crannies. I got myself a coffee and sat at a table in a quiet corner facing a pale yellow wall that was crying out for a lick of paint. The low ceiling made me feel claustrophobic. As the time for meeting my solicitor approached I felt tension in my neck. During our last few telephone conversations rows had broken out between us because of the loss of the crucial motion in the High Court to gain access to US sales documentation from the defendants. After the seven-year battle it had taken to reach this point, I suggested that maybe it was time to throw in the towel, but my solicitor wouldn't hear of it. Two weeks later he was vindicated when the defendants made their first settlement offer of thirty five thousand euro, but when I showed signs of considering accepting this sum my solicitor blew a fuse and told me that I had to hold my nerve and go for what I was owed.

Our scheduled meeting time came and went and still I sipped alone. Ten minutes late, my solicitor, Vincent O'Shea, showed up in a dark suit with a bundle of portfolios under his arm. 'Sorry I'm late.'

In the seven years since he'd taken on my case on a "no win no fee" basis, he had aged visibly. He sat opposite me, refusing my offer of a coffee.

I nodded towards a sheaf of documents under his wing, 'You've come prepared.'

Vincent smiled. 'That's only part of it. One of the porters is following with the rest, on a trolley.'

I finished my coffee and got to my feet. 'I'm ready, if you are.'

Vincent led the way out of the coffee shop. 'We're in a room just down the corridor. Our Senior will be along presently to have a few words with you before the meeting.'

The room I followed my solicitor into was even more grim than the coffee shop. A large wooden table covered in black cigarette burns took up three quarters of the room, surrounded by three iron-framed chairs, one of which almost sent me to the floor when I tried to sit on it. A bare bulb set in a low ceiling lit up networks of damp patches and cracks on the walls (the same sick yellow as the walls in the café), one of which displayed a large framed print of a dark hunting scene from a century gone by. I glanced at one of the dog-surrounded huntsmen who had a brace of snipe in one hand and a slanted rifle in the other, and I smiled. 'The décor leaves a lot to be desired.'

Vincent plonked his portfolios on the table and glanced around the room. 'They've been talking for years about revamping the place. This isn't the meeting room, by the way. SCs use this for confabs with clients before the duels upstairs.'

A quiet tap on the door was followed by the entrance of a teenage girl and a bald-headed porter wheeling a trolley of boxes. After the porter deposited the boxes beside the table, he left. Vincent examined the boxes for a few moments, then glanced at his watch and rushed out of the room, telling me he'd be back presently.

The girl went to sit on the wobbly chair at the head of the table till I alerted her to the fact that one of its legs was askew. 'The chair across from me's probably safer. By the way, I'm Johnny. You must be Vincent's secretary?'

The girl sat opposite me, shaking her head. 'No no, I'm on work experience. My name's Megan. I'm from Boston. My father's a friend of a friend of Mr O'Shea. I've only been with him a few days.'

'And how do you find it, the legal game?'

Megan blushed and shrugged. 'I've only been in the courts once, and I found that, like, very boring. Worse than hospital Emergency.'

I glanced at the boxes containing the bones of my case. 'Have you been filled in on the details of my situation?'

Megan shook her head. 'Not really. Something to do with infringement of copyright, right? You're here for a settlement, I guess. Mr O'Shea doesn't really confide in me. What was the infringement, if you don't mind me asking?'

I hesitated. 'A group of companies made a video featuring a song of mine and released it without copyright clearance. Then they passed on the license of the video to another company who released a CD of the show in America, which sold in the region of a million copies. This company then declared itself bankrupt and I received no royalties. The other companies refused to accept any responsibility for this until they made a recent offer to pay roughly half of what I'm owed.'

Megan tossed back her ponytail. 'Sounds strange – a company declaring itself bankrupt after huge success! What's the name of the song?'

'*The Voyage.*'

Megan's eyes widened. 'You won't believe this but a friend from New York had that song played at her wedding last autumn in Manhattan. She even had the lyric printed in the church service booklet. Wait till I tell her I met the author.'

'I hope she didn't take the words from the Irish Tenors' CD booklet. One American singer did and she had to re-record the proper version after she learned from me that she was singing nonsense.'

'You mean they changed your words?'

'In the CD booklet, yes; they butchered them.'

Our conversation was interrupted by the arrival of Vincent and our barrister, Mr Sreenan, a small gentle character, who had a huge reputation, enhanced recently by the success of a multi-million lawsuit he'd defended for a fruit company in the Supreme Court. This was my first time meeting him. After introductions and handshakes, he looked me in the eyes and smiled. 'Let's hope we can conclude this business without too much fuss. Shall we sit.'

Before we sat, Vincent suggested to Megan that she get herself some lunch in the coffee shop. After she left the room Mr Sreenan sat opposite me in the chair Megan had vacated. Vincent took the wobbly chair at the end of the table and somehow managed to remain upright on it. After some chitchat, Mr Sreenan cleared his throat and announced that he had some bad news for us. 'I've already had a word with their SC upstairs and it seems their preference is to deal directly with me, without a meeting.'

Vincent scowled. 'They're the ones who asked for a meeting. This is just a tactic.'

Mr Sreenan sat upright. 'Tactic or not, this is what they want.' He turned to me. 'I know we didn't achieve access to US sales documentation at the High Court hearing but do you have a rough idea of what you're owed?'

I drew the brown envelope from my inside pocket and produced *The Sunday Times* article. 'Going on the sales figure quoted in this interview – even allowing some exaggeration for PR purposes – I reckon I should have got somewhere in the region of seventy thousand punts. Taking currency conversion and interest adjustment into consideration, it could be as much as eighty.'

Vincent cleared his throat, but didn't say anything.'

Mr Sreenan took the article and gave it a quick scan. 'I will of course mention this but I don't think it would be appropriate to produce it now.' He handed the article back to me and glanced at a sheet of currency calculations I gave him. After poring over my figures for a few moments, he shook his head and informed me that my sums were out somewhat. 'I just need a ballpark figure.'

I glanced at Vincent. He remained silent. I turned back to Mr Screenan. 'Bottom line, I'd accept seventy thousand.'

Vincent shook his head, then got to his feet and had a quiet word with Mr Sreenan while he was leaving the room.

Twenty minutes later Mr Sreenan returned with a solemn expression and told us that the defendants weren't prepared to raise the all-in offer already on the table of thirty-five thousand. 'I tried to push them for legal costs as well but they wouldn't even budge on that.'

Vincent's face grew rigid. 'What are they playing at?' Without waiting for an answer, he turned to me. 'They're trying to humiliate you; trying to break your spirit.'

Mr Sreenan gave me a sympathetic look and shook his head. 'I don't think they're going to budge. They claim their clients can't afford to up the offer. Their hands are tied.'

Vincent gave a false laugh. 'The TV company can't afford to pay a few thousand euro extra!'

Mr Sreenan drew a long breath. 'As far as I can gather, the TV company are not involved in this. The offer is coming from the other defendants, who seem to accept the bulk of responsibility.'

I reminded Mr Sreenan of a clause in the TV company's contract for the show – a contract that he himself had gained access to at the court hearing – which stated that the onus was on the TV Company to obtain copyright clearances for the territory of Ireland only. The task of getting international clearances was up to the other companies.'

Vincent loosened his necktie. 'Yes, but the TV company are still accountable.'

Mr Sreenan sighed. It was obvious he was growing impatient and wanted to conclude matters. He turned to me with a look of sympathy. 'I'm sorry but I really do need a decision. If you decide not to accept, I should warn you that you are going to face an uphill battle that could take years to sort out.' He turned to Vincent. 'Maybe I should give you time to talk it over.'

Without looking at me, Vincent shook his head decisively. 'We don't need to talk it over. We didn't accept the offer when it was made and we're certainly not going to accept it now. Final.'

Mr Sreenan went back upstairs. Vincent started fumbling at the portfolios on the table, even though none of them had been opened, and eventually placed them on top of the boxes of other documents. 'I have to go look for a porter to get these things back to my car. What time's your bus leaving?'

I glanced at my watch. 'There's one at four. Where does this leave us now?'

Vincent went to the door and turned the handle the wrong way. 'Sreenan is flying off for a holiday next week. He had warned me that he might not have time be go on working with us if we didn't reach conclusion today. That gives us another headache. But don't worry, I'll find someone solid to replace him.'

A deep sense of weariness came over me at the thought of ploughing on with the case. 'Maybe we should consider accepting the offer?'

Vincent opened the door but then closed it again. 'No way. Can't you see we have them on the ropes. That's why they made the offer. The reason they scuppered this meeting was to humiliate you and grind you down.'

I drew a loud breath. 'Well, they've achieved their objective.'

'You can't give up now. We've gone too far.' Vincent opened the door. 'After I've had time to digest this I'll phone you. We'll discuss it then.'

I was so confused and disappointed I didn't think of grabbing a bite to eat in the coffee shop before leaving the building. I rushed along the quays trying not to dwell on the humiliation I'd just been through and arrived at the terminal in plenty of time to catch my bus. For the duration of the journey back to Galway I sat by the window in a daze, wondering what I should do.

When I finally arrived home I found Joan watching a delirious puppet turkey on TV performing Ireland's next entry for the Eurovision Song Contest. While I was breaking the bad news to her about the meeting, the raucous puppet, surrounded by strobe lights and scantily dressed lap dancers, brought his manic rap song to a close and a beaming TV presenter took over the proceedings. After making a gag about a 'fowl performance' he introduced the chairman of the committee that had chosen the puppet and song as Ireland's next Eurovision entry. A bearded man appeared on the screen and started praising the puppet and the rap song in the highest terms. I looked at the man's familiar face and cursed. From her couch, Joan turned to me in puzzlement and asked what was wrong. I pointed to the screen and cursed again. 'You'll never guess who that is?' I moved closer to the set while the bearded man heaped accolade after accolade on the turkey puppet. I gave a false laugh. 'That's one of the men partly responsible for the long frustrating day I've just been through, to say nothing of the seven years I've been pursuing him and his colleagues through the courts; a man who neglected to get my copyright clearance, abused my lyric and sold on the performance rights of my song to a company who defrauded me of my royalties. That's him – the guy fawning over the puppet.'

I paused and scrutinised his smiling face, then sighed. 'It wasn't all his fault, but if he only knew half of what he and his cohorts have put me through!'

SUNDAY

That's why my faith in Christ,
God knows, grows and grows.

Darwin & St Paul

Waking at my usual Sunday morning time of seven, I dressed and
went down to my workroom to do some spiritual study. As it was cold,
I slipped into the bed, propped three pillows on top of one another as
a back rest, reached for the *Confessions* of Augustine, and got down to
reassessing a book I'd read a number of times in the past. Focusing only
on select passages that had made an impression on me over the years,
I flitted through Book 2 and lit on Chapter 4 dealing with an orchard
that Augustine had stolen pears from with some 'roguish' friends when
he was a kid. The pangs of conscience he'd suffered because of this
misdemeanor had prompted me during a previous reading to write at
the end of the chapter:

> When I think of all the orchards I skinned as a kid without even a
> twinge of conscience, I must say I find Augustine's scruples over
> stealing a few miserly pears a bit over the top.

The next section I focused on dealt with the beginnings of
Augustine's wayward years as a Manichean, wondering, while I read,
how such an intelligent man could have been taken in by a sect that
believed, among other things, that figs wept when they were plucked.
His mother, Monica, I learned, was responsible for his being saved from
these and other pagan delusions. The intensity of her devotion to prayer
on her son's behalf culminates in Chapter 11 of Book 3, where she is
visited in a dream by a heavenly host who shows her a vision in which
she is joined in spiritual union with her son. Though this prediction
would take years to take effect, the holy bond between mother and son

that would lead to his ultimate conversion is established at this point.

At nine o'clock I put the *Confessions* aside and went to prepare Sunday breakfast for the family. In the kitchen, I plugged in the hi-fi and put on Bach's *Air on a G String*. Though I played this piece often on Sunday mornings, it didn't diminish the pleasure it gave me now. Listening to it was as close as I could imagine the tone of eternity might sound like. Other works of Bach's which I loved had ornamental passages of their time that rankled a little to my ear, but Suite No. 3 in D Major seemed timeless. I enjoyed it so much, I played it a second time and then let the collection play on as I went about cooking eggs and bacon.

When the grill was ready, I went to the bottom of the stairs and called Joan and the kids. Joan arrived down first in her long purple nightgown, yawning. The first thing she did on entering the room was to turn on the radio to Des Kelly's big band show, even though Bach was still playing on the hi-fi in the background. Count Basie and Bach battled it out for dominion of our kitchen until I went over and switched off the hi-fi, without a word of rancour. One of the golden rules of our house was that democracy regarding household music reigned on Sunday mornings, once the family came down stairs. At other times they put up with my dictatorial hold on the hi-fi controls during meal times, but not on Sundays.

After breakfast, Joan went shopping and our son Kevin drove off to a friend's house. Ailbhe and Brian went upstairs, one to study for exams, the other to play his PlayStation. I made myself a mug of coffee and went back to my room and returned to the fourth century and Augustine's journey towards faith.

After reading a very moving chapter on the death of one of Augustine's closest friends who had converted to Christianity on his deathbed (his name curiously isn't given), I skipped to a heavily underlined section of Book 6, Chapter 4, dealing with the huge influence that Ambrose had on Augustine, especially in the area of scriptural reading, which had baffled Augustine till he learned of the figurative approach to such study, an approach that helped his faith enormously.

> I began to believe that the Catholic faith, which I had thought impossible to defend against objections of the Manichees, might fairly be maintained especially since I had heard one passage after another figuratively explained. These passages had been death to me when I took them literally, but once I heard them explained in their spiritual meaning I began to blame myself for my despair . . .

At twelve forty, I put the book aside, went and got my navy anorak and woolly cap for my customary Sunday walk to the Atlantic.

Following the winding path past the playground and down across the iron bridge over the stream, I fell into a steady pace heading towards Barna Woods. It was a lovely clear frosty afternoon – ideal walking weather, except for occasional patches of hazardous melting ice. While negotiating the upward path leading into the woods – walking on the grassy margin to avoid the ice of the incline – a boy coming down the slope slipped and fell. His mother following behind with a Labrador on a leash cried out the boy's name, as though feeling his pain. On the verge of tears, Tommy picked himself up and put on a brave face, while mother rubbed his behind and consoled him.

Going through the woods, the chaotic geometry of the leafless trees took my attention, as they often did. Though there appeared no order to the sprawling mass of branches and trunks leaning every which way, it fascinated me that most of the larger trees grew to exactly the same height, as though by common pact, so that, seen from a distance, the entire wood appeared like a single organism.

Emerging on to the Spiddal road at the far side of the wood, I noticed that the car park of Barna chapel was empty so I went into the church for a spell of quiet contemplation. After saying a few prayers for family and friends at a shrine to Our Lady, I settled into focusing on the single syllable "God". While the drone was humming in my head, thoughts of Augustine interrupted my mantra. Doing some mental calculation, I totted up that I'd read the *Confessions* at least a half dozen times over the past fifteen years. Originally my interest in the saint was connected to his stubbornness at putting off his conversion till he'd extracted all the pleasure he could get out of our world before making his leap of faith (something I had done myself after my swinging '60s days). Later I began to see parallels between the fact that Augustine's parents, like mine, were polarised when it came to religion, though his father, like my father, came to respect the faith of his spouse, realising that it helped their marriage bond and brought order to their household. Again, when I thought deeply about this aspect of my sympathy for the man from Hippo, I detected superficiality and even egotism in my interest in him. Finally, during my last few readings of what is considered the first autobiography ever written, I began to be impressed by the intensity of Augustine's lust for discovering truth, a craving that I began to see was even more potent than his earlier sexual urges.

The sound of someone entering the church broke my thought pattern and made me realise that I'd completely lost the thread of contemplation. The new arrival knelt in a pew a few rows behind me. I was tempted to turn around, but didn't. I tried to get back into my mantra but my concentration was hampered by the sound of whispering prayers behind me. I said a final *Our Father* and got to my feet and left the chapel.

On the sloping road to Silver Strand a white souped-up Triumph sports car whizzed past me at tremendous speed. I cursed the young driver and moved closer to the grassy margin for safety.

As I approached the coastline I noticed three bright coloured windsurfers' sails out in the choppy ocean and a single red kite bobbing in the clear sky above the strand. Rather than make my way to the beach where people were walking dogs and playing ball, I trudged through some wet seaweed, wobbled over a stretch of stones and rocks and came to a boulder I was in the habit of sitting on. Maneuvering myself onto its flat surface, I had a perfect view of the Burren at the far side of the bay and a more restricted view of the Aran Islands out on the hazy western horizon. Noticing the purple colour of the long stretch of limestone hills on the far coast I recalled that they had been slate-grey the previous Sunday. I let my gaze drift along the rocky Connemara coastline and then brought my eyes back to my more immediate surroundings of boulders, rocks, stones, pebbles, shells, sand and seaweed. The array of delicate colours and the variety of stone and pebble shapes held my attention till a high pitched squeal made me look seaward just in time to witness a flock of birds swirling in perfect coordination above the wind surfers.

While I was drinking in Galway Bay, my mind drifted back to the chapter of the *Confessions* that I'd read before lunch dealing with Augustine's bafflement of biblical scripture till Ambrose put him on the right trail. Because my own first readings of the bible after I'd returned to the faith had left me totally bewildered, I took comfort from Augustine's disclosure, and I wondered why church leaders down the centuries hadn't highlighted this crucial aspect of belief for the general public.

A windsurfer hit a high wave that unmanned him from his board. The purple sail collapsed into the choppy grey-green water and the surfer disappeared from sight for a few seconds before re-emerging and pulling himself erect on his board, which was immediately whisked away by the wind.

I got to my feet, collected a few tiny whorled orange shells from the dun coloured sand around the boulder I'd been sitting on, put them in my pocket and started retracing my steps home.

Back at the house I deposited the shells in an ornamental bottle on the window of my workroom (a keepsake that grew prettier and prettier each week in proportion to the rising level of shells added to it).

After establishing that there were no relevant emails to deal with, I went to the kitchen and had my afternoon coffee while Joan went about preparing dinner.

After glancing through a Sunday tabloid that Joan had bought at the shops (I'd long since given up reading Sunday newspapers in detail), I made my way to the living room where I found our son, Brian, and his friend Graham watching a soccer match on TV. I glanced at the set and asked the boys which team was winning. Brian ignored me. Graham smiled. 'Man-U. Two nil.'

'Who are the other team?'

Graham went to tell me but Brian interrupted. 'What difference does it make? You have no interest in soccer! You're just trying to be polite.'

I smiled at Graham. 'Do you talk to your father like that?'

Graham chuckled. 'Yeah.'

Brian looked at me and loured.

A scream went up from the telly and Graham let out a yelp. 'Wow, did you see that? And from such a long distance out! That's three nil.'

Brian looked at the telly and frowned, then turned to me and scowled. 'I missed that goal over you!'

I retreated to my room and resumed reading the *Confessions*:

> I was eager for fame and wealth and marriage, but You only
> derided these ambitions. They caused me to suffer the most galling
> difficulties, but the less You allowed me to find pleasure in anything
> that was not Yourself, the greater, I know, was Your goodness to me.

Moving on to Book 8, I skimmed through many underlined passages dealing with Augustine's struggles to make a definitive leap of faith till I came to the seminal moment of his conversion in Chapter 12, above which I'd written "Crisis and Resolution". In this famous section Augustine – deeply disturbed about his ongoing procrastinations regarding committing himself fully to the Christian faith – hears a child's voice repeating the refrain "Take it and read, take it and read", an injunction that leads Augustine to pore over a random passage from an Epistle of St Paul in his possession that he feels is directed at him: "Not in revelling and drunkenness, not in lust and wantonness, not in quarrels and rivalries. Rather, arm yourself with the Lord Jesus Christ; spend no more thought on nature and nature's appetites."

The confluence of these serendipitous occurrences convince the future saint that his path from here on in can only lead in one direction. At the end of the chapter I found the following observation I'd written many years before:

> The first time I read this chapter I found it a little naive and even silly that Augustine should base his conversion on such a chance happening. But the more you read it – especially after reading the chapters of struggle leading up to it – the more you see that its inevitable outcome was divinely inspired. I've had several similar moments in my life – especially the moment after I wrote my song *The Beacon* when I opened George Herbert's book *The Temple* at random on the poem *Frailtie* (spelt in this old English way) just after reading a chapter of *the Imitation of Christ* by Thomas Á Kempis that ends on the same word, Frailty.

At four o'clock I put the paperback aside and went for a second stroll, around the park. Though the temperature had dropped a few degrees, I sat on a bench overlooking one of the main football pitches where a young team was practicing, being put through a strenuous drill of exercises by an enthusiastic trainer who kept shouting commands in a brash voice. After watching the boys with some sympathy for a few minutes, I turned my gaze towards Barna Woods. Already the sun was beginning to set behind the long stretch of leafless trees in a pink and orange glow. As I watched it's slow descent behind the grey treetops, the thought came to me again that the wood seen from afar looked like a single organism due to the fact that the trees grew to a uniform height. In its leafless state it didn't look as impressive as it did in high summer when the full green growth of leaves gave it the appearance of a single giant shrub, but even without its foliage it looked singular.

Back at the house Joan was busy in the kitchen setting the table for dinner, which she informed me would be ready shortly.

I went to the living room (the two boys were gone), put some turf on the fire and then returned to Augustine in my room. Skipping to a moving account of his mother Monica's death, I focused on a single line which I'd underlined some years before:

> In the flesh she brought me to birth in this world; in her heart she brought me to birth in Your eternal light.

Moving on a few pages I halted at a hand-written heading "Mystical Moment" that I'd jotted at the top of the page during a previous reading. Halfway into the chapter I came upon what for me has become the most important passage of the book, a moment when mother and son, while staying in a town called Ostia not long before Monica's death, experience an epiphany where time takes on a new aspect and Augustine realises that eternity is not in the past or in the future.

> While we spoke of the eternal wisdom, longing and straining for it with all the strength of our hearts, for one fleeting instant we reached out and touched it . . .

At the top of the page on which this is chronicled I had written

> The timeless moment experienced here sets the tone for the rest of the book – a search to explain the substance of the eternal in time.

While I was pondering on my own words, Joan called me for dinner.

THE PRODIGALS @ THE ELECTRIC PICNIC

I felt the world turning, journeying, in the sea of night
and my heart started burning for our returning to the light

To The Light

The bus dropped us close to Stradbally House on a path skirting the festival grounds. The arts officer co-ordinating our contingent of writers and poets pointed towards an area known as The Mindfield, telling us that the tent allocated for our readings and performances was called The Literary Stage. 'Please stick to the timetable you've been given so that we can fit you all in at the scheduled times. Have a great day and see you back here for our departure at ten thirty tonight.'

In groups of twos and threes, the writers and journalists stood awkwardly at the front of the bus, uncertain of what to do next. A vehicle like a golf cab whizzed passed my son Brian and I, as a familiar fuzzy-haired man wearing glasses approached us. The fuzzy-haired man glanced after the cab with a bemused smile and turned to Brian. 'Where would I get one of them?'

Brian shrugged and gave me a puzzled look, as much as to say: Who's this wally?

The 'wally' glanced at my guitar bag and held out his hand. 'I'm Paul Muldoon, nice to meet you.'

Having spotted the poet on the bus earlier, I was fully aware of who he was. I shook his hand, telling him that I was familiar with his poetry and that I'd read a recent article on him in *The Times* of London. 'I was surprised to discover you're a big fan of old Broadway musicals.'

The poet looked me up and down. 'You read that? I didn't get to see it myself. Just flew in from the States this morning for a spot on this festival. Yeah, I love the elegance of some of the old lyricists. I write songs myself; not so elegant, but I enjoy it.' He turned to Brian. 'What band are you looking forward to seeing this weekend?'

Brian tugged at his rhinestone earring. 'Mumford and Sons, but I don't think they're on till tomorrow and we're leaving tonight.'

The poet shrugged. 'Never heard of them. Are they good?'

Brian took out his mobile phone and regulated the dial till a distorted song began to play on the tiny speaker. 'This is them.'

The poet took the proffered phone and put the instrument to his ear and listened for a few moments then gave the phone back to Brian. 'Lively stuff. Mumford and Sons! I'll look out for them.'

The Irish Times columnist and my literary partner for the day John Waters approached us, smiling. I introduced the two writers and explained that John and I were set to collaborate for a performance later in the evening. 'We call ourselves The Prodigals.'

Paul scratched his head. 'There's a rock band called The Prodigals, isn't there?' Without waiting for an answer, he started backing away. 'I'll try and catch your set. Have a good day, Brian.'

John Waters glanced after the poet. 'Nice fella.'

I nodded. 'Fine poet too. But don't be surprised if he doesn't show up for our spot. He has no time for religion. So I learned from an article I read on him a few days ago.'

John shrugged. 'Every man to his own.'

We moved into the Literary tent, where a young novelist was reading to an audience of seven in a seated space that looked like it could hold two hundred. I deposited my guitar at the back of the stage and had a few whispered words with the stage manager regarding technical requirements for later on. Back outside the tent, John Waters and I discussed our programme – which we'd already worked out by email – and then went our separate ways, agreeing to meet up ten or fifteen minutes before we were due on stage.

After checking out several tents in the Mindfield, Brian and I headed off to explore the grounds further afield. We watched a number of bands – all playing in such close proximity to one another that the sound overspill made it impossible to listen with any kind of clarity – then we gravitated towards the main stage where the sound system was a lot clearer. A black funk band decked out in bright caftans were performing to a fairly large audience who were for the most part ignoring the musicians on stage. Brian thought the band was 'cool' but this didn't stop him from growing restless minutes later and suggesting that we check out what was going on in one of the massive circus-like tents out at the periphery of the site.

As we approached the large tent I was forced to stick my fingers in my ears to block out the deafening noise. Approaching the entrance, the high decibels almost had the effect of physically driving me back in my tracks. 'I'm not going in there. My ears couldn't take it.'

Brian grabbed my arm and pulled me in. 'Come on, chicken. This must be the techno tent. Sounds massive.'

Inside, a capacity crowd of five or six hundred teenagers were gyrating in a single mass to a heavy electronic pulse coming from a line of synthesizers on a strobe-flashing, smoke-belching stage. There appeared to be only two people operating the record-decks, computers and machines. Most of the kids flailing their arms about in front of us looked like they were chemically induced. Brian started copying them, waving his arms and bobbing to the heavy beat. I gave him a disapproving look and was about to say something disparaging, but then I had a flashback to a club I performed in myself when I was roughly Brian's age. The memory of my wild antics and the wild antics of our audience made me bite my tongue.

On leaving the Electro tent we headed for the food stalls in the centre of the grounds. A group of young teenagers stumbled passed us sucking on cans of cider, laughing and cursing. I glanced at my watch. 'Not even four o'clock! Can you imagine what they'll be like by midnight!'

Brian grinned. 'You'd need a few cans to enjoy a place like this.'

I scowled.

Brian laughed. 'Only messin'.'

After a quick bite to eat, we headed back to the Mindfield to catch Roddy Doyle and Irvine Welsh being interviewed by Dermot Bolger on the Literary stage. The tent was full to capacity when we got there and the interview was in full flight, with long bouts of audience laughter being ignited by banter from the stage. Given the nature of the work being discussed, the mock library setting with its gaudy backdrop of faded painted bookshelves looked totally incongruous, but the three writers sitting in antique leather armchairs seemed to be enjoying themselves immensely. Soon after Brian and I squeezed into a standing space at the back of the tent, Roddy started reading from one of his books. I tried to take in the expletive-peppered dialogue of his north Dublin characters but bouts of laughter from the audience kept interfering with my concentration.

Irvine Welsh stood up for his reading, telling the audience that he liked to 'get physical' with his characters. In a thick Edinburgh accent he related the story of a young woman living in bleak circumstances in an unspecified Scottish city. Brian was very impressed by his raucous humour.

'Who's he, dad? He's massive.'

'You know the film *Trainspotting*? He wrote the book the film is based on.'

'What do you think of him?'

I looked at the big florid man gesticulating on stage. 'He's a good performer but I have no time for his non-partisan attitude to the drug culture he writes about. He adds to the confusion for young people, I believe.'

Brian eyed the audience drinking in Irvine's every word and turned a blank eye on me. 'They seem to like him.'

I shrugged.

After Irvine's reading, Dermot Bolger threw the proceedings over to the floor for a short questions and answers session. As the two writers gazed out expectantly at their admirers, the thought ran through my mind of asking Roddy why he had ended his TV drama *The Family* (his greatest achievement in my estimation) with the Lord's Prayer, given his staunch atheism. I searched for the courage to raise my voice above the hubbub of questions that were being flung at the stage from every quarter of the tent, but I couldn't find my tongue.

The three writers left the stage to a tumultuous round of applause, then the tent quickly emptied. Brian and I rambled off for a stroll and returned to the literary stage in the middle of readings by three of Ireland's top crime writers. Though one of these was the well-known journalist, Gene Kerrigan, the tent was less than quarter full. The crowd dwindled even further during the next reading. By the time John Waters arrived there were just six people in the tent, plus Brian who removed himself to a shadowy corner to hide his embarrassment at the low turnout for The Prodigals.

John and I took to the stage without the fanfare of an introduction (which would have been farcical under the circumstances). With an armful of books, John made himself comfortable in one of the leather armchairs while I sat on a hardback chair with my guitar on my lap. I opened with a song from my *Just Another Town* album, prefacing it with a brief story relevant to the theme of our performance: 'I received an email once from a guy who informed me that my opening number, *Mary*, had been one of his favourite love songs till his wife tuned into the lyric and suggested that the song might be about the Virgin Mary. After I wrote back commending his wife's perception, the man responded with a curt few lines informing me that, as an agnostic, he felt tricked and no longer rated my song so highly.'

O Mary it's true I loved you
But it's been so long I'd forgotten you.
You dressed in blue and white too

And my memory picks daffodils for you.
In a park in the city I stole them for you,
Now those flowers remind me of you.
When I went to a park when the spring was new
A bunch of those memories grew,
So I picked a bunch and thought of you.

Exotic eastern music (sitar accompaniment for a belly dancer, we later learned) started spilling into our space from the tent next to us. This completely threw my concentration but somehow I managed to keep singing. During the second verse the audience swelled to nine, one of whom I noticed was Paul Muldoon. In an attempt to draw a few more people in from outside, I sang my most popular ballad *The Voyage*, and it worked. Seven or eight new arrivals came in during the chorus and several of them joined in with the singing.

After a loud round of applause (loud for sixteen or seventeen people, that is), I introduced John Waters and filled the audience in on details of our association, going back to an interview John did with me for *Hot Press* magazine in the late '60s, an interview in which I admitted publicly for the first time to being a practicing Catholic. 'That was the last time *Hot Press* did a feature on me, but John has been a great support down the years.'

Looking like a sixteenth-century divine with his long locks pouring over his shoulders and his grey beard adding gravitas to his face, John opened his spot with a reading from his book *Lapsed Agnostic*, which describes the naïve notion that he had of God as a boy growing up in Castlerea, Co Roscommon:

Despite having no body, God managed to have a long beard and was dressed in a kind of long white vestment-type garment. He was bald on top but had long hair down his back and shoulders. He wore sandals, without socks. I'm not sure where the sandals came from, because God usually manifested Himself only from the waist up, the lower half of his body being suffused in fluffy clouds . . .

This standard, anthropomorphic portrait of the Almighty drew laughter from the audience and the atmosphere in the tent became relaxed. After reading another few light passages, John deepened his tone and related a story of an agnostic alcoholic he met at an AA meeting who battled against the idea of turning his broken life over to a nebulous force that he felt didn't exist. In a barrage of swear words that Roddy Doyle would have been proud of, the man railed against a 'fucking God' he didn't believe in. 'In the end the man fought against his own stubborn nature and got down on his knees and, in doing so, inexplicably found a way to live again, without alcohol.'

While the audience was giving John a round of applause, I noticed Paul Muldoon standing up. He bowed towards the stage and then left the tent, waving a backhand over his shoulder in a gesture that I interpreted as: Nice performance lads, but Christian guff's not my cup of tea.

John read a final story about a tragic young couple who jump hand in hand from one of the Twin Towers on 9/11. Though a fictional account of what transpired between the pair in their final moments, the audience was so moved by the piece they gave John a standing ovation. For an encore, I sang *Don't Give Up Till It's Over*, and everyone in the tent joined in on the chorus.

After we came off stage John rushed away to catch a performance by Steve Earle in one of the large tents. I spoke to a few stragglers from our audience while packing away my guitar, then Brian and I headed off to see some of the headline acts at the centre arena.

On the main stage Imelda May was singing to a crowd of thousands. Beneath a medallion moon, she and her band belted out a set of rockabilly songs that had the audience bopping in the grass. Following Imelda, a band called The Frames took to the stage and things cranked up a gear, sound wise. Though I was familiar with some of the band's songs from the radio, the high sound level of their live performance was too much for my ageing ears. After two or three songs, I suggested to Brian that we head off to the food stalls to get some snacks and beverages.

Sitting at a plastic table at a comfortable remove from the main stage, I sipped a beer while Brian drank hot chocolate topped with multicoloured marshmallows. As most of the festival crowd was at the main event, we had a whole seating area to ourselves, apart from a friendly group of happy campers who raised their glasses to us as we sat. Chatting about the day gone by, Brian admitted that most of the music he'd heard hadn't really appealed to his rap sensibility, apart from what he'd heard in the techno tent. 'Oxygen would be more my style.'

I raised an eyebrow. 'From what I hear, the Oxygen festival is just an orgy of alcohol and drugs.'

Brian shook his head. 'They get great bands; Eminem played there this year.'

I shrugged. 'And you know what I think of him!'

'Eminem's a poet, dad. You should listen to his words.'

'Diatribes without melody are not songs. And I don't like the way he rails against women. I know he was born in disadvantage, but that doesn't give him the right to rant on and on in such a misogynistic and aggressive way about the nightmare that aspects of the American dream is turning into.'

'Ah dad, you're brain dead if you can't hear the genius of Eminem.'

I laughed. 'You're brain dead for allowing yourself to be sucked in by the trends and fashions of your time. You need to develop an independent mind about the culture around you.'

Brian shrugged and sipped hot chocolate.

We sat in silence for a few minutes listening to a strident echo coming from the main stage. I looked skyward and noticed a bright object rising above the arena. I pointed it out to Brian. He thought it was a star. I shook my head. 'It's a lantern with a candle inside.'

Brian disagreed. 'You're seeing things! It's a star.'

'Stars don't move that fast.'

'Maybe it's a satellite.'

'It's a floating Chinese lantern.'

Brian drank some hot chocolate and licked cream from his lips. 'I'd say John Waters was disappointed by the small crowd that came to see you, weren't you?'

'I'm used to small crowds. We did okay, in the end.'

Brian smirked. 'Not as good as Roddy Doyle and the Scottish guy.'

I sipped some beer. 'God is out of fashion for a lot of people in Ireland these days, understandably so to a degree because of the cover-up of church corruption, but we're in danger of throwing out the immaculate baby with the slimy bathwater. John has had a tough time since he published his book *Lapsed Agnostic*, and I'd say he's going to have an even tougher time in the years ahead, operating as he does in a milieu that has little sympathetic towards Catholicism, an area I've struggled in myself for the duration of my career. It's happened slowly, but Ireland has become almost a godless place for the young.'

Brian raised his head. 'I believe in God.'

'I know you do.'

'I'm not sure I believe that Communion is the body of Christ, though. My friend Rohit thinks that's a daft idea.'

I looked up at the full moon. 'That's because Rohit's a Muslim or a Buddhist.'

'No he's not. He doesn't believe in any God. Neither does his father. His mother's the Buddhist.'

I searched the sky for the lantern and spotted it as a tiny speck at the right of the moon. 'The Eucharist is the centrepiece of our faith. That's what it's all about. If you don't believe in that, you're not a Catholic.'

Brian shrugged and sipped his hot chocolate.

I glanced back at the sky. 'Look how far the lantern's risen now.'

Brian scrutinised the heavens but couldn't locate the light. I tried to point it out to him but ended up losing track of it myself. 'I can't see it either now. But I know it's there.'

Brian laughed. 'Like God.'

I looked in the sky one night and saw a star,
clear and bright, but so far away from me alone in the dark.
I turned from that distant light and went to bed
And slept for a while with you by my side,
then woke from a dream and looked out again,
and the heavens were all aglow, shedding light on all below,
and I felt the world turning, journeying, in the sea of night
and my heart started burning for our returning to the light.

TO THE LIGHT

Now we're ageing and grey, but the dream hasn't faded away;
our intentions survive, our soul connections are still alive.

Burning Again

As Jack and I made our way under the Whistling Bridge at Cleeves' Bank
and out onto the narrow dirt path skirting the Shannon, I gazed across
the river at the giant sail-shaped Clarion Hotel on Steamboat Quay just
outside the docks and my eyes retreated back across the brown water.
'Limerick's changed a lot since our day?'

Jack glanced at the ultra-modern skyscraper and nodded. 'For the
better, I think. I like that building; it's a brave statement, telling the
city and the docks area in particular that it has a future, despite the
recession.'

I agreed. 'I stayed there soon after it opened. The city looks terrific
from the top floor. The docks are pretty run-down, though.'

Jack looked towards the port area. 'Shannon Airport made it
redundant. But there's great potential there still. Think of London docks!
If it weren't for the fact that your banks and builders are bust, I think
it has the capacity to become the hub of the Limerick arts scene, with
theatres, music centres, art galleries and a maritime museum replacing
those dilapidated buildings overlooking the harbour.'

I smiled at the way Jack – a long time UK resident – dissociated
himself from Ireland's financial meltdown. Since we'd slummed together
in Granny's Intentions back in the '60s, he had gained a reputation as
an astute businessman, and, during our present band reunion for a
series of gigs in the hometown, I could see why.

An elderly couple coming towards us forced Jack and myself to get
in single file. Back shoulder to shoulder, Jack returned the conversation
to the show we'd played at the Belltable Arts Centre the night before, the
first of a sell-out three-night run. 'Those musical hiccups you mentioned

earlier were inevitable – our last reunion was more than ten years ago, and performing seventeen new songs is a lot different than playing the old stuff. I think it went terrific.'

Jack had praised the show already but I was glad he reiterated it now, as one of the reasons I'd asked him to come on this riverside walk was to assess the mood of the band after the first performance of what was essentially a show based on my solo album *To The Light*. 'I thought it worked really well myself, but I sensed unease from some of the lads after we came off stage.'

Jack shrugged. 'I think they all really enjoyed it, Hoggy in particular. There's great scope in some of your ballads for him to shine as the classical musician he is. '

I brought to mind the rehearsal period that preceded the opening night and recalled how Hoggy had acted as the band's musical director, taking on the roll that usually fell to our keyboard player John Ryan, who had opted not to take part in the reunion. It occurred to me during the practice sessions that Hoggy's enthusiasm may have had something to do with the fact that he had recently retired as a music teacher from Limerick's School of Music after a career of nearly thirty five years. Remembering back to when he had gained his musical degree in the London School of Music as a part-time student while still a member of our band, I recalled him voicing an ambition back then of becoming a classical concert guitarist.

Skirting a puddle on the path, I recalled some of the compliments we had received after the show the night before. 'The audience seemed well contented anyway. Three fans down from Dublin kept telling me in the pub after the gig how much they'd enjoyed themselves. They admitted that they'd come to hear our old songs but were won over by the new stuff by the end of the night.'

Jack laughed. 'I know the three you mean. The minute you left the bar one of them came over to Cha and myself and started giving out reams about the fact that we hadn't played enough soul and Motown.'

I chuckled. 'The hypocrite.'

Jack gave me a taste of what the old biddy had said, mimicking a rough Dublin accent: '"Who the fuck does Johnny Duhan think he is, singing all those personal songs about old girlfriends and telling us stories about his wife. What do we care about his bleedin' wife! We came to hear Granny's Intentions singing Motown classics like *If I Were a Carpenter*"'

I laughed. '*If I Were a Carpenter* is a folk song by Tim Hardin.'

Jack tittered. 'I know, I know. But it shows you what we're up against. I love the show. And I realise how important the stories are for bringing the audience into the songs. I have to tell you, though, that some of the lads do feel a bit awkward standing around during some of the longer yarns. Maybe you could tighten them up a bit?'

'I'll try, but some are necessarily long. They help the audience connect with the lyrics.'

A gull attempting to perch on the thin branch of a sally tree down on the mudflats took my attention – its wide grey and white wings flapping madly trying to gain balance. It wobbled on the bobbing stem for a few moments then gave up and flew down river.

When we reached the end of the walkway Jack and I lingered in the grassy recreational area overlooking the Shannon, discussing individual songs from the show that needed tweaking. Agreeing to an impromptu rehearsal when we got back to the arts centre, we retraced our steps to town. On the way Jack predicted that the night's performance ahead would be the best of the three shows.

As we turned into O'Connell Street my mobile phone started ringing in my pocket. It was my sister, Kay, who had contributed backing vocals for the band the night before. 'Just calling to let you know I'm having lunch right now with one of your greatest fans in the Belltable restaurant, DJ Alan. He's just flown in from London with a gold disc of Granny's Intentions' first single, *The Story of David.*'

'Gold disc! We never sold a million.'

Kay laughed. 'I know. Alan had the single gold-plated himself. He feels you deserved to have had a number one. He's quite a character. Wants to know if you'd come and meet him before the show tonight?'

I moved the phone closer to my mouth. 'Jack and myself are on our way to the Belltable right now to run over a few songs. Tell him I'll see him in a few minutes.'

As we entered the basement restaurant at the Belltable I spotted Kay sitting at a table with a small man dressed entirely in black, except for a necktie with the imprint of *Sgt Pepper's Lonely Hearts' Club Band* down the front. As we approached, he jumped up and hugged me. 'Is this Johnny Duhan, the boy I idolised in Cork's Cavern Club back in '65? A life-long dream has materialised before my eyes.'

I glanced around the restaurant at a few bemused customers and tried not to blush. The little man went on speaking so rapidly I found it impossible to keep up with the flow of his Corkonian tinged Cockney twang. He looked into my eyes. 'I'm sorry for this display of emotion, Johnny. But you don't know what it's like to come face to face with someone you've looked up to for so long. This meeting is as significant as my first meeting with Paul McCartney. I've met all the Beatles. George wasn't so nice and Ringo was downright rude, but Paul was a gentleman. I sense a gentleness in you too Johnny. You look so calm, so grounded.'

We sat and Alan started talking about his life-long passion for bands of the '60s, dropping famous names like they were personal friends. Humming one of my old songs, he dipped his hand into a carrier bag and produced a framed gold disc of Granny's Intentions' single, *The Story of David*, with a photo of the band dressed in black velvet slim-line costumes above it. 'You always had a sense of style. You deserved to be stars. And in my eyes you were stars, and still are.'

In an effort to stem the flow of embarrassing compliments, I introduced Jack to Alan and mentioned that he lived in London. Alan took a business card from his pocket and handed it to Jack, inviting him to visit his 'Pop Shop' in Soho. 'You'll have to come and visit me too Johnny when you're next in London.'

Using the acceptance of the business card as an apt moment for bringing the meeting to a close, I told Alan that we'd see him later at the concert and thanked him for coming.

In the theatre, Jack and I spent an hour running over songs from our programme, then parted company till the night's performance. I went to my hotel and had dinner with my son Brian, who was acting as my shopkeeper for the three shows. At six-thirty we headed back to the arts centre and set up our merchandise stall in the foyer, laying out CDs and books on a small table.

The band began arriving around seven – Cha, our second vocalist, and Guido, our drummer, followed by keyboard player Jim (the only non-Granny member of the band) then Jack and our sound engineer, Ado, and finally our lead guitarist, Hoggy. Before going to the dressing rooms we did a quick soundcheck and ran through a few songs. While we were going over a medley of soul and Motown standards that ended our programme as an encore, Cha reminded Hoggy that they had decided to switch one of his soul songs to end the show as a more dramatic finale than one I had finished with the night before. Not having been informed of this change, I was a little taken aback. I looked at Cha and thought I detected a glint of one-upmanship in his eye as he ran through his song, but I said nothing, thinking it fair enough to allow him the final moment of glory in a show that was otherwise dominated by my imprint.

After fine-tuning my guitar, I followed the rest of the band upstairs and went to a dressing room I'd shared with Cha and Guido the night before. The lights were on but the place was empty. I looked at myself questioningly in one of the glowing bulb-fringed mirrors. A humorous incident from the previous night came back to me. Cha was putting on a pair of flame-red trousers and rose-pink sneakers and Guido and I started jibing him about the vivid colours. With a smirk stretching his oval face, Cha (one of my oldest boyhood friends) strutted around the room doing Chuck Berry knee-bends while telling us that we hadn't seen anything yet. "I bought three different coloured pairs for the three separate shows. I'm really goin' ta sock it to 'em."

Curious to know what colour trousers Cha had chosen for the night's performance ahead, I made my way to the other dressing room and found most of the band there – all except Jack. As I entered the room I noticed a lull in the conversation, though most of the guys greeted me with a smile. Cha was wearing bright green trousers. I complimented him on 'going patriotic' and made small talk with Jim for a few minutes. Then I withdrew and went back to the other dressing room. Sitting in front of the lit mirror, I asked myself if I was witnessing a conspiracy but quickly rejected the notion, telling my reflection that I was being paranoid. I thought back on the many days of rehearsal that had gone into preparing the show during the weeks gone by and recalled the camaraderie we'd enjoyed becoming reacquainted after the ten year hiatus since our last reunion back in the '90s. More mature in our attitude now, we seemed to get on as a unit much better than at any time in the past. Encroaching mortality, evident in our grey hair, bald pates, turkey necks and pot bellies, seemed to concentrate minds on getting as much enjoyment out of our time together than ever before. The banter and jokes reached a crescendo one day when, during a coffee break, Cha posed the deadpan question, "What'll I do if one of the ladies in the audience wants me to take her backstage and give her the iron?" The raucous laughter that this question generated grew even louder when I retorted: "Iron! More like lead by this stage, Cha."

A few minutes before showtime I turned off my mobile phone and headed down stairs to take up my position at the side of the stage. On the way I ran into Hoggy, who was having a last minute smoke at an open exit door on the stairwell. As I was passing, he leaned towards me with a tense look and touched my shoulder. 'Before we go on, Johnny, I have to tell you something. Two people walked out of the theatre last night because they weren't happy with the show. They came to see Granny's Intentions but didn't get what they were expecting. I just thought you should know.'

I shrugged. 'Two people! What about the two hundred plus that remained and gave us a couple of encores?! People walk out of shows all the time. You can never please everyone. But you might have chosen a better time to tell me this than just before we go on stage.'

Hoggy took a pull from his cigarette. 'Another thing: Don't include me in any of your stories tonight. I feel like a fool standing around waiting for them to end. They're too long. Shorten them!'

I tried to make allowance for Hoggy's curtness, reminding myself that he was a man of little tact, but I was still stunned by the force and timing of the assault. I walked on towards the stage door in confusion. In the darkened wings I spotted Jack talking to one of the stage assistants. I went up to him and told him that I wasn't sure I was going to be able to go through with the night's performance, explaining what Hoggy had just said and mentioning my suspicions of conspiracy among the others. Jack put his arm around my shoulder and told me that he realised there was 'some shit happening' but he asked me to rise above it. 'You have to go on, man. You can't back out now. The place is full, for Christ sake. I know it won't be easy but, if anyone can do it, you can.'

From where we were standing, I could see the floor manager announcing the house regulations to the capacity crowd, who were just about visible in the dimly lit auditorium. With the preliminaries out of the way she introduced the band and the house lights went down further. A huge round of applause went up in the darkening theatre and the band members started shuffling on to the stage. I made my way to my chair at the front of the amplifiers and drums and placed my guitar on my lap while the band behind me got harnessed into their instruments. A photographer whom Jack had commissioned, Tulla O'Mahoney, took a few shots from the side of the stage and gave us the thumbs up. The show began and over the next two hours the band played a blinder and I put in one of the best performances of my stage career.

At the end of the night we were showered with compliments from every quarter. As I left the stage to go to the foyer I spotted Hoggy signing an autograph for an eager fan. I nodded to him and walked on.

I signed numerous copies of my CD and book *To The Light* before the last stragglers left the theatre. Brian and I then packed away the remaining merchandise in boxes and my sister Kay helped us take it to my car.

Outside the centre, members of the band and their wives and friends were gearing up for a pub party. After saying a quick good night to Jack and Jim I slipped away with Brian and Kay without telling the others that I wouldn't be attending the celebrations.

I woke the following morning – a Saturday morning – just after eight o'clock feeling guilty over shunning the pub-bash the night before. In the pale light of day, my protest seemed petty. Restless, I got up, dressed and went off in search of a chapel, though I wasn't in the habit of going to church on Saturday mornings.

The Redemptorists' and St Joseph's, close to the hotel, didn't have suitable Mass times, so I made my way to the Augustinians' on O'Connell Street. I arrived there five or six minutes before the nine o'clock service was due to begin. Taking a pew near the back of the near-empty church, I went on my knees and started to say a prayer of thanks for the success of the night before. Half way through an *Our Father* I started thinking of the confrontation with Hoggy and the conspiracy suspicions regarding band members. I called to mind the written proposal I had sent out to each one of the band before booking the shows which spelt out the parameters of the programme, specifying that it would be based on songs and stories from my songbook *To The Light* and not on the band's old material. I recalled how John Ryan had rejected participating in the project, predicting that confusion would ensue because the audience would expect our old songs. After the shenanigans of the night before, I had to admit that John was right. In an attempt to vindicate myself, I brought to mind the great success of the show itself, but this, I knew, didn't exonerate me. The mixed motives of using the band's name to promote the songs and stories of *To The Light* had backfired on me.

A bell rang and a grey-haired priest dressed in green vestments came onto the altar and started saying the Confiteor, an age-old confessional prayer that purifies the Mass-goer for the Eucharistic ceremony ahead. Listening to the faint sound of the small congregation droning around me, my concentration went astray and I found myself thinking about a song I'd written for the Granny's reunion, *Burning Again*. A line of the lyric ran through my head: 'Searching for light, not just limelight; something more bright, purer than spotlight.' The song, I recalled, had been inspired by an email that Jack had sent me accepting the terms of the band reunion: "Of course I'll do it. I still think of the guys in the band as family." Another line from the song ran through my head: 'That's how we made our name, burning with an inner flame; in the vein of lovers, through the strain of brothers, now we're doing it as men.' As I reflected on the double meaning of the words 'the strain of brothers', I thought of the strained relationship I had with some of my own blood brothers.

I lowered my head and joined the small congregation and got on my knees as the priest began to lead us into the celebration of the Mass.

THE STORM

Heavy loaded minds tend to travel on their own.

Heavy Loaded Minds

As I pulled in behind my daughter Niamh's Passat, a mongrel sheepdog appeared briefly in my headlights before I switched off the engine. Getting out of the car, I rushed through delving rain towards the back door of the cottage, avoiding puddles while at the same time looking out for the dog. Though the sound of my car would have announced my arrival, I made as much noise as I could going through the scullery and hall to let Denny know of my presence. At ninty-two, not only was his hearing beginning to go but his comprehension had deteriorated to such an extent that often he had to be told something several times before it registered. Pushing open the living room door, I conjured up a smile and made a chirpy entrance. Seated in a low, ramshackle armchair at the side of a newly installed stove, Denny widened his eyes and sat forward, glancing at Niamh sitting at the other side of the room. 'Masha, look who's here. Come in a maneen and take a seat. It's a wild night out there.'

Niamh put a magazine aside and stood up. 'It took you a long time to get here.'

Noticing strain on my daughter's face, I regretted not having set out from home to relieve her earlier. For the past few weeks she, more than any other family member, had been caring for her ailing grandfather. 'I had to stop off for petrol before getting on the motorway. And I'll never get used to the narrow windy roads out here.' I sat on an old chair at the head of the Formica dining table, glancing at the flickering TV mounted on a cabinet in a corner near the back-window. 'You're watching telly, Denny?'

Denny threw a glance at the almost silent set and waved his hand dismissively 'I leave the picture on but don't bother with the blabber.'

Niamh went to the back-kitchen while I made small talk with Denny about the weather. He'd lost a lot of weight since I'd last seen him. Never a big eater, he'd always been of slight build, but now his jaws were beginning to cave in and his eyes were gone so far back in his head the sockets were black with shadow. His disheveled shirt and greasy trousers were hanging from his limbs in such loose folds he reminded me of one of the scarecrows he himself used to erect in the autumn corn fields of years gone by.

A loud gust of wind set the dog barking outside. Pelting rain on the windows rattled the frames. Niamh returned with a glass of water and some pills. 'Here Denny, take these before I go. They'll settle you for the night.'

Denny sat forward and slapped his knee. 'Whatever you say, Dorry. You're the boss.'

'I'm Niamh, Denny, not Dorry. Dorry and David are in Boston, remember? They'll be back on Wednesday.'

Denny gave Niamh a puzzled look. 'What did you say?' He scratched his head and gazed at me with incomprehension, the threads of his recollection unravelling. He'd been having a lot of these memory lapses over the past few weeks. A few nights earlier a neighbour had discovered him walking on the main road looking bewildered. When asked where he was going, Denny had said that he was on his way home to visit his mother in Co Mayo, his mother who had been dead for almost seventy years. On learning of his time warp, the family had called in a medical team who assessed Denny's condition as advanced vascular dementia. The psychiatrist had been quite philosophical about the diagnosis, pointing out that Denny had been lucky that the illness had manifested itself so late in his life. But he stressed that he would need a lot more care and attention from here on in, suggesting that the family consider putting him into a nursing home, for his own good.

Denny put the tablets in his mouth and washed them back with water. 'No bother, no bother.'

Niamh took the glass from him. 'You'll be fine now, Denny. John will be staying here with you tonight, up in the middle room. And I'll call tomorrow after work. Be good now, won't you?'

Denny sat forward, smiling. 'Good night, Dorry, and thank you for coming. You're a great girleen.'

Niamh took her handbag from the table and beckoned to me to follow her into the hall. Before leaving the house, she instructed me to lock the back door after she'd gone and to keep the key in my pocket.

'We don't want him wandering off in the middle of the night again. By the way, you'll find matches hidden behind the blue mug on the second shelf in the press in the pantry. You'll need them tomorrow morning for lighting the stove. Before you leave, make sure you put them back behind the mug where he won't find them. He tried to light a fire in the middle of the night during the week. Ronan found charred newspapers all over the floor the following morning. He could have burned the house down. He doesn't know what he's doing, poor man.'

I nodded. 'The family are going to have to get him into a home. Either that or get more family support for looking after him. It's not fair that you should be doing most of it. Still no chance of Paddy coming on board?'

Niamh shook her head emphatically. 'Not a hope.'

'He'll regret this when he's gone.'

Niamh drew a loud breath. 'What can we do; we can't act as his conscience. Dorry and David will be home from Boston on Wednesday, so they'll be back in the roster for next weekend. But none of us can stay with him twenty four hours a day. And that's what's soon going to be needed.'

'What about the nursing home?'

'There's not enough money left in his bank account to keep him in a home for six months. David used a lot of it on land improvement on the farm.'

I shook my head. 'It's one thing allowing Denny to sign the place over to him but to make land improvements from his savings! Jesus, there'll be war about this when Paddy finds out.'

Niamh buttoned up her jacket. 'I don't want to think about that. Denny is my only concern. He has to be looked after.' She moved towards the back door. 'Don't forget to lock it.'

As I re-entered the living room Niamh's car could be heard revving outside. Denny looked towards the window. 'Is that Joan?'

'No, Denny, that's Niamh. She has to get home to put her daughters to bed. Joan's in Galway. You'll see her tomorrow. I'm staying here with you tonight.'

'Very good, very good.' Denny sat back in his chair. Though he hadn't seen me in several months, he seemed comfortable enough in my company. He beckoned towards the TV. 'If you want to turn up that yoke, go ahead. Don't worry about me.'

'No no, I'm fine, Denny. I'll turn it up later on. I think there's a good film on after the news.'

Denny sank back in his chair and closed his eyes.

THE VOYAGE

The faint sound of throbbing coming from the TV drew my attention. On the screen, a motorboat was ploughing through a choppy sea making it's way towards some rocky headland, an eager helmsman in yellow oilskins narrating to the camera. I was tempted to go over and turn up the sound to hear what was being said but didn't want to disturb Denny. I took a book from my jacket pocket, a paperback collection of Robert Frost's poetry, and read a poem (one of my favourites) that I'd earmarked as appropriate for the occasion: *An Old Man's Winter Night*. When I got to the end of it, I glanced at Denny snoozing in his chair and reread the last lines:

One aged man – one man – can't keep a house,
A farm, a countryside, or if he can,
It's thus he does it of a winter night.

A few days earlier, I had thought of sending a photocopy of this poem to Denny's estranged son, Paddy, in the hope of softening him for a reconciliation before it was too late, but Joan put me off, saying that nothing would move Paddy now. I glanced across the room at Denny wheezing before the stove and brought to mind one of the many rows I'd witnessed between him and his only son while I was living on the farm years before. During a summer vacation from agricultural college, Paddy had driven their tractor at high speed into a low shed in the haggard, dislodging the funnel from the upper part of the engine. Understandably, Denny exploded when he saw the extent of the damage to the vehicle, but the level of insult he showered on his teenage son was disproportionate. After calling him every harsh name under the sun he predicted that Paddy would never make anything of himself. I cringed now thinking about the hurt expression on Paddy's florid face as he suffered the onslaught head on.

A gust of wind rattled the back-window and Denny's head jerked forward. 'What was that?' He looked at me. 'Is that David?'

'No Denny, David's in America. He'll be back on Wednesday with his mother.'

Denny got to his feet and left the room. I waited for a few moments then followed him into the hall. A shuffling sound came from the bathroom. I went to the door. 'Are you alright in there, Denny?'

Denny huffed. 'Why wouldn't I be?'

I returned to the living room and took up my book. Denny returned minutes later and opened the glass door of the stove and threw in a single sod of turf from a bucket at the side of his chair. 'It doesn't really need it at this time but if you're going to be watching that yoke when I'm gone to bed . . .'

I glanced at the stove. 'There's great heat out of the new stove. You must be glad you put it in?'

Denny gave me a puzzled look. 'I didn't put it in. Paddy put it in.'

Knowing that it was his grandson David who had installed the stove back in the summer, I was about to correct Denny's lapse of memory but bit my tongue. 'There's a lot more heat from it than the old fireplace.'

Denny shrugged. 'I miss the open fire; it was cosier.' He sat back in his chair but got on his feet almost immediately and left the room again. I followed him into the hall and found him opening the parlour door, a rarely used room that he and Paddy had built as an extension years before. Looking into the bleak interior, I winced at the acrid smell of mould. Denny pointed to a framed photograph above the tiled fireplace, a family portrait of himself and his brothers and sisters taken during an anniversary get together years before. 'They're all dead now, every one of them. I'm the only one left. I outlived them all.'

I smiled at the hollow boast. 'That photograph used to be in the living-room, wasn't it?'

Denny nodded and pulled a long face. 'I couldn't stick looking at it, so I moved it out here. I'll never see them again, Jack, Tommy, Mick, Paddy and Bridie. They're all gone.' He started sobbing but immediately pulled himself together. Closing the door, he sighed heavily and walked on down the hall to the scullery where he took a carton of yogurt from the fridge. 'Dorry got me these earlier today up at the shop.'

Back in his chair, eating the yogurt with a large dessert spoon, Denny started reminiscing about the distant past, telling a story he'd told me a number of times already about how he'd come to live in Cloonamorris seventy-odd years before. 'I was only fifteen when I went to work in Raftery's bar and grocery shop in Woodlawn. Mr Raftery drove up to our place in Mayo to get me. My mother packed my bag but wouldn't come to the gate to say goodbye, she was that heartsick. My father brought me out to the car with tears in his eyes and handed me over. But what could they do? They had no money. They had Jack and Tommy and Mick and Paddy and Bridie to look after. Tommy was the eldest, but they needed him on the farm. Tommy and myself used to cut turf in a bog eight miles from our place in Ballisnahine, but moving to Woodlawn was like moving to another country. Fifty miles was an endless journey in those days. I used to cycle home once a month till my mother died.' He took a deep breath and sighed. 'Did I ever tell you, I swore to my mother on her dying bed that I'd never drink or smoke, and I kept my word?'

I nodded . 'You did, Denny. And that's probably why you've outlived them all.'

Denny jerked his head affirmatively. 'That and hard work!'

I looked at Denny's lean frame and drew on a memory of him as a vigorous middle-aged man straining behind a horse-drawn plough, the tendons and veins of his neck bulging every time the blade encountered stone beneath the turning sod. 'You certainly did work hard, Denny. I can vouch for that.'

Denny wiped some yogurt from his chin with the back of his hand and sat forward. 'Paddy Mullen down the road died last week and Molly Murphy from New Inn was buried yesterday, and they were in their eighties. There's very few left around these parts to match my age.' A look of pride glittered in his eyes but then he sank back in his chair and his voice grew faint. His eyes closed but he went on mumbling under his breath.

I went back reading but couldn't concentrate. I glanced at Denny snoozing in his chair. A framed photograph on the wall above his head drew my attention, a family portrait that I myself had taken after a meal in Paddy's house seven or eight years before. In the photo, Denny and Mary are surrounded by their five children, Carmel, Joan, Dorry, Teresa and Paddy. Though they're all smiling for the camera, most of them look tense and awkward. This was because a week earlier Carmel had returned for a holiday from her home in Zimbabwe, a ghost of her former self. Though she fully intended returning to her husband and daughters in Africa, she died from cancer a few days before she was due to fly home. In Portiuncula Hospital in Ballinasloe on the day before she passed away, I witnessed Denny taking his leave of his eldest daughter while she was in a coma. He kissed her forehead and left the ward sobbing. Moments later he rushed back and collapsed by the bedside, clutching her bony hands, groaning. "Masha I'll never ever see you again, agirleen. Never! And how are we going to live without you?" Carmel's mother, Mary, who had been too grief-stricken to accompany her husband to the hospital for the final farewell, answered this hopeless question when she herself died a year later.

Thinking of Mary now, my eyes drifted to a framed picture of the Sacred Heart dominating the wall above the table I was sitting at. A votive lamp beneath the gilt-edged picture frame was coated in a thick layer of grey dust, suggesting that it hadn't been lit in years. I brought to mind the many evenings I had joined the family on my knees during recitations of the rosary. Though I considered myself an atheist at the time, I participated in the ritual out of a sense of gratitude to her parents for taking me in and making me feel at home at a time when my career was on the rocks. Though I felt hypocritical reciting the litany of Hail Marys, Our Father's and Glory Be's, I came to appreciate the bonding force of these family assemblies. And at a deeper level, looking back on it now, I could see that the seed was sown during these prayerful gatherings for my own slow return to the faith years later.

Denny stirred in his chair and opened his eyes, looking slightly bewildered. Muttering under his breath he got to his feet and made his way towards his ground-floor bedroom, yawning. 'I'm as tired as an ass; I'm going to bed.'

'Do you need any help?'

Denny gave me a crooked look and shrugged. 'I'm not a baby!'

At nine o'clock I turned up the sound of the TV for the news. Then I watched a gripping film featuring Daniel Day Lewis, *There Will Be Blood*. At quarter to twelve, I knocked off the set and looked in on Denny. His breathing came to me through the darkness in a gentle wheezing sound. Following Joan's instructions, I turned on a lamp near his bed so that he would have light if he needed to go to the toilet during the night.

Turning out the rest of the house lights, I went upstairs and got into a double bed in an attic room with a slanting ceiling, the room I had slept in thirty-odd years before on my first night in the cottage. Switching off the bedside lamp, I looked up at the skylight window but couldn't see a thing because of the pitch-black sky outside. I brought to mind my first night sleeping in the room. The skylight on that occasion had been freckled with stars and a banana shaped moon was beaming through the glass. Joan's mother, Mary, had thrown a party for us earlier that night and I was stuffed to the gills with ham and egg sandwiches, apple-tart, porter cake and milky tea. After our overnight sailing from Hollyhead, Joan and I were exhausted, but I couldn't sleep. The contrast between the bleak bedsit we'd come from in Chiswick and the bright lively cottage couldn't have been greater. The homely atmosphere overwhelmed me. Joan's parents and sisters, Teresa and Dorry, had greeted me like one of the family, though I'd only been in their company once in the past. After the meal, they coaxed me to take out my guitar and sing a few songs. Knowing of the popularity of country music in the area, I sang Hank Williams and Gordon Lightfoot numbers and a few of my own uptempo songs. Joan and her sisters jived around the table. A one-legged family friend, Willie Burns, threw aside his crutches and danced with Joan on his wooden leg. Mary and Denny looked on from their chairs by the fire with beaming eyes.

I turned on my pillow now and started thinking of Denny below in his fusty bed, all alone. I thought of the years he'd put up with me staying in his home while never once questioning my unorthodox occupation as a songwriter. A humorous comment he once made to my son Brian about my profession came to me. "It's a strange job your father has, standing by the window for hours on end waiting for songs to come like last year's swallows."

I got out of bed and went on my knees and started praying for Denny, a fine man.

THE TRIBUNAL

I have looked at the dark side of life;
as well as day I've studied the night.

The Dark Side

Though I arrived at my daughter's house in Loughrea ten minutes early, I wasn't surprised to find her waiting at the open front door with her handbag over her shoulder. Aware of my excessive punctuality, Niamh had inherited the same trait herself. Closing the door slowly so as not to wake her two girls and partner upstairs, she came to my side of the car and suggested that she drive, to allow me relax before my ordeal ahead. Knowing her low opinion of my driving skills, I knew this was a ruse to get me into the passenger seat, but I went along with it, thinking that it might not be a bad idea to read over some of the tribunal documentation during the course of the journey.

As she took off, Niamh noticed a cup of cereal sitting in one of the coffee holders behind the brake shaft. 'What's that?'

'My breakfast. My constitution's so fine-tuned I can't eat before eight o'clock. Any time before that might result in cramps, or worse. One of the penalties of ageing. I'll eat when the eight o'clock news come on. We should be halfway to Dublin by then.'

The way Niamh drove, we were more than three quarters way to Dublin when the news started on RTE radio 1. I hadn't felt the hour go by as we'd chatted all the way, mainly about Niamh's recent dramatic decision to change career from accountancy to Suzuki music teaching, drawing on the seven grades of violin exams she'd passed in her youth to get into the teacher-training course she'd started some months before. Though she hadn't thanked me for the countless hours of violin practice I'd foisted on her as a kid, she was grateful now for the opportunity it afforded her to switch jobs in her late twenties.

Listening to the news, I ate my cereal and deposited the empty cup and spoon on the floor behind my seat. I then located the envelope marked *Tribunal* and took out some documents. Niamh glanced at the pages in my hands. 'Will there be a judge at the hearing?'

'A magistrate of some sort, I expect. My case will be just one of a few and it will only deal with affidavits that my former solicitor is submitting. Given the opportunity to attend, I thought I'd better go to show the tribunal I mean business. I don't even know if my ex-solicitor will be there. He mentioned something about getting another solicitor to represent him in the last letter he sent me.'

Niamh cursed a slow driver ahead of us. There was no traffic in the slow lane so she had the opportunity to go around the car but she didn't take it. 'Remind me again of exactly why you fell out with him. I know he went against you for something but I can't remember why.'

I drew breath. 'He made it impossible for me to consider accepting an all-in settlement offer of fifty grand in my litigation case by refusing to tell me how much of it would come to me, if I accepted. He was determined to take the case to trial, against my will.'

'Really!' Niamh punctuated her anger by jerking the steering wheel suddenly and whizzing past the car in front of us.

As we approached the outskirts of Dublin the traffic increased. Niamh zigzagged in and out of lanes to get past slowcoaches, making it difficult for me to read the documents. I reminded her that we were in plenty of time and asked her to slow down and listen to a section of a speech I intended making at the hearing.

'The substance of my complaint against Mr O'Shea stands on the principle that when an all-in settlement offer is put to a client in a litigation case like mine, the client should have an inalienable right to know within a reasonable period of time exactly how much of the settlement sum will come to the client if he accepts the offer, after fees and costs are deducted. The fact that Mr O'Shea did not supply me with a written cost estimate at the outset of taking on my case – which in itself is a breach of Section 68 of the Solicitors Act – is proof that he was more than obliged to let me know his costs . . .'

Niamh interrupted me. 'You mean he didn't give you a breakdown of what he was going to charge you when you took him on? My God, even the solicitor who handled my house purchase contract two years ago gave me a cost estimate. That would seem a basic requirement.'

I started putting the documents back into the envelope. 'Our original agreement – a verbal agreement – was that I would only have to pay him if he achieved a reasonable settlement, though I would be eligible for his costs, even if he didn't achieve the figure we agreed on

– a figure close to the sum we were eventually offered, as it happened, which I wrote into a page of my pocket phone notebook at the time, and still have. He later denied these terms, after the settlement offer was made, but still refused to supply me with a cost estimate, though his solicitor son suggested on the phone that their costs might eat up the full sum on offer, if I agreed to take it. Eventually I sent him a registered letter demanding an exact breakdown of his costs up to the time the settlement offer was made. Under this pressure, he sent me an estimate for a little over sixteen thousand euro, but emphasised in a follow up email that "an estimate is just an estimate", which again left me in the dark. When I eventually pressed him for an exact costing, he threatened to pull out of the case and let me deal with the defendants myself. At that stage I informed him that I would report him to the Law Society if he didn't provide me with an exact bill for what I owed him.'

Niamh looked at me. 'And?'

'He refused, so I sacked him and reported him to the Law Society, partly on the grounds that he had not supplied me with a cost estimate at the outset of taking me on, which another solicitor I hired informed me is a statutory requirement for all solicitors. To overcome this, O'Shea provided the Law Society with the estimate of sixteen grand that he had sent me a few months before, and, when the Law Society weren't satisfied with this, he miraculously came up with an estimate and an S68 letter with a date corresponding to the time I took him on, and the Law Society accepted this bogus document and threw out my case. I had no alternative then but to take the matter a step higher to the Solicitors Disciplinary Tribunal, where we're heading now.'

Niamh glanced at me, wide-eyed. 'Is he not afraid of being struck off?'

'Apparently not, though in my first affidavit to the tribunal I gave five solid reasons why he couldn't have sent me the early estimate, the strongest being a sheaf of e-mails I sent to him over the years asking for a cost estimate, which he never responded to. If the written estimate that he sent to the Law Society had existed back then he would have referred me to it, if for no other reason but to get me off his back.'

Niamh sighed. 'Still, It'll be your word against his.'

'I realise that, but remember this is a tribunal, not a court of law. If the tribunal read my affidavits and back-up e-mails and letters carefully, I'm sure they'll be convinced that he blocked me from considering the offer and fabricated the S68 letter and estimate. It took me two weeks to write my first affidavit and a month to write the second. During that time I also had to write up a submission to the High Court outlining valid reasons for why I should be allowed to represent myself in the actual infringement case, the main one being my solicitor's refusal to hand over the files of my case, except on his terms. I may have no alternative but to take on the case myself, as my new solicitor won't work without the case files.'

Niamh sighed. 'Won't that be risky, taking on the case yourself?'

I drew a long breath. 'I may have no alternative. At my lowest point, I phoned the State solicitor of Limerick, Michael Murray (an old acquaintance) and explained the situation to him. He advised me to take this route.'

Niamh gave me a sympathetic look. 'My God, I knew by the way you locked yourself away all summer that the case was serious, but I had no idea that it was this complicated. You must be really anxious?'

'Anxious? After O'Shea entered the fabricated estimate that resulted in the Law Society squashing my complaint I had many sleepless nights.'

We arrived at the quays and found a parking place close to the tribunal building. After take-away coffees, which we drank in the car, we made our way to the tribunal offices on Bow Street, an old red-bricked building called The Friary situated at the back of a Franciscan church. At reception, a grey-haired man before us in the queue turned and gave me a penetrating look. Thought I didn't recognise him at first, it was my former solicitor, Vincent O'Shea. As he moved away from the hatch, he handed me a large brown envelope. 'My latest affidavits, copies of which I sent to your new solicitor, who informed me that you are representing yourself here.'

I took the envelope without explaining that my new solicitor had sent me only one affidavit.

Once Niamh and I were given clearance to enter the building, we made our way to the Tribunal Hearing Room.

Behind a long desk facing two small advocate tables, an elderly grey-haired male magistrate was flanked on either side by female magistrates, all three reading documents and consulting one another. Along with three other applicants, Niamh and I sat at the back of the room, as far removed from Mr O'Shea as we could get. I glanced over the affidavits he'd just handed me and passed them on to Niamh, knowing I wouldn't have time to read the new one in any kind of detail before the hearing commenced. While Niamh was skimming through the new documents Vincent looked our way and scrutinised Niamh, wondering, no doubt, if she was some kind of legal representative of mine. Dressed in a neat navy skirt and jacket with her hair tied up in a bun, Niamh returned his stare without flinching while dipping her hand into her leather satchel-like handbag and extracting a biro. I smiled to myself, thinking how glamorous and confident she looked.

Just after ten thirty the main magistrate cleared his throat and called out Mr O'Shea's name as the first applicant to be dealt with. Vincent got to his feet and asked the magistrates for a delay in the hearing of his applications on the grounds that a solicitor he had hired to deal with my complaint hadn't as yet arrived. The chairman frowned, shuffled some papers, and proceeded to call on another applicant. A stout man in a dark suit stood up and said a few words about a faulty affidavit that he had resubmitted. As soon as the chairman ascertained that there was no opponent present, he concluded the issue in a matter of minutes. The chairman then turned back to Mr O'Shea and told him in forthright terms that the board could not afford to wait any longer to deal with his applications. He mentioned my name as the opponent, so I got to my feet and made my way to one of the advocate tables.

Mr O'Shea gave a brief account of the two affidavits he was submitting and the chairman then turned to me and asked if I had any objections to the inclusion of these new documents as part of Mr O'Shea's defense. Suppressing a flutter of nerves, I got to my feet and made a brief apology for the fact that, due to my not being used to public speaking, I was going to read my statement. Putting on my reading glasses, I raised a single A4 sheet and opened with a sharp criticism of Mr O'Shea for sending his latest affidavits with inappropriate postage to a wrong address, resulting in my receiving only one of the affidavits four days before the hearing. Basing my objection on the single affidavit I had received, I pointed out that Mr O'Shea's fresh arguments against my grounding affidavit bore no relevance to my case. After I reminded the board that the main issue of my complaint against Mr O'Shea was that he deliberately blocked me from considering accepting an all-in settlement offer and fabricated an S68 letter and estimate, I suggested that Mr O'Shea's latest affidavits were nothing but a smokescreen. Before concluding, I criticised Mr O'Shea for suggesting in the summing up section of his third affidavit that I seemed relaxed about the issue of my copyright infringement case being put in jeopardy by my tribunal complaint against him. 'I can assure the tribunal that I am far from being relaxed about any aspect of my dealings with my case, and I hope that my appearance here this morning – which entailed setting out from Galway at six o'clock this morning – will attest to the seriousness with which I view these proceedings.'

After I sat down, the chairman reminded me that the present hearing was not the forum for dealing with the main issue of my complaint but merely a channel for accepting or rejecting fresh affidavits. He consulted with his two female colleagues and informed me that he was accepting Mr O'Shea's affidavits, on the grounds that I could make objections to the tribunal in detail in a further affidavit and at the main hearing, if my case was accepted for a full hearing. As I had been expecting this outcome, I asked that my complaint be entered into the records and then thanked the board and made my way back to Niamh.

Niamh stood up, smiling. 'Well done. The solicitor's eyes were glued on you the whole time you were on your feet. And if looks could kill!'

As we were leaving the building Mr O'Shea, who had left just before us, glanced over his shoulder and gave me an anxious look. In the street he looked my way again, and for a moment I thought he was going to approach me, but he didn't.

When we reached my car, Niamh automatically took the driving seat, suggesting that I read the new affidavit during the journey home. Though I was in no frame of mind for reading more legal jargon, I got into the passenger seat.

We were more than half way to Galway when the thought occurred to me to get out the unread affidavit. It wasn't a bulky document, just five or six pages. Quarter way into it I let out a yelp. 'My God, he's admitted that the Section 68 letter that he swore he sent me under oath was never sent.'

Niamh looked at me, askance. 'Are you sure?'

I pored over the clause a second time and then read the most salient lines aloud:

'I no longer have a conviction that I sent the applicant a Section 68 letter. I believe I did not. I do not have a record book of post sent or an equivalent record for that period and can't prove what the applicant denies. More than that, I accept his denial of its receipt and apologise to him and the tribunal for my earlier averment.'

S68

Night can be black, blacker than coal, when there's cloud in the way,
but when that cloud rolls back other worlds unfold
that you can't see by day

The Dark Side

As I waited for the arrival of my new solicitor outside the Four Courts I watched a lone protester plodding backwards and forwards with a placard denouncing corruption within the legal and banking systems. *One Law for the Rich, No Law for the Rest, No rest for the Poor. Bankers – wankers!* While I was pondering on the peculiar wording of the handwritten scrawl a man approached me and smiled. 'Johnny Duhan?'

'That's me. Michael Ring?'

Michael nodded and glanced at his watch. 'I hope I'm not late. I miss-calculated how long it would take to cycle in.'

I smiled. 'I'm always early.'

As we shook hands I scrutinised Michael's lean florid face and neatly cropped hair.

Since I'd taken him on to try and sort out the mess of my infringement case, we had only spoken over the phone, and for some reason I imagined him to be much older than the boyish young man who stood before me.

After some chit-chat about my bus ride from Galway (I hadn't driven up because I gauged that the late afternoon meeting would entail driving out of Dublin in rush hour traffic) we made our way through some narrow side streets and lanes to the Distillery Building on Church Street for our scheduled head-to-head with my former solicitor's barrister, who was now considering acting with Michael on my behalf.

As we walked, Michael outlined the parameters of the meeting we were heading to, which was set to centre on a recent discussion that he and the barrister had had with my former solicitor regarding his terms for handing over my case files. 'Mr Foley made it clear that he wants to keep the focus on the mechanics of us taking over from Mr O'Shea and exploring the possibility of reaching a settlement on better terms with the defendants. He does not want to get involved in discussions about the rights and wrongs of your tribunal case against Mr O'Shea.'

I nodded. 'So you said on the phone. But to move the actual case along you are going to have to get O'Shea to divulge the costs he intends charging me before you can even get the case files. And the way I see it, that's going to be a sticking point.'

'That's why we've arranged this meeting, to discuss ways of trying to get around that obstacle.' Michael raised his briefcase and pointed it towards a glass fronted stone building across the street.

As we approached the Distillery Building (an old whisky distillery converted into a modern block of legal offices), I reminded Michael that I had been in the building once before for a meeting with the barrister we were now heading to meet. 'It must be three years ago. O'Shea set up the meeting at his own expense in an attempt to convince me that taking the case to trial was our only option. The meeting didn't convince me.'

Michael scratched his ear. 'But at least it led to determining that the lodged settlement sum was still available?'

I shook my head. 'No, no, I only learned that through Mr Foley in the last year, with no help from Mr O'Shea. O'Shea refused to tell me whether the lodged sum was still available as part of his strategy for blocking me from accepting the offer. In his final affidavit to the Disciplinary Tribunal he admitted that he hadn't informed me that the lodged sum was still available because – to quote himself – he'd had "a lapse of memory" on the matter.'

Michael frowned but didn't say anything.

Stepping through the revolving glass entrance door of the Distillery Building, we emerged into a wide, high-ceilinged modern reception area. Approaching the reception desk, I told the receptionist of our arranged meeting with Mr Foley SC. She turned to a switchboard and moments later informed us that Mr Foley was held up in a meeting and would be with us as soon as possible. 'You can wait over there (she indicated some seating) or there's a coffee shop further down the hall.'

Opting for the coffee shop, Michael got himself a mug of coffee (I abstained, having had more than my quota of coffee already that day). We took a table at the back of the almost empty space. After some small talk about the difference between the pristine building we were in and the more antiquated buildings attached to the Four Courts, I took a sheet of paper from a plastic portfolio with a list of questions I had typed up to put to Mr Foley regarding the proposal that Michael had come up with for making an attempt to resurrect the settlement offer on better terms. 'I must say, I'm not at all happy that O'Shea seems to be still calling the shots. In one of the affidavits I submitted against him to the tribunal I made the point that it should be mandatory in all-in settlement offers that solicitors should be obligated to inform their clients of exactly what portion of a settlement sum would come to the client after costs and fees are deducted. It seems so logical that this should apply, I can't see how a law isn't already in place regarding the matter. I wouldn't be in this fix if such a law existed.'

I waited for Michael to respond but he remained silent. Though I'd done so before, I reminded him that he had informed me during our first phone conversation that I had a legal entitlement to know how much of the settlement offer would come to me and that Mr O'Shea had been in breach of section 68 of the Solicitors' Act by not providing me with an estimate of his costs and fees at the outset of me taking him on. 'On the strength of that information, I informed the Complaints' Department of the Law Society of the breach. To counteract it, O'Shea produced a Section 68 letter out of thin air and submitted it to the Complaints Department, which resulted in them throwing out my case, leaving me with no alternative but to elevate my complaint to the Solicitors Disciplinary Tribunal.'

Michael put down his cup. 'I realise that this must be extremely stressful for you, but I really can't see any other way out of this conundrum without settling the cost issue with Mr O'Shea before we can deal with the main case. Mr Foley is of the same opinion. Before you can definitively accept any offer from the defendants you have to know what Mr O'Shea's costs are going to be, and he has agreed to allow a taxing master determine those costs.'

I gritted my teeth. 'Yes, but as I've stressed before, I am only willing to pay O'Shea up to the time that he refused to provide me with his costs when the all-in offer of fifty grand was put on the table. Almost four years on he's still not only refusing to tell me what those costs are but he won't even give Mr Foley – his own barrister up until recently – an estimate of what he wants.'

Michael bit his lip. 'I know the man is being awkward, but the taxing master should move things along.'

I gave a false laugh. 'O'Shea dragged his heels for almost ten years before I sacked him and reported him to the Law Society. I wouldn't hold my breath for any promise he might offer about hiring a taxing master.'

'Let's wait and see what Mr Foley has to say on the matter.' Michael finished his coffee and got to his feet, glancing at his watch. 'Will we go back to the reception area? Mr Foley is sure to make an appearance soon. Barristers are generally fairly punctual creatures.'

Soon after we made ourselves comfortable back in the reception area Mr Foley came along, a tall man in a neat grey suit. Focusing on me almost exclusively, he smiled. 'You've changed, Johnny; lost a bit of weight. You look almost Jesuitical in those dark clothes. How long ago has it been since Vinnie brought you along here for that meeting?'

I smiled, taking note of how Mr Foley was still using O'Shea's nickname, though he'd informed me a week or so before that he no longer represented him. 'Must be three, almost four years. Hard to believe that the thing is still dragging on.'

'Indeed, indeed.' Mr Foley glanced at Michael and waved his hand in a directional gesture. 'My office is on the second floor.'

On our way upstairs, I thanked Mr Foley for the trouble he'd taken almost a year before of establishing that the sum that had been lodged in the High Court by the defendants years previously was still available. I had already thanked him in writing for doing this but I repeated it now because I presumed that he had gone against Mr O'Shea's wishes in helping me in the matter. 'I hope he didn't hold it against you?'

Mr Foley laughed. 'Not at all, not at all. It gives us a bit of solid ground for entering fresh negotiations, if that's what we can agree on at this meeting.'

As we entered Mr Foley's small office I took note of bulging portfolios and sheaves of documents piled on his desk and on shelving on either sides of a small window. I tried to recall if it was the same office I had been in years before but couldn't remember. Thinking back on that meeting during the bus ride earlier in the day, the only thing I could recall with precision was the feeling of unease that it had left me with. Though Mr Foley had backed O'Shea's claim that we had the defendants "pinned to the ropes" regarding culpability for copyright infringement and loss of royalties, Mr Foley hadn't appeared at all certain of winning the kind of extravagant sum that O'Shea had in mind, and he pointed out very clearly the punitive consequences that might rebound on me if we couldn't establish conclusively that my royalty losses exceeded the lodged settlement sum. On those grounds alone I had baulked at the idea of allowing O'Shea push the case to trial.

Sitting behind his desk now, Mr Foley gestured to me to take the chair directly in front of his desk and pointed towards another chair at the side for Michael. After some small talk about the recession and the effect it was having on the legal profession, Mr Foley got down to business and asked for my assessment of the case as it stood. 'I read the synopsis you drew up for representing yourself in the High Court – and I must say I was impressed – but I'm not so sure about the case you have against Vinnie in the tribunal. I think it was wise of you contacting Michael here to explore this avenue we're now entering. Lay litigation can be a very stressful and precarious business.'

I gave a false laugh. 'Who are you telling! Dealing with the Central Office alone can be a nightmare. And as for trying to negotiate the High Court website for information on procedures, I wouldn't wish that on my worst enemy.'

Mr Foley glanced at Michael and laughed. 'Luckily, we have secretaries for that kind of thing.'

I leaned forward. 'Until you found out that the lodged settlement sum was still available, I had no alternative but to go it alone. At least now I know there are funds there for covering legal expenses, if nothing else.'

Mr Foley smiled. 'I think we can do better for you than just cover expenses, Johnny. But to get down to business; we made some progress with Vinnie at our meeting last week. I'm sure Michael has informed you.'

I looked at Michael. 'Yes, though the fact that the meeting ended in stalemate regarding his fees and costs doesn't augur well for a beginning. I was surprised that he wouldn't even give *you* an estimate of what he intends charging me.'

Mr Foley turned to Michael, who was keeping notes in a pad. 'You did get back to Vinnie regarding his commissioning a taxing master after our meeting?'

Michael glanced at me. 'I spoke to him on the phone and he assured me that he has set that train in motion.'

I sat forward. 'Regarding this taxing master, I've already told Michael that I am only prepared to pay O'Shea up to the time that he started coercing me into going on with the case against my will. I have no intention of paying him after that time.'

Mr Foley cleared his throat. 'Let's not get bogged down before we even get started.' He looked at me. 'Have you been able to determine if the main defendants who lodged the settlement sum are as broke as they say they are?'

I glanced at my plastic portfolio but decided not to waste time looking up my notes. 'From what I've been able to gather, they're insolvent. And one of the other companies declared themselves bankrupt years ago. That leaves the TV company, whom O'Shea was banking on going after for the bulk of the hundred and fifty grand that he was hoping to gain by going to trial.' I sat forward. 'Having studied the contracts that O'Shea himself gained access to at the one court hearing that took place years ago, I've known for some time that the TV company are only marginally implicated. Their contract was only for the territory of Ireland. They failed to get my copyright clearance for home distribution but they are clear regarding all other territories, including the US, where the bulk of royalties were made.'

Mr Foley raised his head. 'You're sure of that?'

'Positive.'

Mr Foley stared at me. 'They are not responsible in any way for US losses?'

'Not as far as I can assess. That's why I fought O'Shea all the way against going to trial. He got the sum of a hundred and fifty grand into his head because he knew that the TV company could afford to pay, and he was determined to go after them to get it, even when I pointed out that they weren't directly responsible.'

Mr Foley lowered his head. 'What about the expert US copyright witness that Vinnie had lined up to back up his claim that your losses were in the region of a hundred and fifty thousand?'

I shook my head. 'I put him in touch with that witness – Mary Kuehn – and I can assure you that she would never have backed up the sales figures that O'Shea conjured up. O'Shea is delusional regarding this aspect of the case.'

Mr Foley took a pen from his top pocket and started writing in a notebook. I took the sheet of questions from my plastic portfolio and scanned the list. As I appeared to have covered almost everything I wanted to say, I put the page back in the portfolio and sat back in my chair. Mr Foley put his pen down and looked at me. 'As I've said already, your analysis of the case as outlined in your CH54 is impressive, but the tribunal case you have against Vinnie isn't nearly as solid. That's part of the reason I proposed to Michael that the only way to settle this whole mess was to include Vinnie in the overall settlement. I can't see how we can accept any settlement offer without knowing what costs and fees Vinnie is going to pursue. Michael and I are agreed on that.'

Michael stopped writing. 'I've explained that to Johnny.'

I turned to Michael. 'Yes, but I wasn't happy with the explanation. Just as I wasn't happy with being told that on the one hand Mr O'Shea had breached the S68 requirement and later being informed that there would be no legal consequences to him doing that. What's the point of having such an act, if there's no teeth in it?'

Michael shifted in his chair. 'I didn't say that there would be no consequences to his not having provided you with an S68. I just made the point that it won't affect your having to pay him what he is owed in fees and costs for the work he has done for you. Those costs and fees will have to be paid.'

Mr Foley nodded. 'We're both agreed on that.'

I glanced at Mr Foley. A suspicion that he had been given access to the affidavits from my tribunal case had entered my mind when he'd offered the opinion that my case against Mr O'Shea wasn't solid, and it came back to me now. 'When you say that you're not convinced that I have a case against O'Shea at the tribunal I'm not exactly sure what you mean. I have provided dozens of emails and letters that prove categorically that he did all in his power to block me from considering accepting the all-in settlement offer by refusing to tell me what his fee and costs were.'

Mr Foley rubbed his mouth. 'I'm not saying you don't have a case against him, but proving these things can be difficult.'

I sat forward. 'I've already proved that he didn't send me an S68 letter and estimate.'

Mr Foley laughed. 'My God, if you knew the amount of solicitors who don't send S68s to their clients, and get away with it! It happens all the time.'

I froze in my chair. 'Really?'

'Really.'

I glanced at Michael and drew a long breath, then turned back to Mr Foley. 'The thing is that O'Shea sent the Law Society a copy of an S68 that he purported to have sent me – a document that resulted in the Law Society throwing out my complaint against him – and then he entered the same bogus S68 as part of his defense evidence to the tribunal, in a sworn affidavit. That means that he has all but confessed to perjury as well as forgery. I can't see how he can get out of that.'

Mr Foley got to his feet and cleared his throat forcibly. 'I can't and won't get involved in adjudicating between Vinnie and yourself regarding your tribunal situation.' He glanced at his watch. 'We need to keep the focus on the main case and the lodged settlement offer. In the light of what you've told me, it would appear that the main defendants will not be in a position to up the offer. If that's true, and if the TV Company are not directly responsible for the bulk of your losses, I must put a hard question to you, Johnny. If it's a thing that I go back to the defendants' JC and he informs me that the main defendants have no more money to increase the offer, how will you feel about accepting the lodged sum as it stands?'

I hesitated. 'That's a hard question. It will depend, I suppose, on how much of the sum will come to me.'

Mr Foley glanced at his watch. 'I understand that. But now I'm going to put a scenario to you that I want you to think about after you leave here. Supposing the lodged sum of thirty five thousand is all we can get, and you end up having to pay Vinnie and Michael most of it, how would you feel about being left with less than ten thousand euro yourself?'

I forced a laugh. 'How do you think I'd feel?!'

Mr Foley started buttoning his jacket. 'I'm not saying that's going to happen, Johnny. I'm just giving you the worst case scenario, if negotiations drag on for another year or more.'

Mr Foley's body language indicated that he wanted to bring the meeting to a close, so I got to my feet. After agreeing to reflect on the substance of all we'd discussed, I left the office, followed by Michael.

Out in the dark street Michael asked me how I felt the meeting had gone. I found it hard to find words to explain the state of puzzlement and confusion I was in regarding some of the things that had been said during the hour or so gone by, so I gave a false laugh. 'I'm not sure.'

We shook hands and Michael smiled. 'Sleep on it and we'll talk on the phone tomorrow.'

We parted and I rushed off to catch my return bus to Galway. Before I reached home three hours later I had decided that my only option was to revert to taking the case to the High Court myself, as a lay litigant.

CARRAUNTOOHIL

*We struggled on and upwards
and rose above ourselves.*

The Beacon

Niamh was sitting in the hotel lobby, poring over a brochure, when I arrived down just before five in the morning. A receptionist glanced at me from his desk and went back reading a newspaper. Sitting opposite my daughter, I looked at my watch. 'Ronan and Siobhan will be down soon. I phoned them before leaving our room. How about Padraic; is he up?'

Niamh threw the brochure onto the table. 'He's gone to the kitchen to see if he can get tea and toast. Here he comes now, empty-handed.'

Niamh's tall partner came towards us, yawning. 'The kitchen staff haven't arrived yet. A porter told me of a petrol station where we'll get stuff on the way.'

I picked up the brochure that Niamh had been reading and discovered that it was an area map of the MacGillycuddy Reeks. 'I thought you knew the route?'

Niamh glanced at Padraic. 'We do. It's about six miles out the Tralee road, then there's a turn off for the starting base at Brennan's Yard.' She glanced at the flyer in my hands. 'I was just checking that for other routes. But I think we'll go the way we know.'

Padraic shook his head. 'The way *you* know, you mean. I remember little or nothing about that trip, except that the climb was hell on earth.'

Ronan and his partner, Siobhán – both togged out like the rest of us in anoraks, jeans and boots – arrived just in time to hear Padraic's description of the ordeal that lay ahead of us. Without a word of greeting, Ronan eyeballed Niamh. 'It better not be *that* hard. I have a big match coming up next weekend. I don't want to knock my bad knee out.'

Niamh got to her feet. 'I told you already Ronan, it's the highest peak in Ireland. Much higher than Croagh Patrick, but still only a hill in comparison to Kilimanjaro.'

Ronan groaned. 'Don't start on about Kilimanjaro, for Christ's sake.'

Niamh smiled at her brother and apologised for her boast about her greatest climbing achievement. 'You're as fit as a fiddle, Ronan. It's Siobhán I'm worried about.'

Ronan gave me a crooked look. 'You're the one who got us into this; you and your tribunal promise! I hope we don't end up having to carry you down. What age are you now, father, sixty five, is it?'

'Sixty four, actually, but then I'm not a big smoker like you, son.' I looked towards the front door. 'Will we get going?'

Outside the dawn was breaking but there was no sign of the sun, just some pearly patches in the grey sky above a stretch of cloud-covered mountains on the eastern horizon. In the car park Niamh zapped open her car and nodded to me. 'You sit in the front with me, as you're the oldest.'

'Fine, but please stop alluding to my age.'

A few minutes after we got moving we came to the garage that sold hot drinks and snacks. Back on the road, munching a breakfast roll, Ronan brought up the topic of the tribunal again. 'Any more articles in the papers about your big win, Father?'

I glanced over my shoulder. 'Declan Lynch has something lined up for next Sunday's Indo but the biggest feature is going to be in *The Irish Examiner*. I sent Michael Clifford the full transcripts and affidavits. He worked on all the big tribunals. I was lucky he attended the main hearing.'

Niamh glanced at me and frowned. 'I thought we were going to have a moratorium on the tribunal for these three days?'

I smiled. 'That was your mother's idea. But you're right. Let's change the subject.'

Ignoring my suggestion, Ronan swallowed some food and cleared his throat. 'What are you going to do if your solicitor doesn't pay the award?'

'I've already written to the Law Society about the letter he sent me. It's not so much the award I'm worried about; it's the threat he's still making that he's coming after me for fees and costs, even though I won the case against him outright.'

Padraic cursed. 'He must have a neck like a Jockey's arse.'

I smiled back at Padraic. 'Or as a friend of mine, John MacKenna, put it: balls of iron.'

Niamh clutched the steering wheel. 'I'll never forget the final day of the hearings while we were waiting for the verdict to come in, he started chatting out loud to his barrister about a vacation he had just booked somewhere on the Continent, as though the tribunal was done and dusted in his favour.'

I laughed. 'The worst part of that final day for me was when the evening deadline approached for the journalists to get their copy in for the next day's dailies and there was still no sign of the judging panel coming back with their decision. At around half six *The Irish Times'* reporter, Ronan McGreevy, started tapping on his laptop right behind us and Niamh asked me what he was up to. To confirm a suspicion that was going around in my head, I turned and asked him if he was writing two scenarios. His grin put the shivers down my spine.'

Niamh glanced over her shoulder at the others. 'It was at that point that Daddy told me that, if the verdict came back in his favour, I could name any mountain in Ireland and he would climb it with me.'

Ronan laughed. 'And of course you would pick the highest peak in the country!'

Niamh glanced at me. 'After all he'd been through, Carrauntoohil seemed the most appropriate.'

Ronan grinned. 'It's a wonder you didn't go for Kilimanjaro.'

Niamh missed the turn for Brennan's Yard and had to reverse on the main road. The boreen she turned into was so narrow we would have been in trouble if we'd encountered a bicycle on the bumpy way. While negotiating the bends and potholes, Padraic brought our attention to a valley of cloud-covered mountains up ahead. 'The MacGillycuddy Reeks!'

I leaned towards the windscreen. 'Which one's Carrauntoohil?'

Niamh laughed. 'None of them. They're only hills compared to Carrauntoohil. It's further back the valley.'

We arrived at a white cottage and parked in a yard close to an outhouse, which Niamh informed us had toilets and showers.

Ronan and Padraic went off to use the toilets. When they returned Ronan had three walking sticks with handle grips and steel points that he found in the outhouse, one he gave to Siobhán, another to me. Niamh and Padraic had their own ash poles.

Following a narrow winding footpath past a camping site and through several gates and stiles, we eventually emerged onto an open rocky plain that stretched ahead for miles. Because the path was so rugged and uneven we were forced to walk on the grass margins. Trudging along in single file, I took the vanguard while the others chatted behind me about football and hurling. After walking for a half an hour, Niamh pointed ahead towards an enormous escarpment of black rock enveloped in a mass of seething grey cloud. 'Carrauntoohil! You can just see the base section.'

Ronan scanned the dark prospect and cursed. 'By the looks of it, there's at least another mile or two to go before we even start climbing, and I'm shagged already.'

We crossed a stream and came to an even stretch of path. Niamh and Siobhán went on ahead while Padraic and Ronan came shoulder to shoulder with me. Again, Ronan reminded me that I was the one responsible for the ordeal we were putting ourselves through. 'Wasn't the tribunal tough enough for you without inflicting this on yourself?'

I drew breath. 'It wasn't just the tribunal I had in mind when I made the promise. It was the ten years of the case leading up to it. The idea for the mountain climb was kind of symbolic, to get it out of my system.'

Ronan's eyes softened 'I didn't realise it had been going on for that long till Mother told me after your day in the High Court settling the case itself. That must have been nerve-wracking?'

'Having to learn the legal procedures for getting there and dealing with the defendants' legal teams was a nightmare, but the actual day in court was a breeze.'

Padraic looked at me. 'Niamh explained the case to me but I got lost in the detail.'

I laughed. 'It's not that complicated. I hired a solicitor to try and reach a settlement with a group of companies who infringed my copyright. After years of following them through the courts the main company made an all-in offer of fifty thousand. When I asked my solicitor how much of this would come to me if I accepted, he refused to tell me but implied that it might be the full fifty. After a year of following him for an exact breakdown of his costs, he responded to a registered letter with an estimate of just over sixteen thousand, but emphasised that it was "just an estimate". When I pressed him for exact costs he threatened to resign and send me a bill for full costs, and then let me pick up the pieces of trying to deal with the case myself.'

Padraic drew breath. 'So what did you do?'

'I got legal advice and learned that, because my solicitor hadn't given me a written estimate of costs at the outset of taking me on, he was in breach of a legal requirement known as an S68. I used this against him as part of an official complaint to the Law Society. To offset this, he sent the Law Society an S68 that he hadn't sent me but which resulted in my complaint against him being thrown out. At that stage I elevated the case to the Solicitors Disciplinary Tribunal. And my victory there is the reason we're heading for that black craggy mountain now.'

Padraic laughed. 'Jesus, you're the one who must have had balls of iron to take on a thing like that. Were you not scared shitless that you might lose?'

'After the solicitor submitted the bogus S68 in a sworn affidavit to the tribunal, I didn't sleep for a week.'

Ronan looked at me. 'I would have buckled at that stage.'

I stepped over a jagged rock. 'I had no alternative but to go on. Had I allowed my solicitor to take the case to trial I might have ended up with a bill from him of over fifty grand, win or lose. And, if I lost, I might also have had to pay the defendants' costs. I tried to hire another legal team to sort out the mess but they refused to take me on unless I agreed to settle with the solicitor first.'

Ronan scowled. 'They won't go against one of their own.'

Padraic frowned. 'Thick as thieves.'

Niamh and Siobhán slackened their pace and waited for us to catch up with them. Niamh glanced at her watch. 'We're running way behind schedule.'

Padraic laughed. 'What schedule? What's the rush?'

Ronan looked up the valley. 'The old fella was just explaining to us why we're here.'

Niamh pointed her long pole towards the cloud-shrouded mountain. 'I don't want to be up there if it starts raining. Let's get it over as fast as we can.'

We forged ahead, poking at shale and grit with our walking sticks. The nearer we drew to the mountain the more onerous the climb began to seem. Finally, when we reached the first boulders and rock-shelves that needed to be scaled I looked up at the jagged incline rising into the clouds and my heart sank. 'Jesus, it's almost perpendicular.'

Standing on a huge rock above me, Niamh laughed. 'They don't call this section the Devil's Ladder for nothing!'

A group of climbers descending above us came into view. Pebbles and stones dislodged by their feet created miniature landslides that threatened to come down on our heads. As they clambered past us, slipping and sliding on the wet muddy rocks and stones, one of them informed us that the descent was even tougher than the upward slog.

A third of the way up we stopped for a breather and took photographs with our phone cameras. The view of the valley below was spectacular. We all managed to smile for group shots but as soon as we started trudging upwards again Ronan started griping. 'Jesus, this is murder. How in the name of God did I ever allow myself be roped into it!'

As I groped for crevices to cling to and ledges for foothold, Dante's *Mount Purgatory* came to mind and I recalled how my paperback copy of the famous poem had come in handy as an item of evidence at the tribunal. After my first meeting with my solicitor ten years before I had jotted the financial terms of our verbal agreement in a pocket diary, terms he later denied. Though there was no date on the entry, a few lines from Dante's poem that I'd written on the back of the terms page in conjunction with a note I'd written on the flyleaf of the paperback corresponded with the date of our first meeting, which helped prove that my original expectations of a financial settlement were way below what my solicitor claimed. Thinking back on it now as I breathlessly struggled upwards, I thought of the appropriateness of the poem that had helped me in my struggle to attain justice. I also remembered a joke that the chairman of the tribunal had made while he was examining the Dante exhibit, a joke that raised a heckle among the journalists in the chamber: "At least we can be grateful to Mr Duhan that it's not the *Inferno* he wishes us to consider."

By the time we finally reached the top of the Devil's Ladder the mist had become dense cloud and the five of us were soaked from head to toe in sweat and grime. Gasping for breath, we slumped down on a flat rock and remained silent for a minute or so. Finally, Ronan sat up and sighed heavily. 'At least it's over.'

Niamh got to her feet, laughing. 'Over! We're not even half way up yet.'

Ronan cursed. 'You're joking?'

Padraic smiled. 'She's not. And the next part is going to be really tricky as it's very easy to go astray in this kind of mist.'

Niamh took off her blue anorak and placed it on a flat rock with a couple of stones on top. 'I'm leaving this as a marker so that we'll be able to get our bearings on the way back. It's so easy to get lost up here.'

The second leg of the ascent wasn't quite so strenuous, but the higher we went the more difficult it was to see because of the cloud. Breathlessness was also a problem on account of the decreasing level of oxygen near the peak.

As there was no discernable track to follow, we took our directions from a series of cairns set at fairly regular intervals as landmarks on the slope. After half an hour or more of pushing ourselves to the limit, we reached a flat layer of rock that fooled us into thinking we were at the top when in fact there were further heights to be scaled. Wet with sweat and gasping for breath, we finally gained the summit after almost two hours of walking and climbing.

I was the last to mount the final ridge. Before me a towering iron cross took me by surprise. In a windbreak enclosure at the front of the crucifix, Siobhán, Ronan, Niamh and Padraic were huddled together sheltering from the breeze. Dehydrated and trembling, Niamh was sucking on a water bottle. Beside her, Padraic and Ronan were sweating and panting. In her red anorak, Siobhan was the only member of the group who looked anyway composed. I joined them on my hunkers and gathered my breath for the descent.

Before heading down, we said a prayer at the front of the cross. As well as thanking the almighty for getting me through the tribunal, I prayed for family and friends, and, at the last minute, I overcame some resistance and said one for the man who had driven me to these heights and the limits of my endurance.

Before the descent, Niamh and I posed with our backs to the cross while Siobhán trained her Samsung lens on us, and took a snap for posterity.

> How did this cross, emblem of loss,
> become such a potent symbol
> for so many people on earth?

THE DARK

I have looked at the dark side of life;
as well as day I've studied the night;
while others slept and dreamed it was bright,
I have looked at the dark side of life

The Dark Side

Not being a regular visitor to Dublin, I gravitated to John Street at the side of John's Lane Church off Thomas Street because I'd parked there several months before when I participated at a benefit show for the guitarist Henry McCullough in a venue close to the chapel. The gig I was due to perform this evening – a testimonial concert for the songwriter Philip Chevron (terminally ill with cancer) – was in the Olympia Theatre, a good ten-minute walk from where I now parked. After getting my guitar bag from the boot, I dropped into the church to say a quick prayer for a steady nerve before heading to the venue. While on my knees, the chorus of a song written by Phil that I'd agreed to sing at the show came into my head, a song I'd thought about deeply and practised extensively, but was still apprehensive about singing it live for the first time.

O Lord, Your ocean's so big and my boat's so small;
I can fly if you want me to, catch me if I fall.

When I reached the Olympia, I couldn't remember where the stage door was. I tried the front entrance, but it was locked. Displayed on the red framed glass doors, posters advertising the night's show caught my attention: *'Philip Chevron Testimonial Concert – Songs written by Philip Chevron and Others.'* Among the twenty or so acts listed in alphabetical order, my name was seventh from the top, just above Gavin Friday. Having been sent a PDF of the poster a week or so earlier, I surmised that Phil had been responsible for the diplomacy of the running order, which didn't extend to the timetable of the programme I'd received the day before. The fact that my name had been moved to third in the rota of opening acts didn't surprise me, as it tallied with my low profile in the music scene.

In a narrow lane beside the theatre, I noticed a group of people emerging from a side entrance so I made my way there and found an intercom at the side of a black door. A minute later I was inside the building shaking the hand of a member of the stage crew who directed me to a narrow stairway, telling me that the dressings rooms were on the next floor. At the top of the short flight of stairs I ran into a female administrator who gave me a stage-pass attached to a black and white ribbon, which she placed around my neck. 'You'll need this for getting in and out of this area. There's very strict security on account of the large number of acts participating.' She pointed down a hallway. 'The solo acts' dressing-rooms are that way; the nearest one for females and, just beyond it, the male room.'

As I made my way down the corridor I noticed a number of framed photos of famous entertainers who had performed in the Olympia over the years – Maureen Potter, Danny Cummins, Twink, Christy Moore, Rory Gallagher and Phil Lynott (my old flat-mate), to name a few.

A familiar face came towards me in the hall. 'Johnny Fean, fancy meeting you here?'

Johnny smiled. 'I saw you were on the bill. Good to see you.'

'Same here. Are the other Horslips champing?'

Johnny laughed and pointed past my shoulder. 'We have a dressing room back that direction.'

'I'm sharing with a gang down here somewhere. I came early in the hope of getting a soundcheck.'

Johnny smiled. 'I'll let you go so, and see you later.'

The male dressing room turned out to be empty. Bulb-bordered mirrors took up one wall above a shelf ranged with bottles of wine, beer and water. There was also a tall fridge with a glass front stacked with more booze. Two well-worn couches triangled at one end of the room and there were a number of hard-backed chairs positioned against the wall facing the glowing mirrors.

I took my guitar from its bag, tuned it, sang a song and then headed out for my sound check.

Downstairs I ran into Barry Devlin, bass player and vocalist with Horslips. 'Another Lip. I met Johnny upstairs.'

Barry smiled. 'Great to see you.'

We chatted about Philip's medical condition and I mentioned the song of his that I had chosen to sing at the concert, *The Dark At The Top Of The Stairs*. Barry's eyes lit up. 'A daring choice. I love the chorus – the bit about the boat.'

Surprised that he knew the song, I nodded. 'Phil informed me that that section's a prayer that President Kennedy kept on his desk during the Bay of Pigs.'

Barry's eyes widened. 'I didn't know that.'

I gave a brief account of the countless emails that had passed between Phil and myself regarding the complex lyric after I agreed to sing the song. 'Though we've never met, I feel I know Phil by this stage. The only part of the lyric that he refused to clarify was the section about the boy in the dark. He referred me to Beckett's *Waiting for Godot* for clues on that, but all I could find there was a reference to a boy's fear of human cruelty.'

'You did your research.'

'The song deserves it.'

Parting from Barry, I wandered around the stage area where a number of stage hands and roadies were setting up microphones and amplifiers. I went to the most authoritative-looking one of the crew – a tall man reading a sheet on a clipboard – and wasn't surprised when he informed me that he was the stage-manager, Paddy, who had emailed me regarding my stage requirements a few days earlier. After some small talk, he directed me to a microphone and chair centre-stage and gestured towards a screen between two monitors in front of a mic stand. 'The autocue you asked for. Test it while you're doing your soundcheck. The monitor man, Jimmy, will work the device for you.'

After I settled myself on the chair and established a decent guitar and vocal sound, I started singing the lyric rolling on the screen in front of me.

In the sanctuary of a minute's silence
My thoughts turned to the falling man.
In the final seconds of his short life, the century began . . .

Apart from the song's title, it had been the poetics of these opening lines that had attracted me, and my curiosity deepened when Phil explained that the 'Falling man' was one of the unfortunates who had jumped from the Twin Towers on 9/11.

No Zapruder movie or TV reality show ever felt like this,
I feel like an intruder but can you tell me, mister, what it's like
    at the precipice.

Though Phil informed me that he'd written the song around the time he was diagnosed with cancer, he insisted that the 'precipice' had nothing to do with his medical condition, though I remained doubtful about that.

> Was it like the dark at the top of the stairs
> When you were a boy, and you couldn't go back
> And you couldn't go on, did you ever hear those final prayers:
> I love you Daddy; were you sleeping while the others suffered?
> Are you sleeping still?

The lyric rolling in the autocue was running slightly ahead of itself but I didn't need it, as I knew the words by heart, having sang them countless times since I'd volunteered to sing the song. After inhabiting the lyric for a few days, I came to the conclusion that the nub of the narrative was the cruelty that the boy (possibly Philip himself) had found hard to face in his youth. The possibility that sexual abuse might lie behind the boy's fear occurred to me, but, as Phil refused to explain this section of the song, I compensated by drawing on my own experiences as a kid in relation to familial disturbances that I was in the dark about till I faced them creatively in my work as a songwriter over the years.

> Oh Lord, your ocean's so big and my boat is so small;
> I can fly if you want me to, catch me if I fall . . .

After I completed the second half of the song – which dealt with cruelty coming from both sides in the political conflict that ensued in the aftermath of 9/11 – I thanked the sound engineers and had a quick word with Paddy about my set. As I was leaving the stage a guy with a grey quiff approached me and held out his hand, telling me that he was a member of Phil's old band, The Radiators from Space. 'That was a fine interpretation. You almost had me in tears.'

'I believe the song was on your reunion album?'

'That's right. I think it's one of Phil's best.'

I nodded. 'I was reluctant to sing it at first – I never do covers – but I'm glad I put myself out. It's the real thing.'

Back upstairs I found the singer Duke Special and a journalist from *Hot Press* magazine chatting in the dressing room. I introduced myself and explained that I was on the bill but neither of them seemed to connect with my name. We chatted about the show while Duke changed out of a wrinkled set of clothes into an even more tatty stage costume, the feature item of which was a grimy pink shirt with a dead frill down the front. Noticing me gaping at the limp garment, Duke laughed. 'It could do with a wash. I've been gigging all week and haven't had a chance to get back to base up North. It won't be noticed in the dark, hopefully.' He tossed back his dreadlocks and asked me if he should know me. I shrugged. 'You might know some of my songs?' I mentioned a few titles and Duke and the journalist smiled. We chatted about Phil and the song of his I was due to open my set with. Duke explained that he was doing two originals as he hadn't been able to find any suitable songs by Phil that weren't already spoken for by other artists.

Other songwriters, musicians and performers started arriving. I went downstairs for a coffee and sandwich and when I returned to the dressing room I found Roddy Doyle, Patrick McCabe, Luka Bloom, Conor Byrne, Declan O'Rourke and others chatting about the new Bob Dylan album, *Another Self Portrait*. All eyes turned to me as I made my entrance. Luka Bloom mentioned my name and came and hugged me, while most of the others gestured with hand-waves and smiles. I chatted with Luka and was surprised to discover that, like Duke Special, he wasn't including any of Philip's songs in his spot either. 'I tried grappling with *Lorelei* – a great song – but couldn't get a handle on it.'

Knowing that Luka was scheduled to open the show, I wondered how he felt about going on first, but kept my thoughts to myself. 'How's the brother?'

'Christy? The finest.'

I thought of mentioning a controversy that had blown up between Christy and myself after I publicly criticised him for suggesting in a newspaper article that the Catholic Church had no right to hold its Eucharistic Congress in Croke Park after the plethora of abuse scandals, but again I bit my tongue. Instead I turned to Conor Byrne, Luka's nephew, and reminded him of some gigs we'd played together some years before in Donegal. 'Near Mount Errigal.'

Conor looked at me askance. 'I don't remember that.'

I laughed. 'You should. I kicked up a stink because there was a mix up over who was topping the bill. Your name had been put above mine on the poster, remember?'

Conor laughed. 'Jesus yeah, now it comes back.'

'I've written a chapter on it dealing with my ego. I'll have to send you a copy of the book, if it ever gets published.'

'I'd like that.'

I got myself a bottle of water and sat on a couch beside Roddy Doyle. 'I have a crow to pluck with you. As the former lead singer of the first soul band to come out of Ireland, Granny's Intentions, I must tell you that your group from the Commitments weren't the trail-blazers you made them out to be.'

Roddy smiled. 'I was a big fan of yours in the '80s, when you brought out your *Current Affairs* album. I used to go see you in the Buttery in Trinity.'

I was about to admit that *Current Affairs* was the worst record I'd made, but again I bit my tongue. While I was thinking of complimenting Roddy on his television drama *The Family*, Pat McCabe interrupted our conversation with a cutting remark about some songwriter whose name I didn't get. 'He's no Dylan, that's for sure . . .'

Roddy concurred. 'But who is?'

I glanced from Roddy to Pat, wondering if I should throw a spanner in the works and admit that, for me, since his magical heyday in the '60s, Bob was an Emperor without clothes – or at best an Emperor scantily-dressed – but once again, I bit my tongue, which by this stage was becoming quite sore.

As the time approached for the commencement of the show, a stage administrator arrived and conducted Luka and Conor downstairs to open the concert, telling me that I should follow in ten minutes. I got my guitar and went to a nearby toilet to fine-tune my instrument. I sang a few bars and then headed towards the stairs. On the way, I glanced into the female dressing room – the door was ajar – and spotted the singer Mary Coughlan standing by a mirror brushing her long auburn hair. Noticing me, Mary put down the brush and invited me in. As I entered, I noticed a girl in a corner buttoning her floral blouse. Mary came towards me with her arms extended. 'Johnny Duhan. I'm on after you, I'm told. Tell us, what depressing song have you got for us tonight?' As she said this, Mary glanced over her shoulder to see what effect the remark had made on the girl in the flowery blouse and then, clasping me in a limp embrace, she kissed me on the cheek. I conjured up a weak smile, swallowed some ire and retreated, explaining that I was expected on stage soon.

Because Mary had recorded a couple of my songs – to say nothing of the fact that she'd built her career singing blues dirges – I was surprised that she had allowed herself engage in stereotype casting. But then, knowing Mary, I realised that her remark was just an off the cuff slip of the tongue. Before I reached the bottom of the stairs I found myself making allowances for her on the grounds that she was possibly suffering from ego trauma, having to follow Luka and myself so early in the bill.

At the bottom of the stairs I ran into the singer Gavin Friday, who once duetted with Mary Coughlan on one of my songs. A stage administrator introduced us. Gavin showed no sign of recognising me but shook my hand in a friendly gesture and walked on. Going through the stage door, I stood in the wings and watched Luka and Conor perform. At the end of their set they received a huge round of applause. As they came off stage I clapped Conor on the back and congratulated Luka.

Glancing out at the restless crowd standing at the front of the stage, I waited for the compére, Aidan Gillen, to announce my name.

While making my way into the spotlight a favourite prayer of my mother's ran through my head: *Sacred heart of Jesus, I place all my trust in Thee.*

Once I was settled in my chair with my guitar on my lap, the butterflies settled and I became conscious that Philip was somewhere out in the theatre, probably seated in one of the ornate tiered boxes in the upper floors. Gazing out into the murmuring darkness, I drew a breath and leaned towards the microphone. 'I was first attracted to this song of Philip's – *The Dark at the Top of the Stairs* – by the title and the opening line "In the sanctuary of a minute's silence my thoughts turned to the falling man." I was intrigued when Philip informed me that this falling man was one of the unfortunates who had to jump from the Twin Towers on 9/11. The song also deals with other violent incidents like President Kennedy's assassination. The heart of the song, however, is this kid who's in the dark regarding some personal family matter that isn't revealed in the song. I can relate to that boy because I was similarly in the dark regarding a disturbing family situation when I was young.'

While I was singing, you could hear a pin drop. Towards the end of the final chorus my confidence surged and – as often happens at such cocky moments – I hit a wrong chord. The audience luckily didn't notice, judging by the level of applause that went up as I drew back from the mic. For my second song, I played it safe and broke into *The Voyage*, but half way through the first verse I was sorry that I hadn't performed a new song, *Wings*, which dealt with facing death stoically. To compensate, I sang the final verse of *Don't Give up till It's Over*, and gave a gentle shout out to Phil before starting it:

> Watch the full moon rising like a ghost of the sun;
> Dawn will be more surprising when a new day's begun.
> Don't give up till it's over, don't quit, if you can,
> The weight upon your shoulder will make you a stronger man.

Though the audience joined in on the chorus and gave me a great round of applause, I felt out of sorts leaving the stage on account of the chord blunder. I ran into the singer Damien Dempsey upstairs, who gave me the thumbs up. Other performers who had heard my set over the intercom congratulated me back in the dressing room, which was now almost full to capacity. I drank a bottle of water and chatted for a few minutes with other singers, then began to feel a bit of a spare. My job was done, I told myself, so I packed up my guitar and slipped away without saying goodbye to anyone. Earlier I had been told that there was a possibility that Phil might appear on stage at the end of the night, but it was a long journey back to Galway and something was pushing me towards the exit door.

It wasn't until I was halfway home that I realised that what was bothering me was not only my bruised pride over what Mary had said but also the alienation I felt from the musical fraternity overall due to my years of self-imposed exile from the Dublin music scene. I didn't fully understand the emotion, but I knew it was partly ego-driven and partly driven by forces within the industry who didn't like my ethos.

It was well after midnight by the time I got home. I went straight to bed but didn't sleep for hours. Groggy, I rose at my usual Sunday morning time but, before going to the kitchen to cook the habitual family grill, I went to my computer and found a number of congratulatory emails and messages on my Facebook page regarding my performance of the night before. Someone had also posted a photo album featuring photos of many of the artists that had performed at the concert, including a few of myself. Browsing through the series, I noted many of the acts I'd missed due to my leaving early, including Paul Brady, Brush Shiels, Shane MacGowan, Hothouse Flowers, and others. The final image sent a shiver down my spine – a portrait of Philip Chevron dressed in a red plaid suit, similar to plaid hipsters I wore myself back in the '60s. Bathed in a glow of coloured stage-lights, Phil looking terribly emaciated. I baulked at the image at first but was drawn back to it by the expression of joy on Phil's sunken face, which was lit up by a gleam in his eyes. Remembering a compliment he had paid my old band Granny's Intentions in the first email he sent me, I smiled, then regretted that I'd missed the real beam in his eye the night before.

THE QUOTA

You need some time to think on things that I say;
we need to know the truth, you and me.

We Both Need to Know

Because he was the only man with a beard in the lobby (a long white beard, it transpired), I recognised Danny straight away when I entered Buswells hotel, across from Dáil Éireann. Dressed in grey trousers, dark blazer and brown shoes (the type of nondescript outfit I was wearing myself, apart from my red bomber jacket), he looked incongruous in a room otherwise occupied by men in dark suits. As I made my way towards his armchair, I smiled. 'Danny McCarthy! When you told me I'd recognize you by your beard I never imagined it would be so bushy and white. If you were wearing my red jacket, I'd almost expect a sack of toys to be sitting beside your chair instead of that briefcase.'

Danny got to his feet, smiling, and gave me a firm handshake. 'Funny you should say that. I've just taken a job as Santa in a big department store in Belfast starting in a couple of weeks. The pay is good and I have to supplement my earnings somehow now that the gig market has dried up due to not being able to get my songs played on Irish radio. Take a seat. Pat and Phil should be here soon.'

I ordered a coffee from a passing waiter and sat opposite Danny, small talking about the bus journey I'd just made from Galway. When my coffee arrived, Danny got down to business. 'The meeting with the Minister, as I emailed you this morning, was put back half an hour on account of the Irish Water crisis. Pity the government wouldn't apply the same kind of urgency to the crisis in Irish radio. But then I guess the Irish musical community have only ourselves to blame for that, as we must rank as one of the most disorganised industries in Ireland when it comes to protecting our interests.'

I sipped some coffee. 'Hopefully the meeting today with the Minister will begin to address our concerns. It's great that you managed to set it up. And great too that Pat managed to get Phil Coulter to come along as part of our delegation.'

Danny smiled, obviously pleased by the complement. 'Those articles you wrote for *The Sunday Independent* were a great help. Alex White would never have agreed to meet us if they hadn't highlighted the issue for the general public.'

I nodded. 'You can thank the deputy editor Willie Kealy for that. As a lover of Irish music of all kinds, he stuck his neck out and got them published.'

Danny leaned towards his briefcase. 'I've brought along lots of stats to show the minister exactly how much the Irish economy is losing because of the amount of royalties that are leaving our country year by year, and I also have letters from EU officials who are fully behind Ireland introducing a quota.'

I glanced at the briefcase. 'It's great that you have those figures, Danny, but I reckon we'll be given twenty minutes max to make our pitch this evening, so there's going to be little time to bombard them with statistics. And regarding your EU contacts who are behind the quota, I don't have to remind you that the broadcasting authority itself – which the minister's department set up – obtained full sanction from Brussels many years ago for an Irish music quota, which was blocked by the Irish radio sector. The thing we need to get to the bottom of is, why the government allowed that to happen.'

Pat Egan and Phil Coulter arrived, both dressed in smart suits, Phil with a crombie overcoat draped around his shoulders and a paisley cravat inside an open white shirt. Being acquainted with all three of us, Pat conducted the introductions.

Throwing his crombie on a nearby chaise longue, Phil shook Danny's hand and sat in the chair beside me. 'Johnny Duhan! After hearing so much about you – and helping to promote your music in the US over the years – it's great to meet you at last.'

'Likewise. Strange how our paths haven't crossed till now.'

Phil fixed his cravat. 'Strange indeed, seeing as we're both dinosaurs from the '60s, I a wee bit further back in the Paleolithic line than yourself.'

I smiled and sat forward. 'I did try to contact you some years back when I got into a legal entanglement over the infringement of the copyright of my song *The Voyage* when it featured on an album that also featured two of your songs. I thought you might be able to give me some advice. I phoned your office but you were out of the country.'

Phil hesitated. 'I remember that. One of the companies went bust. I lost a fortune. But I heard you did okay?'

I gave a false laugh. 'After a tribunal case against a solicitor who tried to stop me accepting a settlement offer was resolved. It's a long story, well documented in the papers at the time. And still online, if you care to look it up.'

Phil nodded. 'I heard about it. You went up against a barrister and three solicitors, and won. No mean achievement.'

'A nightmare I'm still recovering from.'

Phil laughed. 'Solicitors are slippery creatures. And music publishing is a minefield, if you don't know the no-go areas. But I'm sure the experience has taught you a thing or two. You certainly seem to have got to the nub of the ills that beset Irish radio in your Indo articles. I've read them and they make a very convincing argument, concise and to the point.'

'From my dealings with the tribunal, I learned that the most important aspect of defending a principle is to expose the fault lines of your opponent and keep the focus on them while hammering home your certainties.'

Phil smiled. 'The John Hume approach! I sensed that from your articles. Before we head across the street to meet the governor, give me a quick refresher on the main points we should keep the focus on at this meeting?'

I glanced across the coffee table at Danny. 'We were just discussing that when you and Pat arrived. Danny and I are of one mind that a quota can only be effective if enshrined in legislation. When independent radio was granted its license to operate in Ireland a broadcasting edict was promulgated that thirty percent of airplay was to be apportioned to Irish music, but almost straight away that rule was flouted. A former chairman of the broadcasting authority is on record as stating that some of the Dublin radio stations lowered the levels of Irish music in their schedules to three percent, which had a knock-on effect of lowering levels all over the country. In an effort to halt the slide, the Irish broadcasting authority itself went to Brussels and gained sanction to introduce legislation to enact a quota, but the Irish radio sector vetoed the move and threatened to take legal action to block any amendment to the Broadcasting Act.'

Phil's face grew rigid. 'I read that in one of your articles and it incensed me. How did the government allow that to happen?'

I drew breath. 'Because the radio sector's legal team, no doubt, put the wind up them with the red herring that it would be unlawful to discriminate against other European artists. But the French introduced legislation to enforce a forty percent quota of French music on French radio more than twenty years ago and no one batted an eyelid.'

Danny leaned forward. 'The Irish radio sector claim that the only reason the French were allowed their quota was to protect their language and culture, which it's claimed we can't do because we sing mainly in English. But my EU contacts say that this obstacle can be surmounted with a proper amendment wording.'

I sat upright. 'If anything, the language issue should work in our favour as all European countries, including France, still have an appetite to hear a high percentage of their songs in their mother tongues, an advantage we don't have.'

Pat glanced at his watch and got to his feet. 'We'd better get moving. Dáil Éireann is probably like Fort Knox. It might take time to get through the cordons.'

I followed the others towards the door. 'By the way, there is one other major point that one of us should make during the course of the meeting. According to a recent PPI statistical report, only three or four Irish acts made it into the top 50 songs played on Irish radio last year. That needs to be hammered home to the Minister.'

Danny laughed. 'And all three of them sing with American accents.'

Phil sighed. 'Jesus, when I started out in the business half of the music played on Irish radio was Irish. What happened along the way?'

I cursed. 'Vultures took to the air.'

Pat's concern about security holding us up at the entrance to Leinster House proved unfounded, but we did have to queue at a hatch to sign for identity badges once inside. While we were pinning our ID discs on our jackets in the vestibule close to a portrait of Michael Collins, a young woman approached Phil and had a few friendly words with him. When she departed, Phil informed me that she was Seán Ó Riada's daughter, which struck me as serendipitous, given that the mission we were on centered on Irish musical culture and Ó Riada was the chief exponent of Irish music in his time.

An official guide led us up a wide flight of stairs and through some narrow corridors, where we brushed shoulders with a few familiar politicians. The brightly lit office we were eventually shown into was quite small and sparsely furnished, with just a long desk that had three swivel chairs behind it and four steel-framed chairs out front. Soon after we took our places in the steel chairs, the Minister entered the room briskly with two officials and seated himself in the centre chair facing us while his team sat flanking him. Cordial introductions were exchanged and the Minister opened the proceedings by assuring us that we were all singing from the same hymn sheet in wanting to maximise the levels of Irish music on Irish radio. Directing his attention mainly at Phil Coulter (probably because Phil's face was familiar), he reminded us that the official broadcasting authority, accountable to his department, was doing all in its power to insure that high standards were being maintained in Irish broadcasting for everyone's benefit, including Irish musicians and composers. He acknowledged that the ever-expanding broadcasting landscape, with its diversity of new technologies, was becoming more and more difficult to police and regulate, but this, he insisted, was a growing problem for broadcasters worldwide. 'And believe me, it's going to become more and more of a challenge for all of us in the future.'

Phil nodded in agreement and leaned forward, pinching his chin. 'We're fully aware of that, Minister, and we can assure you that we are not expecting miracles here. But if I may, I would just like to outline for you in very simple terms the level of change that has taken place in Irish radio since I started out in the business, and that wasn't today or yesterday, as you well know.' He paused to give the Minister time to smile. 'Back in those cradle days of Irish radio when Radio Éireann had a monopoly on Irish broadcasting, almost half of the music they played was home grown, with a diverse range of tastes being catered for. Contrast that with recent statistics that show that just three Irish acts managed to make it into the top 50 songs played on Irish radio last year. No industry could possibly sustain that kind of a reduction in support. Is it any wonder that most professional Irish musicians have to earn their living outside Ireland now, including myself!'

Pat Egan sat forward and cleared his throat. 'As a long-time musical promoter in Ireland, I can verify that those airplay statistics are correct. During the past decade Irish radio has all but eliminated Irish music of all types from their primetime programmes, which has made my job of trying to promote Irish acts in venues around the country almost impossible.'

Across the room, Danny leaned towards his briefcase. 'I have documented statistics here that clearly demonstrate that more than ninety percent of broadcasting royalties – and revenue generated from recordings and live performances – have been leaving our shores for years. This is due to the fact that international acts mainly from the US and Great Britain – have a complete monopoly on our airwaves.'

The Minister glanced in my direction, but I held my fire, waiting to see how he was going to deal with what had been said already. After a long pause, he sighed. 'We know there's a problem, but our hands are tied by EU regulations that demand that all citizens of the union be treated equally. Introducing a quota on national grounds would violate that ruling.'

Danny took some documents from his briefcase. 'Excuse me Minister but I have some letters here from some top EU executives who have assured me that there is no EU law blocking Ireland from legislating for an Irish music quota. I also have an article written by a former chairman of the broadcasting authority who describes how he and his CEO went to Brussels and gained approval to introduce legislation to enact a quota many years ago, but the Irish radio sector vetoed the move.'

The Minister waved his hand dismissively at the pages Danny held out to him, and scowled. 'Who are these top EU executives advising you, and what business have they meddling in our affairs? I'm the Minister in charge of this department and I make the decisions on matters of broadcasting without interference from outsiders. This is an internal Irish matter and has nothing to do with your EU contacts.'

Cowed, Danny sank back in his chair.

After a tense silence the Minister glanced at Pat and me and then turned to Phil. 'I'm sorry but it's been this department's assessment for many years that an Irish music quota cannot be secured, for the reasons I've already outlined.'

I took a deep breath. 'How come the French have a quota?'

The Minister sighed and turned to the official on his left, his secretary-general, and gestured that he should answer. The secretary general looked at me and sniffed. 'The French are the French! They tend to get their own way in many matters.'

I knitted my brow. 'What kind of an answer is that? Why didn't Ireland fight for a similar quota when the French were granted theirs?'

The other official cleared his throat. 'Because we weren't entitled to one.'

The Minister sat bolt upright and looked me straight in the eye for the first time. 'The French used the legitimate argument that their language and culture were under threat from the proliferation of English language based popular music at that time. We couldn't use that argument, as most of our songs are sung in English.'

I looked the Minister straight in the eye. 'Our songs may be sung in English but the best of them have a unique Irish cultural value separate from Anglo-American popular music.' The secretary general raised his finger, but I ploughed on. 'Furthermore – and this is crucial – we Irish have a much more legitimate argument than any European country for needing a quota because most of our EU counterparts have a clear advantage over us because radio audiences throughout Europe, including France, still have an appetite to hear a high proportion of their songs in their mother tongues, which means that their radio playlists are automatically made up of a high percentage of their indigenous native songs.'

The Minister conceded that this was a valid point but insisted that there were complicated legal obstacles hampering any amendment to the Broadcasting Act, not only coming from Europe but from "other" quarters also. 'As things stand, my hands are tied in this matter.'

I stared at the Minister and took a deep breath. 'A former board member of the Irish broadcasting authority – a well-known journalist – told me recently that the Irish radio sector has the government "all stitched up" on this matter, to quote his exact words.'

The Minister dropped his pen on the floor and the official on his right bent to pick it up. After a tense silence, the Minister wrote something in his notepad, glanced at his watch and got to his feet. 'I wish we had more time to explore these matters further, but unfortunately we have a crisis on our hands with Irish Water that must be attended to. But I'll tell you what, if you can come up with a written proposal with a wording defining the uniqueness of Irish music that will be acceptable to all concerned, then I can assure you that I will give it my closest consideration.'

LOVE IS A BOAT

Life is an ocean, love is a boat,
in troubled waters it keeps us afloat.

The Voyage

As we drew close to Derry on the N13, Kate, seated in the back of the car, pointed through her side-window towards a billboard advertising the festival I was due to participate in the following morning. 'Look, there's the boats that came to Galway a few years ago. Remember Mammy, you took us to see them?'

Behind the wheel, my daughter Niamh glanced at the hoarding headed *The Legenderry Maritime Festival 2014* and confirmed that the Clippers displayed on the giant poster were the same type of yachts that had visited Galway two years before. 'I'm not sure if they're the actual boats that we saw but it's the same Volvo Ocean race they're participating in. Derry is putting the event on this year. And your grandad's due to sing *The Voyage* while the boats are leaving for the next stage of the race tomorrow.'

We arrived in the city just after three o'clock and spent twenty minutes navigating unfamiliar, busy streets till we located the hotel that had been booked for us, a mile or so from the town centre. After we settled in, I suggested walking to the river before dinner to check out the marina port location of my first performance scheduled for the next morning.

When we got to the river we found the place teeming with sightseers strolling in a two-way stream along the Foyle walkway, skirted by food stalls, vending booths and merchandise stands. A strong smell of barbecued meat was wafting from spits and grills and a loud babble of voices was contending with distorted pop music coming from speakers mounted on banner and bunting-festooned lampposts along the riverside. Going with the flow of walkers heading towards the famous

Peace Bridge in the town centre, we bypassed a number of moored sailing vessels, including a tall ship in full mast with a black skull and crossbones flag flying from it's top sail. Stopping at a crepe stall across from the pirate ship, Niamh bought Kate a flat pancake coated in chocolate, and, while she was nibbling it, a couple of buccaneers decked out as Long John Silver and Jim Hawkins approached us and asked Kate to feed the puppet parrot on the captain's shoulder. 'Give 'im a crumb and 'e'll sing for ya, matey.' With a nervous laugh, Kate broke off a wedge of pancake and proffered it to the inanimate beak. The parrot remained mute but Long John adjusted the black patch over his eye and started to hum. 'Ho ho ho and a bottle of rum. That'll keep 'er chirping for the long night ahead.' Niamh took a small camera from her handbag and took a snap of the colourful pair with Kate smiling beside them, then the swashbuckler hobbled back to his galley on his peg leg with his young companion beside him. As we resumed walking, I glanced at Niamh and smiled. 'For the heart's treasure together we set sail.'

Niamh gave me a puzzled look. 'What?'

'My song *The Voyage* was inspired in part by my boyhood love of the story *Treasure Island*. Those two buccaneers are the main characters from the book.'

Niamh laughed. 'A nice coincidence.'

Because the line of strollers we rejoined was moving at a snail's pace, it took us twenty minutes to walk the short distance to the port marina, which a passerby pointed out to us. A black iron gate leading to a wooden jetty was locked but a number of sailing boats were visible through the bars, lined up along the inside of a berthing area at the end of the jetty. On the outside of the long berthing ramp one of the Clipper yachts participating in the ocean race was moored with its pristine black mainsail aloft, outshining all the other sailing vessels in the vicinity. Niamh pointed to the craft through the bars. 'I think that's one of the yachts that came to Galway as part of the ocean race a few years back. It's a fabulous looking boat, isn't it? I wonder where the others are?'

I looked down river. 'Probably moored somewhere beyond the bridge. But it's from here they'll be setting off in the morning, while I'll be singing *The Voyage*.'

Niamh smiled. 'I still can't get over you getting this commission after the way you failed to get it in Galway. Serendipity, I think they call it.'

'No, serendipity involves chance. I don't think chance had anything to do with this. Fate more like, connected to faith.' I glanced around the quay but couldn't see any sign of a performing platform anywhere in the area. 'I wonder where I'll be singing when the boats are leaving? I don't see any stage setup, do you?'

Niamh surveyed the surrounding quayside. 'Maybe they'll erect something in the morning.'

I nodded. 'Probably.'

Kate drew our attention to a pontoon decked out with a blue and white crenulated canopy floating in the choppy water of the enclosed berthing space, moored to a poll at the end of the jetty. 'Maybe you'll be singing on that?'

Looking out at the bobbing raft, I laughed. 'I don't think so, Kate. You need to sing into a microphone and I don't see any microphone out there.' I glanced at my watch. 'Come on, I'm starving. Let's head back to the hotel for dinner.'

While we were having our meal, the waiter tending our table informed us of a fireworks display that was planned to take place at midnight on the quayside near the Peace Bridge as part of a concluding ceremony of the festival, an event that the whole town was expected to turn out for. All through dessert, Kate pestered us till we agreed to take her along to the extravaganza later that night, but back in her room an hour later she fell asleep as the nine o'clock news was starting on BBC One television. Glad to be off the hook of attending the midnight spectacular, Niamh and I turned in ourselves soon after ten-thirty and had an early night, in preparation for the day ahead.

Waking at my usual six o'clock and knowing I wouldn't sleep again because of the early night I'd had, I got up and dressed and went off in search of a Catholic church where I might get early Sunday Mass. After a short walk, I found a red-bricked chapel in a leafy street a couple of blocks away from the hotel, but the first Mass wasn't till nine o'clock. Returning to the hotel, I found Niamh and Kate showered and dressed and ready to go down for breakfast. Back in our room after we'd eaten, Niamh unpacked her violin and I got my guitar and we ran over some songs we intended playing together at a lunchtime concert, after the main event at the marina.

At eight-thirty we checked out of the hotel and drove through empty, silent streets till we found a parking spot close to the river. After we took our instruments from the boot, Kate insisted on carrying my guitar bag strapped on her back while we made our way along the empty quay towards the marina. As we approached the gate leading to the jetty, we could see no sign of a performing platform anywhere in the vicinity. Our attention was drawn to the line of Clipper yachts lined up in full sail along the outside of the berthing ramp. There were no crews on board the boats or any officials around the quayside, except for a lone gatekeeper with an identity badge standing by the open port gate who nodded when I asked for directions to the performing area. Turning to the river, he pointed towards the blue and white canopied pontoon floating a little way out from the jetty – the raft that Kate had suggested might be my performing platform the evening before – and he smiled. 'As far as I know, that's where you'll be singing. There was a man out there early this morning setting up a PA system. Look, you can see the microphones and speakers from here. But you're early. The proceedings aren't set to get underway till ten-thirty.'

The surprise of having her inkling realised delighted Kate so much she broke into a fit of the giggles. As for me, when I got over the shock of discovering that I was going to be singing on a floating raft, I began to feel light-headed and giddy. 'When I was a kid, I used to love floating on rafts. Singing on one should be amazing.' I smiled at Niamh. 'Maybe you'll play with me?'

Niamh shook her head emphatically. 'No thanks. I'm nervous enough about playing with you on a stage later on.'

To pass the hour that lay ahead, Niamh decided to ramble down the quay to check out the stage we were scheduled to perform on together at lunchtime, taking Kate along with her. On the pretence of returning to the car to get my guitar stand, I walked three blocks back to the little chapel I'd visited earlier and arrived there just after nine o'clock Mass had started. Putting my mobile phone on silent, I took a pew near the back of the church and concentrated as best I could on the service. After receiving Communion (my mainstay), I said a quick prayer for a steady heart and left the church before the end of the service.

On my way back to the river I took out my phone and discovered that I'd had two missed calls from Niamh. I phoned her. In a quiet voice, she informed me that the agent I'd arranged to meet at the marina at ten o'clock was looking for me. I glanced at my watch and pointed out that it was only ten to ten. Niamh laughed nervously. 'I know what time it is, but he's here beside me now, waiting for you. Get here as quickly as you can.'

Breaking into a run, I arrived at the marina out of breath five minutes later and found Niamh and Kate talking to a young man in a yellow tee-shirt by the gate leading to the jetty. After some introductions, the agent informed me that an engineer was waiting to do a soundcheck as soon as I boarded the pontoon at the berthing area. I asked Niamh and Kate to accompany me but they decided to remain on the quayside, where people were already beginning to congregate.

I made my way down to the jetty and had a quick consultation with the sound engineer (his desk was on a platform at the end of the jetty). Then boarding the pontoon, I did a sound-check, seated between two monitor wedges, while the bobbing raft was being pushed away from the berthing ramp. As well as being wired to some speakers mounted at each side of the floating pontoon, the PA desk was connected to lamppost speakers running all the way down the quay to the Peace Bridge. When I was satisfied with my guitar and vocal sound, I gave the engineer the thumbs up and then sat back and let my eyes drift along the long line of expectant faces on the waterfront, spotting Niamh and Kate among them.

As the ten-thirty deadline for the departure of the Clippers approached, the MC interviewed a few local dignitaries (including Derry's Lord Mayor) on the topic of the success of the festival, then started communicating to the growing crowds of quayside onlookers, preparing them for the imminent ceremony of the undocking of the yachts. A recording of *Danny Boy* came over the intercom and the Derry air began to vibrate with an almost palpable tone that eventually merged with a rumbling sound that turned out to be the Red Arrows' flying squad, which appeared in the sky out of nowhere and swooped down in chevron formation above the Clippers, leaving a trail of red, white and blue arching in the sky above the yachts.

When the aerial display came to an end, the Clippers began to move away from their moorings and file out into the centre of the Foyle in slow formation, one behind the other. After the speed and noise of the jets, the slow silent drill of the departing yachts seemed an anticlimax until the crowds along the quay began to cheer and wave. The crews on board the yachts in turn waved back at the quayside onlookers from the decks of the Clippers, and the whole riverside area became animated. While this was going on I heard my name being introduced over the intercom by the MC, who asked the crowds to sing along with the 'famous ballad' I was about to perform. Though I hadn't planned a preamble before starting to sing, I found myself thanking the city of Derry 'as a Limerick man' for the honour of singing my most popular song for the departing crews. A tremor entered my voice as I started to sing but my nerve steadied during the opening verse. When I reached the first chorus I looked along the quayside and noticed that many of the onlookers were singing with me, though I could barely hear their voices. By the end of the second chorus the whole stretch of the crowd as far as the eye could see had joined in and were singing and swaying to the rhythm I was strumming on my guitar. As a final flourish, I glanced over my shoulder and gave a nod in the direction of the departing yachts while hitting a final chord and raising my vocal tone to a higher pitch. 'Love is a boat. Bon Voyage!'

A loud cheer went up from the crowd and the MC thanked me for a 'sterling performance.' Disembarking from the pontoon, I thanked the MC and the sound engineer and made my way up the jetty to the open gate. Niamh and Kate were waiting for me with beaming eyes. My granddaughter took my guitar and strapped it on her shoulders, while Niamh clapped me on the back. 'You won't forget that in a hurry. Did you hear the way they were all singing along with you?'

Giddy from adrenalin, I laughed. 'I could see mouths moving but I couldn't hear much.'

A number of people approached me and offered congratulations. I spoke briefly to a couple who were eager to tell me that they'd had *The Voyage* played at their recent wedding as their theme song. I congratulated them and turned back to Niamh. 'Did you find out where we're doing the lunchtime gig?'

Niamh looked down the quay. 'It's not too far from here, a three minute walk. But you're not on until twelve thirty. You have lots of time.'

'What do you mean *you*? It's *we* from here on in, kid.'

While we were making our way along the path, a man with a grey mustache and a camera around his neck came towards me out of the crowd with his hand out. 'Johnny Duhan! How's about you? I'm Danny McGilloway, the guy who got you this gig. I didn't know they were going to have you singing so early. When I heard *The Voyage* over the speakers back at the bridge, I knew your voice straight away.'

I took a step back and smiled. 'Danny McGilloway! We finally meet. I had no idea you'd be such a handsome devil. Here, let me introduce you to my daughter and grandaughter.'

By way of introduction, I gave Niamh a brief account of my association with Danny, explaining that he was a long time admirer of my work, going back years. 'Danny is the man I was telling you about who approached Derry City Council and suggested that they book me for one of the shows at the festival. At a single stroke, he did what I failed to do after months of petitioning to perform *The Voyage* at the Volvo race when it came to Galway.'

Niamh shook Danny's hand. 'You must be well in with someone in high places in the Council?'

Danny laughed. 'I'm not, actually. I just did it on spec – phoned the department dealing with the festival and used the popularity of *The Voyage* to reel them in. They knew the song – everyone knows *The Voyage* – so they took it from there.' Danny turned to me. 'I had no idea they were going to feature you singing it while the boats were leaving. That was quite a coup. How did you organise that?'

'The agent who booked me for the show we're heading to phoned me a couple of days back and asked me to consider doing another spot while the boats were leaving, adding five hundred pounds to my original fee as an enticement. Without hesitation, I agreed. But even then I had no idea they were going to have me singing on a raft on the Foyle! I only found that out this morning.'

Danny smiled. 'Well, everyone will be talking about you now, that's for sure. And don't be surprised if it shows up in the national papers tomorrow. But here, before I forget, I want to have my photograph taken with you, before fame comes your way.' He took the large camera from his neck and handed it to Niamh. 'It's easy to operate; just press the button above the lens. Your wee girl will hold your violin for you. She's a great little roadie, isn't she.'

After Niamh took a few shots of Danny and myself standing by the railing with our backs to the Foyle, Danny accompanied us to the location of the outdoor concert, which was already underway when we got there, with a ten-piece pipe-band dressed in kilts playing Scottish marching music to an audience of a hundred or more seated in front of a wide black stage. An hour later I took to the boards myself and opened my set with *Your Sure Hand*, a song I wrote for Niamh, which was an ideal way of introducing her as my accompanist for the rest of the performance. Niamh received a warm round of applause and played a blinder, despite her nerves. We finished with *The Voyage* and added *Don't Give up till it's Over* as an encore.

The following morning a front-page feature in the *Belfast Telegraph* headed 'Legenderry send-off as thousands bid farewell to Clipper yachts' described how 'local singer-songwriter Johnny Duhan performed his hit *The Voyage* during the Parade of Sail.' After the way I'd emphasised my Limerick origins while introducing the song on the pontoon, I'm not sure how the journalist got his facts wrong, but, given that the city of Derry afforded me one of the highlights of my career, I felt more than happy with the adoption.

THE CLADDAGH BAND

As part of a tribe, we respected each other;
the law was inscribed that we love one another;
and though it wasn't always applied, the law never died.

Part of a Tribe

I picked up the singer Jan Nagle in Salthill and, as we drove through morning rush-hour traffic to get to the motorway, filled her in on some of the details of the Dublin event we were heading to perform at (the launch of St Vincent de Paul's annual collection appeal), following the recent release of our SVP charity single, *Part of a Tribe*. Though I'd been in communication with Jan and other members of The Claddagh Band (an association of some of Galway's finest musicians, singers and composers) over the past weeks and months by email and phone while recording *Part of a Tribe*, the line-up committed to the gig we were heading to kept diminishing. 'At this stage we'll be lucky if a third of those who performed on the recording make it to the launch. Dolores and Sean Keane won't be there. Neither will Máirtín O'Connor, Frankie Gavin or Carl Hession. In fact none of DeDannan are coming, not even Eleanor Shanley. The whole thing has turned into a fiasco. Once *The Late Late Show* backed out of considering us for a spot and the head of music in RTE radio refused to playlist the song, the singers and musicians, one by one, began to lose interest. But it's not their fault – they have careers to be getting on with. It's mine, for taking on more than I bargained for.'

Jan glanced at me as I pulled up at a set of red traffic lights. 'You're being hard on yourself. Without you the project would never have got off the ground.'

'That's just it, it never really did get off the ground.' I drew breath as an old man hobbled across the street in front of me on a walking-stick. 'When I think back on all the obstacles that had to be overcome to record one song – more sessions than it took me to record a full album myself last year – I feel like kicking myself for taking on the project.'

Jan alerted me to the lights turning green. 'Getting DeDannan to record together was a great achievement. After the public row they had in the media last year it was widely believed they'd never play together again. Getting them back in the studio was a coup in itself.'

I nodded. 'You know of course that they didn't actually play together at the same time; I had to record each one of them separately. It took five sessions just to put down the backing track. That's one of the reasons it took so long to record the damn thing.'

Jan smiled. 'But the main thing is that we did it and now the song is out there for everyone to hear. It was on RTE radio again this morning, bright and early. It sounded terrific. Even if it isn't playlisted, it's still getting played.'

I glanced at Jan, wondering if I should burst her bubble and fill her in on the low statistics for early morning and late night radio listenership, but I opted to remain positive. 'This launch we're heading to always makes it on to RTE television's main news bulletins. Maybe we'll get lucky and our spot might get highlighted. That would be a great boost.'

We reached the motorway and made good time till I diverted to Ballinasloe, to pick up my daughter Niamh, who had agreed to stand in on violin, with another violinist from Bray, to make up the shortfall of Frankie Gavin. Punctual as always, Niamh was waiting at the rendezvous point in her Audi when I got there. Transferring her violin to the boot of my car, she took over the driving wheel while I moved to the front passenger seat and Jan slipped into the back.

After introductions (Jan and Niamh hadn't met before), Niamh took off at speed and was soon skirting in and out of traffic on the motorway in her usual rush to get ahead of herself. As she overtook a silver Merc, she glanced at me and raised her chin. 'You'll be glad to know I spent two hours last night playing along with the CD of the tribe song, learning Frankie's parts. But I'm still glad you've got a second soloist to play with me. Together the two of us might add up to one Frankie, though I doubt it. What's her name anyway, the fiddler from Bray?'

'Pat O'Connor. She came to see me perform at the Mermaid Arts Centre last year and gave me a CD and book of her own music, which impressed me. She's also played with some of Ireland's top trad musicians, so I presume she knows her stuff.'

Niamh started overtaking another car. 'I hope our tones match. Who else is coming?'

'Sean Tyrrell, Tony Maher and Mary Coughlan, if she can make it.'

Niamh frowned. '*If* she can make it! What does that mean?'

'I had a text from her last night saying she might have a problem.

One of her kids is in trouble at school so she has to meet the school principal this morning for a meeting on the matter.'

Jan leaned forward from the back. 'She's always in trouble, Mary. Fingers crossed that she'll make it or I'll be the only female singer in the band.'

In an effort to take our minds off our worries and concerns regarding the gig we were heading to, I took a copy of The Gloaming's first album from my CD compartment and put it in the CD player, forwarding to track eight, the highlight of the collection.

After a mere hour-long drive, we arrived at St Vincent de Paul's national headquarters on Sean McDermott Street in Dublin's city centre two hours before show-time and were conducted upstairs for a complimentary lunch before doing a soundcheck. There was no sign of Mary Coughlan or Tony Maher anywhere in the building but we found Sean Tyrrell and Pat O'Conner in the canteen, chatting at a table in front of a stainless steel kitchen.

While we were having soup and sandwiches, Niamh and Pat O'Connor talked fiddle while Jan read a newspaper. At a separate table, I broke the news to Sean Tyrrell that he was going to have to sing some extra verses in the absence of Sean Keane.

'No bother, as long as they're written out I should be able to tackle them. How's it doing anyway, the single? I heard it the other night on *Late Date*. Fiachna Ó Bráonáin played it.'

I swallowed some soup. 'Fiachna' s been a great support. But at this stage – after weeks of failed attempts to get it playlisted on primetime radio – I've almost given up on it. Without repeated daytime airplay, you're dead in the water. And the nail in the coffin was being turned down for a spot on *The Late Late Show*.'

Sean held back from biting into a sandwich. 'I don't understand that. With the line up you put together – Sean and Dolores Keane, Mary Coughlan, Eleanor Shanley, and the whole of DeDannan including Ringo and Alex, for God sake – how did they turn it down?'

I shook my head. 'I don't know. But it's going to be very awkward today because Ryan Tubridy is hosting this SVP launch and he was the first person in RTE I sent the song to.'

Sean nearly choked on his sandwich. 'Shit, that might be awkward alright.'

'To be fair, Ryan might not have the full say on what acts make it onto his show – a full production team no doubt decide that – but he must have some input.' I swallowed some soup. 'I'm beginning to think that I might be blacklisted in RTE and in other stations. A series of articles I wrote for *The Sunday Independent* recently on the need for an Irish music quota to be enacted through legislation may have got up the noses of some radio and TV bosses.'

Sean stopped eating. 'I read a few of those. They're spot on. I get more airplay in Germany and America now than I get in Ireland!'

I groaned. 'Don't get me started! I got involved in the campaign when I learned that it isn't the EU who are blocking the introduction of an Irish music radio quota but the Irish radio sector itself.'

Sean dropped his spoon. 'That's outrageous! How did the government allow that?'

I hesitated. 'A former board member of the broadcasting authority told me that the radio sector have the government literally in their pocket.'

Sean cursed. 'And we're supposed to be a republic. As always, money rules!'

After our torrid lunch, we made our way to the hall designated for the launch and were pleasantly surprised to find Mary Coughlan at the front of a small bunting-festooned stage chatting to Tony Maher, who was setting up his keyboards in front of an SVP logo banner. Because of the subdued lighting in the room (ambient blue predominating), Mary didn't recognise me as I approached the stage, but, the minute she heard me calling to Tony, she came and kissed me on the cheek. 'Johnny Duhan, the man of the moment! Well done on getting the project this far. It's a terrific song. And fuck the begrudgers!'

'I'm relieved you made it, Mary. How'd you get on with the school principal regarding your wayward boy?'

Mary turned and pointed towards some rows of seats disappearing in shadow at the rear of the hall. 'He's back there somewhere, the little fecker. Expelled for a week. I had to bring him along or I'd have been late getting here for the run through. But come on, we'd better get on stage and practice the song. I don't know how I'm going to cope with the additional verses you've heaped on me because Dolores couldn't make it.'

The band assembled on stage and tuned their instruments behind a copse of microphone and music-stands, with the four vocalists to the fore, myself seated with guitar on lap. We ran through *Part of a Tribe* several times, while the singers acquainted themselves with their additional verses and the musicians brushed up on the song's chord structure. A number of musical blunders were made and many lines of the lyric were fluffed, but there wasn't time for further rehearsal, as a stream of invited guests – including an RTE camera crew and other media people – started pouring into the room. After we received notification that our spot was scheduled for directly after the screening of the ad for the SVP campaign, we left the stage and went our separate ways, mingling with the gathering crowd.

The official proceedings got underway bang on time with an opening performance by a kiddies' choir of Christmas carols. Ryan Tubridy then appeared on stage, mic in hand, and chatted to a few of the little singers dressed in green elf costumes with red pixie caps with bells on top. Well used to engaging with toddlers on his famous *Late Late Toy Show* (which had only recently been screened to great success on RTE television), Ryan conducted the interviews with the little folk with great sensitivity and humour.

After the choir was led rumbling off stage, Ryan introduced the screening of the SVP campaign video for 2014 (one of the highlights of the launch programme), which was due to be broadcast on nationwide television during national collection week. Unlike some very effective SVP ads from previous years which focused on anguished families sitting around bare tables in darkened rooms, the present ad, narrated by Ryan himself, turned out to be quite upbeat, opening with a close up shot of a smartly-dressed elderly lady facing the towering peak of Croagh Patrick, which she and a group of other smartly dressed individuals (the new poor, perhaps) were about to climb. As the metaphor unfolded, a wash of synthesised pop music accompanied the climbers on their ascent, with a teasing vocal line distorted by a vocoder. Despite the gimmicky nature of the production, the video received a large round of applause from the audience.

When the clapping died down, Tom McSweeney (veteran RTE broadcaster and SVP magazine editor, as well as life-long SVP member) took over the microphone to wind up the proceedings while Ryan Tubridy went and sat at the front of the stage. Taking this as our cue to assemble for the performance of the charity single, the musicians and singers made their way to their instruments and mics, while Tom made an impassioned speech on the community aspect of SVP's mission to support the poor and needy in Irish society, linking his theme to the song we were about to play. 'The stark lyric of *Part of a Tribe* illustrates how adversity and even despair can be surmounted with the right support systems, the kind of support systems that SVP have in place.' Rhyming off the long list of top singers and performers who contributed to the recording of the single, he ended his introduction with the concluding line from our PR flyer, with a caveat of his own: 'Though the sound that The Claddagh Band produce conjures up the salty tones you might hear reverberating around the stony walkways of the Claddagh region of the tribal city, we're sure that the song will reverberate in the hearts and minds of townspeople and city dwellers through the length and breath of Ireland, *if* our radio stations get behind this song.'

Before Tony Maher gave the count in, Jan, standing beside my seat, nudged me and threw her eyes towards an empty chair where Ryan Tubridy had been sitting less than a minute before at the front of the stage. I smiled. 'Not to worry. It's Friday; maybe he needed to get to Donnybrook to prepare for *The Late Late Show* tonight.'

Part of a Tribe

How did we survive the last forty years with all those trials,
going round in circles for all those miles,
how did we ever survive?

As part of a tribe, we respected each other;
the law was inscribed that we love one another;
and though it wasn't always applied,
the law never died.

How did we revive when we despaired when our faith died,
when we lost our courage, when we wept and cried,
how did we ever revive?

As part of a tribe, we respected each other;
the law was inscribed that we love one another;
and though it wasn't always applied,
the law never died.

How did we thrive, with all the confusion going on in our minds,
and all the destruction that we left behind
how did we ever thrive?

As part of a tribe, we respected each other;
the law was inscribed that we love one another;
and though it wasn't always applied,
the law never died.

ST WERBURG'S

Set on a hill with a spire like a mast and a regular bell,
our church is like a ship gone aground in a swell

The Chapel

Stepping inside the tall blue door of St Werburg's church with my son Brian – both of us laden down with musical accoutrements – brought to mind Philip Larkin's poem *Church Going*, as we entered the 'tense, musty, unignorable silence, brewed God knows how long.' Because the place was in darkness, except for the altar-cum-stage which was lit by a white spotlight and red and blue ambient lights, we didn't notice a young man perched behind a glowing sound- and lighting-desk at the back of the row of enclosed wooden pews to the right of the main isle until he cleared his throat. 'Johnny, is it? My name's Jim, your sound engineer for the evening. Everything's ready for you up there – DI box, two mics, small table and chair. I'm ready to go for a soundcheck as soon as you are.'

While my eyes were adjusting to Jim's shadowy face, I introduced Brian as my CD and book salesman and asked where he might set up his stall. 'I feel awkward selling merchandise in a temple, but at least the church is no longer in use.'

Jim shook his head. 'Who told you that? I have to have my gear out of here tonight for a Sunday service at nine in the morning.' He pointed towards a small wooden table at the back of the church. 'The trad band who played here last night sold their CDs from there. It's handy, as it's close to the entrance and exit door. It's a bit dark but I can lend Brian a torch.'

Brian got the torch and went off with his bag of albums and books to set up shop while I went to the altar and unpacked my guitar and other essentials. Before settling in behind the microphones, I unrolled a life-sized vinyl banner of the sketched figure from the cover of my album *To The Light* and set it up to the left of the main microphone, asking Jim to focus another spotlight on the image. 'I like to remind my audience of the fictional character I feel most in tune with, Don Quixote.'

Jim laughed. 'I saw the film *Man of La Mancha* with Peter O'Toole years ago, but all I remember is the theme tune, *The Impossible Dream.*'

'One of the songs I'll be singing tonight is called *After the Dream.*'

While I was running through part of my programme, allowing Jim scope to regulate the sound frequencies suited to my voice and guitar, an official in a dark suit arrived and turned on some lights in the higher reaches of the chapel, illuminating the full sweep of a surrounding wooden balcony that took up most of the upper building and brought into view a magnificent pipe-organ stretching the full length of the top part of the back wall. The added light filtering down from above also exposed an ornate wooden pulpit close to the right hand side of the altar that I hadn't noticed till now.

As soon as I was satisfied with my sound, I thanked Jim and went down and introduced myself to the new arrival. 'A beautiful church you have here. I didn't realise how nice till you turned on the lights up there.'

Without mentioning his name, the man shook my hand and offered his credentials. 'Welcome to St Werburgs. I'm just a caretaker, a stand in for our sexton who's on holiday. I'm afraid we don't have a dressing room as such, but you can use the sacristy on the right of the altar, if you wish. But be warned, the lavatory in there is the only toilet in the building . . .' He paused and cleared his throat . . . 'and both genders use it. It's adequate for our services – our congregation is small – but these TradFest concerts have been putting a strain on the facility. Part of the reason we've started renting out the building for concerts is to get finance for renovations, including new toilets.'

I smiled. 'I'm not fussy about dressing rooms. I can change at our hotel around the corner. I just need a place to wait before going on stage and a place to park during the interval. By the way, who was St Werburg, if you'll excuse my ignorance?'

'Patron saint of Chester, a princess who became a nun back in the seventh century. There are a few churches dedicated to her in England. Legend has it that she once restored life to a goose. Other tales suggest that she banished all the geese from Northhamptonshire, just as St Patrick banished the snakes from Ireland.'

We both laughed.

After I received clearance from the caretaker for Brian to sell CDs and books during and after the concert, I checked out the sacristy, a non descript room with minimal furnishings – a small table, a wobbly chair and a glass-framed cabinet with shelves of musty books, ledgers, and hymnals. The single toilet was in a damp recess just off the main space. After a quick look around, I decided that the place was fine for my needs.

While making my way back along the black and white tiled centre aisle of the nave of the church, Brian came towards me, smiling. 'You should see upstairs. It's fabulous. I've never been in a chapel like this before. It's like the ship from the *Pirates of the Caribbean.*' '

'It's a Protestant chapel. Church of Ireland. Different architectural structure to your common day Catholic church. More stolid. More austere. No statues or holy pictures.'

Brian glanced around the bare walls. 'It's strange holding gigs in a church, isn't it?'

'All the shows in the festival are being held in old churches. I don't know who thought of the idea, but they're ideal musical venues for folk and traditional music.' I glanced around the chapel and another line from Larkin's poem ran through my head: 'when churches fall completely out of use what we shall turn them into.'

Brian looked up towards the balcony. 'You should see the organ up there. It's massive.'

'I had a good view of it from the stage. But come on, we'd better get back to the hotel and get something to eat. It's pushing on.'

Before leaving the building I thanked Jim and told him I'd see him thirty minutes before show time.

Back at our hotel we had a quick meal and went to our room on the second floor, which we'd booked into earlier that morning, prior to a songwriting workshop I gave in the afternoon for the royalty collection agency *IMRO*. The minute Brian stepped inside the door he turned on the TV and threw himself onto my king sized bed. 'This is the life! When you asked me to come along to sell your CDs and books this morning, I had no idea you were going to be staying in a four star place like this. Are the festival people picking up the tab?'

'No, I'm paying for it myself. Because of the workshop, I needed a comfortable place to relax in before tonight's show. The double fee warranted the expense of a good hotel.'

Brian sat up in the bed. 'How are the bookings going for tonight?'

'Haven't a clue. I'm on a set fee, so the size of the crowd won't affect me. But I'm hoping for a good turnout. It should be okay as the festival seems to be very well run.'

'How much are you getting for the two events?'

I touched my nose and grinned. 'Quite a lot.'

Brian frowned. 'Well, if I make a bundle on CD and book sales, you'd better pay me well. Not just ten euro like last time. And remember, you promised to take me to the Temple Bar after the gig, to show me what it's like.'

I laughed. 'I told you already; the Temple Bar is a den of iniquity.'

Brian smirked. 'I know, that's why I want to check it out.'

While Brian watched a sitcom, I changed into a pair of black denims and black shirt, and then slouched on Brian's single bed reading a book of Philip Larkin's poetry. At ten past seven I began to feel giddy, so I got up and walked around the room, going over in my head some opening remarks I might use on stage. At twenty past seven I put on my jacket and turned off the TV. 'Come on, we'd better get going. I want to be backstage before the crowd arrive. And you'll need to be at your stall to ensure that stock doesn't walk when they start coming in.'

Brian followed me. 'I told you before, people who come to your shows aren't the kind of people who steal.'

Back at St Werburg's, Brian took charge of his stall while I had a word with Jim and then went to the sacristy and did some breathing and meditation exercises to calm my nerves. At five to eight the MC for the evening, Mike Hanrahan (one-time IMRO boss and brother of the event's organizer, Kieran Hanrahan), came and surprised me with the good news that a full house was already settled in their pews. After we worked out my introduction, Kieran went on stage and informed the audience that my programme would centre on highlights from my four main song collections. 'Johnny is the only songwriter we're aware of who has written a full autobiography in song. And tonight he is going to take you on an intimate journey through the four stages of his song cycle. Ladies and gentlemen, please put your hands together for the man who has written one of the most popular ballad of modern times, *The Voyage* – Mr Johnnyyy Duhan!'

The round of applause that went up as I came on stage was so loud and prolonged it unnerved me, but as soon as I settled in behind the microphones and looked out at the rows and rows of smiling faces, I relaxed and the momentum carried me effortlessly into the opening songs from my *Just Another Town* collection. Because several of these ballads have a religious theme (*Benediction, Mary* and *Two Minds*), the church setting added gravitas and poignancy to my performance, which the audience appreciated, judging by the high level of applause that followed each song. By the time I moved on to the more romantic ballads from *To The Light*, I had the place in the palm of my hand. Before announcing the last song of the first half of the show, I glanced at the image of Don Quixote on the banner beside me and smiled. 'Back in the '60s I became so dazzled by the limelight of pop culture, I lost my way, but in my twenties I found my bearings through folk music when I started searching for a purer light. This final song before the intermission, *To The Light*, marks a moment when I found evidence that I was finally on the right track to achieving my aim.'

The heavens were all aglow, shedding light on all below;
And I felt the world turning, journeying, in the sea of night;
And my heart started burning for our returning to the light.

While I was catching my breath in the sacristy during the break there was a timid knock at the door and a young freckle-faced woman entered and shyly asked for directions to the 'loo'. While I was pointing towards the recess, she congratulated me on my performance and told me that she was really looking forward to the second half of the show. Almost on her heels, another woman in a red dress appeared and praised several of my songs while awaiting her turn to use the toilet. Within a minute several others were filing passed me – male and female – and soon there was a queue stretching all the way back to the door, and beyond it. While bypassing me, many of those in line made witty remarks about the absurdity of the situation we found ourselves in, and one joker gave me a nod and a wink. 'You might make a song out of this sometime, Johnny, eh?'

Back on stage I laughed into my microphone. 'Now that I've met most of you in person, I feel like we're almost family, so it's appropriate that I'm kicking off part two with a few songs from *The Voyage*, starting with the title track, which you might care to sing along with.'

Almost everyone in the chapel took me up on this offer, which culminated in the final chorus sounding like it was being sung by a full choir. Though some of the darker ballads that followed deal with the more raw side of family life, the audience stayed with me right up to *In Our Father's Name*: 'In the long shadow of our family tree that darkened once the heart of me, I found good reason to believe in our frail seed . . .' Following this with *The Storm* (a homage to my father's tenacity) and *Song of the Bird* (a paean to my mother's faith) attuned the atmosphere for my song *Flame*, which I announced as one of my proudest songwriting achievements. 'The struggle to forge a marriage between poetry and melody that I've been engaged in for almost fifty years culminated when I completed the final verse of this song.

> O when my first flame died and you became my love,
> a fresh breath of air made sparks appear,
> and my heart like coal lit up and my soul took fire,
> while out on your bed you grew blushing red my flower.

I introduced my penultimate song *The Beacon* by relating the story of the mountain climb I made with my daughter and other family members after I won the tribunal case. The huge round of applause that followed this set the tone for my finale *Don't Give up till it's Over*, the chorus of which the crowd joined in on with the gusto and verve of a full Welsh choir.

After a two-song encore, I thanked the crowd for one of the most memorable gigs of my career and left the stage to one of the loudest rounds of applause I've ever had.

Back in our hotel room, Brian totted up his CD and book sales and was so staggered by the calculated sum, he threw bundles of twenty and fifty euro notes in the air above my bed like confetti. 'Now let's go to Temple Bar and celebrate!'

I lay on my bed and groaned. 'I've been on stage for almost five hours today. I'm knackered. Give me time to catch up with myself, then we'll go.'

Brian frowned and went to switch on the TV, but I stopped him. 'If you turn that on, no Temple Bar! I want a bit of peace and quiet for a while. Here, read this book of poetry while you're waiting.' I leaned for the book on my bedside locker and tried to hand it to Brian but he pushed it away.

'You know I don't like poetry. It's boring!'

I opened the book and read aloud one of my favourite Larkin poems, *Deceptions*.

Brian listened with a look of growing perplexity. 'What in the name of God is that about? Why do poets have to write in such a puzzling way?'

'There's nothing puzzling about that; it's just concentrated thought. Larkin is trying to console a destitute man with a nugget of wisdom that has a sting in its tail. He's a pessimist, Larkin, but he has great sympathy for the human condition. That's one of the reasons I love him.'

Brian shrugged and sat on his bed. 'How long more are you going to be?'

I flicked through the pages of the book and came to the poem

Church Going. 'I'll just read you this last one and then we'll go. It's kind of appropriate.'

While I was reading the long poem Brian remained attentive, right up to the last words about the graveyard.

'That reminds me of the church we've just come from. But what does it mean?'

'Larkin was an atheist. But if you read between the lines, it's obvious he would have liked to believe. Though he does a fair bit of sniggering, his respect for what he perceives to be a crumbling institution comes out in the last verse in the line 'A serious house on serious earth it is . . . proper to grow wise in.'

Brian got to his feet. 'If only it wasn't surrounded by the dead. I listened to it! Now let's get a move on to Temple Bar!'

'Do you know why it's called Temple Bar? . . . Because the area is full of churches.' I put the book back on my locker and got to my feet. 'Let's go so. But remember, we're not staying long. One or two drinks and then back to bed.'

While the lift was taking us down to the lobby a few lines I once wrote about Larkin came into my head, but I kept them to myself, knowing that Brian had other things on his mind.

> Before he died, Philip Larkin read the bible from cover to cover,
> then tossed it aside. On learning of his reverse doubt,
> the *pang* of his old despair came back to me:
> *"What can be said, except that suffering is exact*
> *but where desire takes charge, readings will grow erratic."*

CREATION

In thoughts of others, we gain like lovers
who put one another first

First

In preparation for producing a video of the pivotal opening track from my album *Creation – The Fallen Tree –* I rose early on the morning of the shoot (a fine Saturday morning in spring) and went to my workroom to read over the hand-written entries from my song journal dealing with the gestation of the work, in the hope of finding something relevant to say on camera as an introduction to the song cycle. As the air in my room was sharp and damp after recent rain, I got under the covers in the bed across from my computer desk with my copybook and highlighter, propping three pillows behind my back for comfort. Going to the first entry in the journal related to the new collection, dated the 6 January 2015, I was surprised to discover how dejected I was at the beginning of the year, just a few months earlier.

> Due to the failure of many of my aspirations in 2014 (the rejection of part two of my autobiography by several publishing companies who initially showed interest; the failure of my song collection *Highlights* to sell due to lack of national and regional airplay and the consequent low attendance at most of my autumn shows; followed by the collapse of The Claddagh Band's Christmas charity single after radio and TV bosses refused to support it; to say nothing of my aborted efforts to get an Irish music radio quota established in legislation through several articles I'd written on the subject for *The Sunday Independent*), I start into 2015 in very low form . . .

Despite this despondency, by the end of the entry my spirits have rallied and I'm already beginning to draw on resources that will sustain me during a period of inspiration that I hadn't experienced since I wrote the songs for *Just Another Town* in my mid-twenties.

> . . . Many aspects of my Christian faith have no relevance in the reality
> of our world, but there is another world (I feel it in my heart and I know
> it by the hints and sacred evidence I'm given from time to time) and I'm
> going to cling to that belief in Christ's message of Love till the end, come
> what may . . .

This affirmation is followed by the entry of a song lyric that ignited
the inspiration for writing the collection *Creation*, a lyric that I'd been
struggling with for months but hadn't been able to complete, until now.

Advent 2013

All through December, I made my way to the chapel in the bay.
Drawn like the Magi, I left my car,
walked the dark shoreline without a star.
The wind was against me, the ocean was wild,
when I made the journey for the child.

Black on black as ebony, the clouds and the rocks
and the spread of the sea, with only shadows guiding me.
The narrow path, the town up ahead; a forest of lights
and the holy bread, and the deep hunger by which I'm led.

All through the winter, I kept on going while the storms were blowing.
Drawn like a moth to the candle flame
that burned on the altar to the infant's name.
The time was against me, where few now conceive
how anyone can still believe.

Black on black as ebony, the clouds and the rocks
and the spread of the sea, with only shadows guiding me.
The narrow path, the town up ahead; a forest of lights
and the holy bread, and the deep hunger by which I'm led.

All through the season till Christmas day I struggled all the way.
Lured by an instinct and the fear I might fail
the little life in the stable tale.
Now light pours upon me here in the spring,
where under the sun I sing.

Below this lyric, an explanation for the motivation behind the song illustrates something of the complex nature of a faith that has compelled me to attend daily Mass to receive the Eucharist for the past 30 years and more:

> God be with the days when I viewed my faith in Christ simply. This is as good as I can do now. It's a struggle, I know; even the melodic form wavers. But it may lead on to a song vibrant with a more muscular strength by the end of the series.

Already it's quite clear from this extract that the completion of *Advent 2013* stimulated a desire in me to write a 'series' of songs that will attempt to explain the substance of the faith I have lived by for most of my adult life, a faith that is not only related to religious practice but is also inextricably linked to family and community, and to the creative part of my nature.

In a rushed attempt to get started on the project, I began to write a song on that fateful day (6 January 2015) based on a snippet of conversation I'd had with my wife the evening before on the thorny subject of ageing. In the post Christmas lull of our empty house (after all our kids and grandkids had gone back to their own lives), while we were watching a stale repeat programme on TV, Joan turned to me with a look of dejection and groaned. "Isn't getting old bloody awful?" In an attempt to cheer her up, I suggested that there were positive aspects to being over sixty that needed to be taken into account, but Joan wasn't convinced. "What are they?"

In an effort to answer that question, I started working on a new lyric the following morning and was still working on it late that night.

Winter

O winter never seemed so cold;
It's bitter and we shiver
but if the truth be told,
it's not just the weather,
the harsh weather that has us in its hold,
And though we're together as ever
together we're now growing old.

O winter never seemed so stark;
It feels forever since a summer left its golden mark

And pleasure on pleasure
ignited from just the spark
Of being together as ever,
Now together we face this dark.

O winter never brought us so low.
Still as a father and mother we've watched our children grow
And reap a treasure beyond measure -
Grandchildren who glow
When we're together as ever;
This, together, we know.

O winter ever season of demise,
This ghostly weather we'll survive
together for bright-eyed surprise.

The "bright-eyed surprise" came in the form of *Hold Your Horses*, an up tempo fairytale song written for our five granddaughters, Aoibhean, Allana, Saoirse, Hannah and Kate. And on its heels I wrote *Missing You*, a lament for our daughter Ailbhe, working in Australia. What took my breath away about these compositions was that they were directly linked – through the conduit of the lyric of *Winter* – to my song *The Voyage*, in that our children and grandchildren were, when I thought about it, the "treasure" that Joan and I had set out to attain when we "coupled our fate" over forty years earlier and journeyed for "the shores of the heart."

To avoid being preachy in the lyric of *Hold Your Horses* (something all kids disdain), I drew on my own youthful passion for pop music for a chorus that I knew would appeal to the girls: "Don't get me wrong, you're hearts will belong in the dizzy regions when the pulse in your blood is as strong as the beat of the rhythm of your favourite pop song."

These new songs didn't exactly ameliorate Joan's fear of ageing, but they did bring a beam to her eye and a smile to her lips when I sang them to her. What pleased me also was that my friend and fellow songwriter Paddy Houlahan gave the lyric of *Winter* the thumbs up which bolstered my confidence and gave me the impetus to go on digging for more songs. As a mark of gratitude to Paddy himself, I came up with a song to mark our enduring friendship – *Avoiding Tyranny* – that included the line "I have a friend more like a brother."

By the 11 February (four weeks after I'd started the project) I was brimming with enthusiasm.

Suddenly I have a trove of new songs, two or three of which I'm excited about recording, but will hold off till I've exhausted the seam. I'm hoping and praying for one more major song that will convey the central place that Jesus holds in my heart. The core of Christianity is probably no more and no less than the message of Love (Christ's passion and self-sacrifice being the heart of the matter). All else is probably only window dressing to get that vital message across to the world. Without love and concern for others, we inhabit a dog eat dog Darwinian landscape . . . Christ's message of love is probably the key to the mystery of life.

A book I was re-reading at this time – *the Phenomenon of Man* by Teilhard de Chardin – stopped me in my tracks one morning when I came upon a line that dredged up a memory of a mysterious incident from my boyhood that I'd pondered on many times while growing up without mentioning it to anybody, for fear of being thought loopy: "Man only progresses by slowly elaborating from age to age the essence of the totality of a universe deposited within him."

In Me

When I was just a boy,
One dark night I
Woke with a sound in my head,
A low drone that drove me out of my bed.

Standing there on the floor,
Mary on the wall near the door,
My brothers' soft breathing in sleep
And I gripped by something mysterious and deep.
Though I was partly afraid, I acted brave
And stood firmly absorbing the sound.
It deepened and spread inside like a rising tide;
It absorbed me, yet I stood my ground
And then I found
A place free mystically of gravity,
Like a vast galaxy, only this galaxy was in me.

Now that I'm growing old
The memory needs to be told
In the tone that once mystified me
When I was touched by the epiphany.

While I was struggling to complete this lyric, I came upon a fallen tree one morning while strolling in nearby Barna Woods. It made such an impression on me I jotted the details of the encounter in my song journal.

A recent storm knocked a number of trees in Barna Woods. One in particular – a huge ash tree – now blocks the pathway up the incline I usually take on my walks, so that now I have to swing around the exposed massive root structure that was wrenched out of the ground by the high winds. All around the fallen tree, other similar trees – some not so sturdy – survived the tempest, which made me wonder why. Studying the root section I noticed that the tree had grown on a shelf of rock, which meant that it hadn't scope to root properly. Whatever the reason, the felled tree is down for good, laid low at the prime of its life. Like that tree, we are all exposed to the winds of time, one way or another.

The Fallen Tree

O the pathway, the narrow pathway on the slope in the winter wood,
was blocked to me by a tall tree that had fallen in the way,
and as I wound around the sorry ground where the roots had come undone
by the high winds, the stormy winds that had blown all night till day,
I saw the birthplace of that tree where the seed had sewn unnaturally
on a shelf of solid rock where the full roots couldn't lock;
how on earth did it ever grow such a long long time ago?

O the tree trunk, such a wide trunk flat on the forest floor,
like a fighter, a brave fighter knocked by a mighty blow;
and its branches, its sturdy branches, like extended arms
held out in love to one above who had helped it survive and grow;
and I stood in the birthplace etc.

O the fallen tree spoke to me straight to my old heart
through a scar mark on the dark bark of the pain that we all share;
and I felt the sap rise for one last *surprise* coming in the spring
when the buds break and the leaves awake for the full bloom of the year.
And I stood in the birthplace of that tree where the seed had sewn unnaturally
on a shelf of solid rock where the full roots couldn't lock;
how on earth did it ever grow and thrive so long ago?

Like a bolt out of the blue, this song literally wrote itself. After jotting it into my copybook, I was on high doh.

> I'm over the moon regarding the wave of inspiration that has come over me since Christmas. In just a few short weeks I have amassed the flesh and bones and spirit and soul of a new album, possibly the best song collection I've ever written. *Just Another Town* (the full collection) came to me in a similar overwhelming wave of inspiration, but I didn't have the kind of skill I now have to fully shape some of those songs.

The next day I was setting my sights even higher:

> . . . The Christian subject I would most love to bring alive in song is the Transfiguration. It glows with wonder, supernatural wonder. It's as though Christ needed to be infused with God's Holy Spirit – in the same way that an engine needs fuel – before He could willingly and lovingly journey towards His natural end and His supernatural beginning. But where in my life might I stand to achieve that kind of illumination and transcendence? If there is such a place in my own paltry life, guide me towards it God, so that I might attempt my song of praise.

On the day I made that entry, I woke in the middle of the night and jotted this line into my song Journal: "It's just dawned on me that *The Fallen Tree* is me." During the following days I began to associate *The Fallen Tree* with the cross of Christ and the Calvary of my own voyage to find Him, through song. As well as writing a series of lyrics on His life – most notably *The Three Temptations* and *The Cross* – I found a way to put a positive slant on the Passion of my own calling as a songwriter:

> When I reached the bottom of pure desperation,
> right there at rock bottom, on solid foundation,
> I found Creation.

I was so overwhelmed when I came to the entry describing how I wrote the song *Creation* (one of my favourites of the collection), I felt compelled to get out from under the blankets and get my guitar and sing it, not once or twice, but three times.

A couple of hours later I headed out for Barna Woods to rendezvous with Tony Walsh (my video producer) and his assistant and wife, Caroline, at the site of the felled tree, where we spent two hours filming in glorious sunshine while a choir of birds serenaded us from the surrounding branches. During the course of setting up one of the shots, I spotted hundreds of lime-green shoots in the rocky soil around the exposed root structure of the toppled tree and reminded Tony that the lyric of the song specified that winter was the season we were dealing with, so the fresh slips shouldn't be focused on. Glancing at the myriad sprigs in the shallow earth around us, Tony took my point and observed that few, if any, of the countless shoots we were gazing at would survive the months ahead. Caroline brought our attention to a more positive aspect of the awakening spring by pointing to the supine branches of the felled tree, which were already beginning to bud, despite the tree being down. 'A sure promise of the summer ahead.' This prediction, coupled with the natural transfiguration of the season we were going through set the seed in me for the final song of *Creation*.

Resurrection

Fresh shoots of spring are here again
in woodlands, gardens and parks;
and from bushes and trees we hear a hymn/amen
of linnets, blackbirds and larks;

And in the open heavens a resurrected sun
is shining like a halo over everyone
and there is so much wonder still to come
in the endless summer of the Kingdom.

Bright flowers on stems are bowing,
bending to the prayer of the wind
and like flames petals are glowing
as rays of light descend

from the open heavens where the risen sun
is shining like a halo over everyone
and there is so much splendour still to come
in the endless summer of God's Kingdom.

In the run up to Easter 2016, I submitted *Resurrection* to a number of Irish radio stations for playlist consideration, but none of them picked up on it. Carl Corcoran was one of the few radio presenters to play the song on air in his popular programme *Blue of the Night* on Lyric FM. I didn't hear the spin myself, but on the morning after its airing I received a brief text from a Margret Geaney from Castleisland, Co Kerry, which put a smile on my face: "I heard your song *Resurrection* on the radio last night. Thanks for being you."

Soon after I released *Creation* I started rereading Martin Buber's *I And Thou* and came upon this passage in a section headed *I Consider a Tree*:

> ". . . in considering the tree I am bound up in relation to it. The tree is now no longer *It*. I have been seized by the power of exclusiveness . . . The tree . . . is bodied over against me and has to do with me, as I with it."

The coincidence of having just written a song on this subject took my breath away.

THE BILL

Let this song flow from the radio to the heart
of all who care for the welfare of those who start
to live on air

We Live on Air

A van with the Riverdance insignia on its side pulled up beside us as my daughter, Niamh, backed into a tight parking space on the Leeson Street side of St Stephen's Green, three quarters of an hour before I was due to team up with Willie Penrose and a delegation of musicians and composers for a meeting in Dáil Éireann on the issue of enacting legislation for an Irish music radio quota. Getting out of the car, I gestured towards the line of long-legged tap dancers as I helped Niamh get her son, Dylan, into his buggy. 'That's a coincidence. I was telling you on the way up about my visit to Bill Whelan's house in Roundstone the other day before my show at the Clifden Arts Festival. I wonder is this a good or bad omen?'

Fastening Dylan into his buggy, Niamh fished in her handbag for coins for a parking meter. 'Why would it be an omen, one way or another?'

I took my guitar from the car. 'While Bill was playing me some of his latest compositions in his recording studio, he reminded me that he had made the same journey to Dáil Éireann on the same mission we're on today thirty years ago, soon after the French successfully legislated for a forty percent quota for their broadcasters. The French did it without a blink of protest from other EU countries but Bill and his team were blocked from getting their proposal past the Oireachtas committee stage by Fianna Fáil, who insisted that legislating for special privileges for Irish musicians and composers went against EU law, by discriminating against our EU musical counterparts, even though the French had just done it.' I tapped Dylan on the head. 'I hope the same thing doesn't happen today.'

Niamh started pushing the buggy in the direction of the Shelbourne Hotel. 'It's a wonder Bill didn't come along and support you?'

'Once bitten twice shy, maybe. He still supports us, and his signature is right at the top of the list of Irish musical artists – along with Paddy Maloney, Brendan Graham and Christy Moore (to name a few) – who endorse our manifesto document S.H.I.P., which I showed you when I was trying to get *Comhaltas* on board. They never got back to us, by the way.'

When we arrived at Kildare Street, I invited Niamh into Buswells hotel for a coffee (our delegation's rendezvous point) but she declined, as her main reason for accompanying me to Dublin was to visit a friend who had been rushed to a maternity hospital close to Dáil Éireann a couple of days earlier after giving birth to premature triplets, who weighed into the world at just two pounds each. 'Pass on my good wishes to Siobhan. And when you get back, come straight into the Dáil building and tell the security guards that you're with the Willie Penrose delegation. I'll leave your name at reception, so you'll have no bother getting in.'

Waving goodbye to my grandson, I crossed to Molesworth Street and entered Buswells thirty minutes before schedule. Phil Coulter and Pat Egan (two of our team) were there before me, sitting in a lounge just off the lobby, being attended to by a waiter bringing them coffee. Ordering coffee myself, I sat opposite Phil, commending him and Pat for being so early. Phil picked up a page from the coffee table and fluttered it. 'I came early to pore over these bullet points you sent us.'

Pat dipped into a satchel and produced a sheaf of laminated fold-over A3 sheets with the S.H.I.P. logo on the cover (a harp-shaped hull & shamrock-encased anchor beneath the title *The Shamrock & Harp Irish Playlist*), our manifesto which spelled out in concise detail the criteria for introducing an Irish music radio quota. Designed by the Athenry artist Francis Kennedy, the document looked very impressive. I praised Pat for getting such a professional printing job done at short notice, with a pun. 'It's sure to make a big splash when it's handed out at the meeting.'

Other members of our delegation began to arrive, including long-time stalwart, Danny McCarthy, John Sheahan, Tony Allen, Michael English, Pete Cummins, and a whole crew of young musicians and composers from a diverse range of styles, with little in common except a united grievance with the Irish radio sector for ostracizing Irish music from the airwaves in our time.

In the middle of the growing hubbub, Willie Penrose (the politician most committed to our cause) arrived and approached Phil and myself with burning eyes. 'We'd better get the show on the road. There's a media circus across the street and they're growing impatient. They've asked for a few tunes and songs at the gate before we go in. Unfortunately, we've been blocked from allowing the media into the meeting, so we'll have to make do with whatever publicity we can get at the gate.'

With no time to dwell on this downturn in our expectations of impressing the media with our carefully choreographed musical programme for the afternoon, I followed Willie out into the packed lobby where, in his most rugged Westmeath accent, he called the assembly to attention while pointing towards the front door. 'Come on lads, get yer banjos and fiddles and follow me. Some of my Labour colleagues are waiting outside to escort you to the Promised Land.'

As we trailed out the front door after Willie, we were met by other representatives of the Labour Party who had survived the last general election, fronted by their leader, Brendan Howlin, who, Moses-like, stretched out his hand towards Kildare street and led our procession through a halted sea of traffic to the black gates of the Oireachtas, where a virtual army of journalists and cameramen were waiting like a firing squad with aimed lenses, ready to shoot. As we shuffled towards them, I glanced at Willie and recalled that it was as a private member's motion that he had got his amendment bill for an Irish music quota through the first stage of the Dáil, not with the help of his Labour colleagues (Alex White included) but with the support of Fine Gael's Frances Fitzgerald. But this was politics and, under the circumstances, allowances had to be made.

The media mayhem that ensued was part of politics too, with an added crazy dimension that only the music business can drum up. As I was being jostled towards the main group of celebrities that the cameras were focusing on, an old musician friend stuck his head over my shoulder, telling me that he needed exposure for a new album he was about to release. At that stage it dawned on me that the sea of faces around me – all contorted with crooked smiles – were clamouring for nothing more than a place on a newspaper page or a television screen. I tried to back away from the cameras, but Willie Penrose called out my name and asked me for a song. I fumbled my guitar out of its bag but couldn't tune it in the crush. In a half stupor, I broke into an Acapella version of *Don't Give up till It's Over* and the whole assembly joined in on the chorus.

The singer Sibéal Ní Chasaide was called on next and sang an impassioned version of *Mise Éire*, in Irish. Despite the noise of passing traffic and the chaos of the surrounding crowd, her performance – in the context of where she was singing – personified the essence of what our whole campaign was about.

To wind up the musical proceedings, the Doyle sisters performed *The Parting Glass* and John Sheehan joined one of the hottest young trad bands in the land, Moxie, for a set of jigs and reels. A number of individual interviews were conducted for TV and then we were ushered into a Dáil chamber with tiered seating.

As I took my place behind a long table beside Willie Penrose – Phil and others from our group were at his other side – I scanned the room and was pleased to note that an almost capacity crowd had shown up for the event, some musical supporters, but mostly politicians from various political parties.

Willie started the proceedings by reading an introductory speech that brought a hush to the room.

> If a nation is defined by its culture – and it is – it's hard to grasp why we Irish have allowed one of our greatest cultural assets – our music and song – to be banished from our primetime airwaves during the last few decades. It happened gradually – that's why we didn't notice it – but happen it did. And that's why representatives from the Irish musical community have come here today to support a bill I introduced in the Dáil last Christmas to pass legislation to enact a forty percent Irish music radio quota. To accept that we Irish don't have a legal entitlement equal to the French to protect our musical culture through a radio quota is an insult not only to our musical forbears – from O'Carolan, Thomas Moore and Ó Riada to The Chieftains, Bill Whelan and The Gloaming – but also to those who sacrificed their lives to establish our cultural independence in 1916 – men like like uilleann piper Éamonn Ceannt who set up the Pipers Club at a time when the music was in danger of being lost. The Irish musical community represented here today – old and new proponents of several different musical styles – will give you a sample of the type of music that is no longer deemed worthy to be broadcast on primetime Irish radio in 2016, one hundred years after the men who established Dáil Éireann died for our cultural independence. But first, we'll have a few words from a few members of the delegation who will outline some of the key aspects of their case.

Willie handed the proceedings over to Phil Coulter, who spoke eloquently about his long history in the music business – referring to himself as the 'granddaddy of living Irish songwriters' – then honed in on just one aspect of modern Irish radio that riled him, stating that, since he had started out in the early '60s he had seen airplay for Irish music plummet from fifty to three percent in our time. To put the statistic in cast-iron context he glanced across the table at me and frowned. 'If Johnny Duhan wrote *The Voyage* today or Pete St John *The Fields of Athenry* or Paul Brady *The Island* or I *The Town I Loved so Well*, I can assure you ladies and gentlemen that not one of those songs would have a chance of getting on Irish radio today.' He paused and took a white handkerchief from the top pocket of his fawn jacket and wiped his brow. 'I rest my case'.

Willie glanced at me and chuckled. 'Follow that!'

Though I had helped with Willie's speech and had drawn up the bullet points for our delegation, to say nothing of writing the five *Sunday Independent* articles on the Irish music quota issue that fed into our manifesto document, which many of the politicians before me had been dipping into since Pat Egan had distributed them at the outset of the meeting, I suddenly realised that I had made no preparations for what I was going to say myself. For a few minutes I winged it and spoke about why an Irish music quota needed to be established in law rather than in just edict, but, while I was improvising, I noticed a blank look on a few faces before me, so I changed tack and reverted to a story: 'Thirty years ago this year the composer of *Riverdance*, Bill Whelan, came into this house soon after the French and Canadians successfully introduced national musical quotas and warned the Irish government that, if they didn't follow suit, the Irish music industry would go down the toilet. The Irish government didn't listen to him. Using a spurious argument dreamed up by the independent Irish radio sector that an Irish music quota contravened EU law, they vetoed the move, and they're still doing it today. Youth radio in Ireland in 2016 play little or no Irish music in their schedules.' I paused and gestured towards the line of young musical acts seated before us waiting to perform. 'These young Irish musicians and singers who will soon play and sing for you will never get on primetime Irish radio unless you politicians take the bull by the horns and get behind Willie Penrose's bill to enact a forty percent Irish music radio quota.'

Danny McCarthy spoke finally about the huge loss to the Irish economy that was a direct consequence of the Irish government's intransigence on the Irish music quota issue, and pointed out that the Irish broadcasting authority had gone to Brussels as far back as the '90s and were given clearance by the EU to enact legislation to bring in a thirty percent Irish music quota under a specific wording of what constituted Irish music at that time. 'What happened to that initiative is a scandal that needs to be exposed'

A short debate ensued during which our motion appeared to be supported by all in attendance, except Fianna Fáil. Their chief spokesman offered the opinion – not once but several times – that quotas were 'blunt instruments'. Because of the mantra-like way he kept repeating this, I suspected that he was merely mouthing the official all-party line passed down through the corridors of power by the same lazy civil service department that had blocked Bill Whelan thirty years earlier. After the third 'blunt' comment, I was tempted to tilt my guitar at the man and make light of the matter by informing him that 'all our instruments were finely tuned', but I let him off the hook, deciding to go above his head at a later stage and appeal to the better sense of his leader, Micheál Martin, who I suspect is his own man and wouldn't want the stain already on his party's conscience to remain there for another thirty years.

The debate was followed by performances by all the young musical acts who had come to support the cause, ending with a stunning instrumental piece by Moxie, a rip-rousing set by Ruaile Buaile and a new version of *Mise Éire* by Sibéal Ní Chasaide, composed by her uncle, Patrick Cassidy, which was the highlight of the occasion.

As the meeting was breaking up, Willie Penrose invited our team to lunch in the Dáil canteen but, as we were heading there, I had a call on my mobile phone from my daughter Niamh, who informed me that, having attended the final part of our meeting, she was heading back to her car as her allocation of parking time was about to run out. Knowing that she needed to get home to pick up her kids after school, I told her I would make my apologies to Willie and the others and be with her as soon as I could. Before I let her go, I remembered her friend whom she'd visited in hospital. 'By the way, how are the triplets doing?'

'Great, thank God.'

With Niamh behind the wheel, we were back in Loughrea just after four in the afternoon. Two hours later RTE television ran a feature in their six o'clock news bulletin highlighting the musical extravaganza outside the Dáil. Instead of focusing on the primal moment of Sibéal singing *Mise Éire* at the Oireachtas gate they opted to portray the Paddywackery aspect of the gathering. Though this was ameliorated somewhat by a clip of Phil Coulter and John Sheahan making salient points on some of the key aspects of our cause, the feature ended with a dry statement issued by a spokesman for the Broadcasting Authority of Ireland admitting that an Irish music quota had at one time been submitted to the EU but, following a complaint to the European commission, it was withdrawn because it 'wasn't compatible with legislation'.

This short rebuttal of our campaign was worded in such a way as to hide the fact that it was the independent Irish radio sector that had made the complaint to Europe that had derailed the quota in the first place. To make sure I was a hundred percent correct on this crucial point, I went to my files and located the *Hot Press* interview written by onetime chairman of the broadcasting authority of Ireland, Niall Stokes, and focused on these highlighted lines:

> In my new role with the IRTC, I succeeded in winning support of the board for the introduction of a thirty percent Irish music quota. The first response of the Association of Independent Radio Stations was to make a complaint to the EC, on the basis that the measure was anti-competitive . . . We knew, however, that there were quotas in effect in France and Portugal . . . so we began a lengthy dance with the EC to establish terms on which a quota could be introduced here . . . The chief executive of the IRTC, Michael O'Keeffe, and I engaged in lengthy negotiations with Brussels and we prevailed in the end on the basis of a cultural exception and it was accepted by the EC that music was an essential part of Ireland's cultural heritage and its natural resources and therefore it was valid to put measures in place to protect it. And we agreed a definition with the EC on what constituted Irish music.

Some time after our day in Leinster House, a Dail debate on the issue of enacting legislation to introduce an Irish music quota was voted down by both Fianna Fáil and Fine Gael. Soon after this fait accompli an article by Colin Coyle in *The Sunday Times* headed "Irish Music Quota Stymied" explained what had brought this about:

> Denis O'Brien's Communicorp, which owns Today FM, 98FM, Newstalk and Spin 1038, lobbied against a proposal to introduce a 40% Irish music quota on radio. The lobbying register shows the company wrote to 43 TDs, including ministers, to encourage them to vote against a bill tabled by Willie Penrose, a Labour Party TD, seeking a music quota because "it did not recognise listener preference".

THE TREE

Now that you've outgrown my tallest tales

Hold Your Horses

I had spent an hour or more in my room re-reading Teilhard de Chardin's *The Phenomenon of Man* and became so engrossed in its speculations about where God-driven Evolution is leading mankind, I lost track of time and ran ten minutes over schedule before putting the book aside and getting into my wellington boots and anorak for my customary second walk of the day. My earlier walk to Silver Strand through Barna Woods had been spoilt somewhat by rain, but now I was glad to see through my workroom window that the sky was invitingly blue, so I was looking forward to a trek around the park, without my umbrella.

After popping into the kitchen to see how Joan was getting on with preparations for dinner, I put my head around the living room door and asked our visiting granddaughters, Kate and Hannah, if they'd care to accompany me on my walk. Hannah tore her eyes away from the TV and glanced down at her pink socks, grimacing. 'My ingrown toenails are at me again! I'm not able to walk.' Her sister Kate, reading a teen magazine (though she's only nine), looked up from a picture of a handsome teen idol and blinked behind her red glasses. 'I'll go. I want to see are there any chestnuts under the chestnut tree for a school project. You know the tree with the low branch that Han and I used to play horsey on when we were small.'

I laughed. '*When* you were small! You're still small – too small to be reading those magazines. Does your mother know you're reading that?'

Kate smiled, coyly. 'Of course.'

Hannah backed up her sister. 'One of the twins left it here last weekend. Mammy doesn't mind us reading them. There's only pictures of pop stars in it and dating advice.'

I frowned at Kate. 'That's what I'm worried about. I'll ask your mother when she gets back from the shops. Meanwhile, get your wellies and we'll head out. It's very mucky after the rain.'

Taking the narrow path past the children's playground across from our house, I set off at my usual swift pace, which meant Kate had to skip along to keep up with me. Approaching a fork in the walkway, I let my granddaughter decide which way to go, knowing that she would opt for the downward slope towards the small iron-railed bridge fording the stream rather that go the other way towards the sports' amenity centre. She did this instinctively, following a habit set years before when she and Hannah and our other granddaughters first started accompanying me on my walks. Back then Kate's natural leadership instinct (or obstinacy, as her mother termed it) came to the fore and she dictated the course of our stroll, which set the pattern we were still following today.

Our pace naturally slackened on the decline, so Kate caught her breath. Observing that the line of blackberry bushes skirting the walkway were completely bare of fruit, she pointed towards the withering briars. 'Look, all the blackberries are gone and the leaves are all spotty and smudgy.'

I glanced at the thorny entanglements of withered vegetation coiling among nettles and weeds along the border of the path. 'Autumn is doing its cruel work. Hard to believe only a few short weeks ago you and the girls were filling jam-jars with berries from these sorry looking ramblers.'

Kate laughed. 'Remember Saoirse found the worm in the berry she was going to eat? That's why mammy makes us steep them in hot water.'

We came to the bridge. A holly tree overhanging the grey railing caught my attention. I stopped and examined the fronds between the shiny prickly leaves for buds, but there weren't any. 'By the looks of it, there'll be no berries on this tree this year.'

Kate got up on her toes and studied the spaces between the leaves. 'How do you know?'

'There're no buds. Some years berries don't come on some varieties of holly trees. Maybe because of the weather. There's a different variety of holly at the far side of the bridge full of berries already, not as red as the ones that grow on this tree, but they'll be gone before Christmas. They always are. I'll show you when we get across the bridge.'

The stream flowing under the bridge was swollen because of recent torrential rains, making a thunderous noise. Glancing up stream I observed the mad rush of muddy water cascading over rocks and eddying around tree trunks close to the flooded bank. 'The water can't wait to get back to the sea.'

Kate smiled. 'Then it will be sucked back up into the sky by the sun to form clouds that will rain down on the land again.'

I tapped Kate on the head. 'You have a good memory. I told you that a long time ago. That's why we call nature Mother Nature, because she looks after the world.'

'Why don't they call it Father Nature?'

I thought of Kate's father, separated from her mother and living in England. 'I suppose because a mother's love is really special. Fathers are important too, of course. God is our father and he loves everyone. And your own father also loves you and Hannah, though he doesn't live with you anymore.'

Kate lowered her eyes. 'He forgot to phone me for my birthday. Mammy was mad.'

I patted her on the head. 'Men can be forgetful sometimes. That doesn't mean that he doesn't love you. He does.'

Making our way up the slope at the far side of the bridge, I pointed to another holly bush growing among a copse of sally trees, its emerald spiky foliage heavy with bunches of crimson berries. 'Little robins will have a great times dining on them when winter comes.'

Kate laughed. 'You don't say *dining* for birds.'

'Why not?'

Kate smiled, shyly. 'Because they're creatures not people.'

'There's a thing called a poetic license which allows us to bend the rules.'

Kate blinked behind her glasses. 'Like in the nursery rhyme *Hey Diddle Diddle* where the cow jumps over the moon?'

'And the cat runs away with the spoon. Exactly. You're a bright girl. Do you remember the day I was telling you and the girls the story about *The Wedding Dress Flower* – as white as the moon – and you asked me if the moon could talk?'

Kate lowered her eyes. 'I didn't say that.'

'You did, I swear. You were only five or six at the time. No need to be embarrassed. I explained that while the moon couldn't speak with words it could communicate with beams of light, and you were satisfied with that.'

Kate laughed. 'How come you don't tell us stories anymore?'

'Because *you* found me out, remember? I was telling you about Mr Goosegog and the Talking Fish one Sunday back in the summer and you said it was all made up. My goose was cooked as a storyteller after that. But I don't mind. You read books now, don't you. That's good enough for me.'

We came to another fork in the walkway. Turning left and then sharp right, we skirted a wide muddy puddle and made our way along a stretch of path by a soccer pitch. Two boys kicking a football midfield were shouting at a mongrel that kept running after their ball. While I was watching them Kate directed my attention to a nearby goalpost where a single magpie was perched on the top bar. When I spotted it, Kate laughed. 'One for sorrow!'

I feigned a frown. 'Why'd you have to show me?'

Kate grinned. 'You do it to Hannah and me all the time.'

We walked on, watching the boys following the mongrel who had managed to get the ball in its mouth. One of the boys caught up with the dog and grabbed it by its collar. The dog dropped the ball and ran away. The boys resumed their game.

'How are things going at school?'

Kate smiled. 'Good. The reason I have to get the horse chestnuts is because we're doing a nature project.'

'What's your favourite subjects?'

'Maths, English and Art.' She glanced at me. 'I like Religious class too.'

I gave a false laugh. 'Religious class, you?!'

'I do, really. Mammy often reads us the Kids' Bible that you gave us last Christmas. I love the stories in that. Hannah loves them too.'

'Which ones?'

Kate hesitated. 'Noah and the Ark, Moses in the Basket, King Solomon and the Baby he was going to chop in two. We love lots of them.'

I nodded. 'What about *The Garden of Eden?*'

'It's scary when the snake comes and tempts Eve to eat the apple from the forbidden tree – the tree of knowledge.'

'Why do you think the tree of knowledge was a forbidden tree?'

Kate gave me a puzzled look. 'I don't know. Was it because it was evil?'

'The bible says it was good as well as evil.' I glanced at the boys who were shouting at the dog because it had run off with their ball again. 'Some people think the tree of knowledge is just a metaphor or a symbol for the mystery of life. A metaphor is something that stands for something else, to make it easy to understand. God's ordering Adam and Eve not to eat this fruit meant that they weren't to try and figure out what God's plan is for our world. But of course they broke the rule and committed original sin. That's why they had to leave paradise.'

Kate frowned. 'The angel used a sword to drive them out of the garden. And he told the snake that he must crawl on his belly forever.'

I smiled. 'Scary stuff alright. Luckily it's only a myth. The early stories in the bible are like fairytales. All good fairytales have something real in them, something that we can learn from. But unlike fairytales, bible stories were inspired by God, so they're very special indeed.'

Kate frowned. 'But myths aren't real and Adam and Eve were real.'

I hesitated, thinking that I'd overstepped the mark; wondering if Kate was old enough for a dip in such deep waters. 'Some people believe Adam and Eve were real and others think they were just mythical characters, invented by God to teach us the message that we mustn't disobey His will.'

Kate looked at me. 'Which do you believe?'

I laughed. 'Snakes can't talk! I'm on the myth side. I think original sin might have something to do with the aggressive nature that is in all living creatures, especially man. The instinct to survive makes us hurt one another. That's why wars have been going on since the beginning of time. Jesus came to stop that carnage.'

Kate gave me a baffled look. 'What does carnage mean?'

I pointed towards the dog out on the pitch who had got his teeth into the ball and was tearing it to shreds while the two boys looked on agape. 'That's carnage.'

Kate laughed. 'It serves them right; they should have stopped playing till the dog went away.'

Relieved at the tangent our conversation had veered in, I directed Kate's attention to a blackbird perched on the low branch of one of a group of sally trees that lined the walkway on our right, after we left the football pitch behind. 'Look at the orange beak of that bird; isn't it beautiful? And it's a beautiful singer too.'

Kate admired the bird as we passed the tree. 'My favourite bird is the robin. They're so cute. I don't like big birds, like jackdaws. They make too much noise. Magpies make a lot of noise too, like they have a baby rattle in their mouth.'

A canopy of leafy branches overhead darkened the pathway ahead. After walking in silence for a few minutes we came to a line of very old trees growing at the bottom of a slope behind a stone wall. Most of them had massive moss-covered trunks with multi-shaped branches spreading out chaotically every which way. Some of the trees had gaping scars where branches had been torn from the boles by storms and gales. The final tree at the end of the line was a tall chestnut with a low curling branch resting on top of the wall. Kate pointed towards the arc of the branch sitting on a flat stone and smiled. 'That's where we used to sit and play horsey when the branch wasn't so low.'

I laughed. 'It was you, Hannah and Saoirse who collapsed the branch from all the bouncing you gave it.'

Kate chuckled and started rummaging among the yellow and ochre leaves on the ground around us. 'I can't see any chestnuts, just a few empty shells.'

I looked up through gaps in the branches overhead and spotted clusters of lime-coloured spiky shells among the pronged leaves still on the tree. 'Most of the chestnuts haven't come down yet. Not ripe enough, I guess. We'll come back next week and maybe you'll find a few.'

Kate kept searching and suddenly let out a yelp. 'Found one. It's very small, but it's lovely and shiny and brown. Look.'

I looked at the little pristine object in Kate's palm. 'It's certainly too small to play conkers with. More like a hazelnut, though a hazelnut has no sheen and that has a lovely gloss.'

Kate smiled. 'It's so perfect looking, isn't it?'

I looked again at the little nut in Kate's palm and recalled another nut that features in one of my favourite spiritual books, *Revelations of Divine Love*. 'Hundreds of years ago in England a lady called Julian of Norwich had a vision that a nut no bigger than that contained the whole universe. In God's eyes, she said, our world is just a speck.' I tapped Kate on the head. 'Life is full of mystery. Maybe when you grow up you might crack the nut and find the code.'

Kate laughed and went on searching among the leaves for other chestnuts, but there were none to be found. We resumed walking, homeward, by a different route, one that led us by a section of the same roaring stream we'd encountered earlier crossing the bridge. Eventually we came to a curving path on a hill rise that I called 'Dogshit Row' because of the dog pooh that almost always befouled it. 'Watch out for turds, Kate, or you'll have to clean your sole when we get back to the house.'

Kate tittered. 'You mean the sole of my shoe, not my holy soul?'

'No, not your holy soul. That'll stay clean if you keep saying your prayers.'

We came to a wooden seat that I often sat on. I suggested taking a rest before the last leg of our journey home. While we were sitting there in silence gazing at Barna Woods in the distance, our earlier conversation on the forbidden tree came back to me and I wondered if I had confused Kate in any way in what I had said. 'I used to meet an old man called Paddy here on this very seat fairly regularly before he died last year at the age of ninety-four. He loved music. That's how we became acquainted. Every time we met he used to ask me if I'd written any new songs, and that always started a conversation. He loved Bing Crosby and Frank Sinatra. He was a very religious man. As well as going to Mass regularly he told me that he spent a lot of time praying every morning when he got up.'

Kate looked at me. 'How did he die?'

I hesitated. 'To be honest, I'm not sure. Old age, I guess. I lost contact with him when he got sick and stopped coming for walks to the park. I suppose I should have gone to his apartment to find out, but I didn't. Anyway, when I heard he had died I remembered a conversation I'd had with him before he grew ill which was very similar to the one I had with you earlier about the Garden of Eden. I told him that it was just a myth and he was very disturbed because he believed that it was a true event that happened in history. When I insisted that it was just a story like a fairytale, he shook his head and grew angry. When he died I remembered this and I felt sorry that I'd upset him.'

Kate gave me a penetrating look. 'And well you should. It was cruel!'

'I know.' I drew a loud breath and sat in silence for a moment. 'I hope my telling you the same thing a while back didn't upset you?'

Kate squinted through her glasses. 'It's different for me; I'm just a kid. But for an old man, it wasn't nice.'

'But do you not think that everyone should know the truth? At one time most people thought that the sun, moon and stars revolved around our world. Now we know better, even though lots of men still think that the stars, moon and sun revolve around them.'

Kate gave me a puzzled look and got to her feet. 'Come on, we'd better get home. The dinner will be ready and Momum will be mad if we're late again.'

THE CROW & THE GULL

My songs are my guide

We Both Need to Know

I arrived home from my usual Monday night St Vincent de Paul duties earlier than usual, not just because I'd handed in my resignation at the Conference meeting before going out on one of my final runs of home visitations, but because I'd planned to watch a TV debate on *The Claire Byrne Show* on the forthcoming referendum on the repeal of the Constitutional 8th Amendment after the 9 o'clock news. Though the subject had been ventilated ad nauseam in all strands of the media (I even published an article on a new song related to the subject myself in *The Sunday Independent*), tonight's RTE "Special" was hyped as being the forum that would decide one way or the other whether abortion would be legalised in Ireland in our time. I had a personal interest in the programme also because a live version of my song prerecorded and filmed for RTE was due to be broadcast as part of the show.

After I deposited my SVP notebook in my workroom, I went upstairs for a quick chat with Joan, who had opted to watch the programme on the bedroom TV rather than risk any embarrassment of viewing it with me downstairs in the living room. She was aware that I'd been very ill on the day I went to Dublin to prerecord and film the song, so she was as nervous as I about my imminent performance. Already in bed, watching the news, she propped herself up on her pillows when I entered the dimly-lit room and listened distractedly to a brief account of the SVP meeting I'd just come from. 'I'd already told them last week about the resignation letter I'd sent to our national president because of the neutral position the organisation has taken on the referendum, and two or three of our members had read my article, but still a few of them seemed shocked by the stance I've taken. It surprised me how many of them are on the repeal side.'

Joan shifted in the bed and glanced at her watch. 'You must be getting nervous? Just fifteen minutes to go.'

I glanced at the TV. 'I keep wondering how they've edited and spliced together the various takes we did. I told you, they had only one camera, so they had to film me singing it a half dozen times.'

Not interested in technicalities, Joan gave me a knowing look. 'Relax and go and have your cup of tea. I'm sure it'll be fine.'

Downstairs, I dropped into my workroom and checked my computer for emails. Among the spam, I spotted a Facebook notification. Clicking on it, I was taken to my Timeline and a card with the lyric of *Could Have Been Me* printed beside a photograph of a French student, Victoire Listeman, whose story of abortion survival my song was partly based on. I glanced at the comment below the card – "*Aborting a healthy unborn baby of three months is liberalism gone crazy*" – and then read through the lyric of the song to check for typos, as I'd changed a few words on the advice of a friend before republishing it earlier in the day.

Could Have Been Me (for Victoire Listemann)

My heart went out to an infant pumped from its mother's womb
through a cannula where the tiny life was consumed,
and as it seeped away molten tears came to my eyes
and burned me up for the countless souls like this who die.
That innocent life could have been me, but for my mother's sensibility,
in thinking things out with me in mind, her living child.

Now I've come to view each newborn baby as unique,
irreplaceable as the love we give and the love we take,
and as I make my way through life I often kneel and pray
for the silent ones whose voiceless tongues have no say.
That innocent life could have been me, but for my mother's bravery,
in thinking things through with me in mind, her grateful child.

It could have been me, it could have been you,
It could be any one of a few lining up in a voting queue.

For the lonely girls who cannot cope and give in
to the pressure of their own fear or another's will,
my heart goes out to you in deepest empathy
for in you I see my mother before she had me.
That innocent life could have been me but for my mother's sensitivity,
in thinking with her heart pounding to find her loving child.

Before putting my computer to sleep, I linked to a YouTube video of the song produced by Francis Kennedy and was held by the visual imagery of youthful faces that featured as abortion survivors and young mothers alongside the printed narrative of their unfolding story on the screen. The calm sweep of Tony Maher's keyboard arrangement also pulled me in, without impinging on my vocal performance. But the crowning achievement of the musical production was undoubtedly the natural percussion of the infant heartbeat that tugged at the emotions for every beat of the song. As its pulsating rhythm gripped me, I wondered how the live acoustic version recorded for television would hold up without the vital pulse.

I went to the kitchen and made a mug of tea and took it to the living room, where Joan had left the TV on, tuned to RTE. A little behind schedule, Claire Byrne's signature tune started and Claire's attractive face appeared on screen in a darkened set with low ambient lighting showing up her two panels of guests in silhouette in the background, separated by her empty chair. After welcoming the audience and viewers, she gave a brief résumé of the night's proceedings, mentioning my name and the name of rival singer, Rosin O, in her preamble. She then went and sat between the trios of opponents and the discussion commenced.

As I knew the fixed opinions of most of the rival guests inside out, the stream of arguments cascaded in and out of my concentration till the end of part one, without leaving much of an impression, except for when Savita Halappanavar's name was introduced as a hard case for legalising abortion. This brought to mind the wife of the recording engineer who helped me record my new song, Eileen Maher – a retired nurse from the hospital where Savita had died – who told me that the tragic death of Savita had nothing to do with the restrictions of the 8th Amendment.

A flutter of butterflies rose in my stomach at the beginning of part two as my name was mentioned again as a forthcoming guest, but, when my song failed to follow, I put my anxiety on hold and tried to get back into the discussion. The debate grew contentious and got bogged down in a series of rancorous exchanges between members of the panel and members of the audience. I tuned out and started thinking about an email I'd received from the French student, Victoire, a few days earlier, thanking me for dedicating the song to her and complementing me on the "beauty" of the lyric. The word *beauty*, I recalled, had stopped me in my tracks because of the graphic description of an abortion operation that was outlined in the first verse, but then I remembered that several of the earliest comments left by YouTube viewers of the video were also complementary regarding the esthetic quality of the song, one going so far as to describe it as "poignant and lovely". Thinking on this now, while the debate on the screen was turning brash and ugly, I reflected back on how the inspiration for the song had come to me after a very disturbed period in the days leading up to Ash Wednesday gone by. During my weekly stroll to Silver Strand on the previous Sunday, a crow flew out of a black cloud over Galway Bay and perched on a rock in front of a boulder I was sitting on, and remained staring at me while cawing and flapping its purple-tinged black wings. To avoid its brazen gaze, I looked away and spotted a seagull gliding in from a stretch of pearly-grey clouds on the western horizon. As it got closer to me the cloud-veiled sun above its outstretched wings became partly visible and reminded me of a pearl in an oyster shell. A few days after this, on Shrove Tuesday, I remembered the contrasting birds and jotted an account of my encounter with them in my song journal. Using a strong melody that had been haunting me for some weeks before this (melodies always precede and shape lyrics for me) I tried to write a song about the birds, but it refused to rhyme. The following day, Ash Wednesday, I tried again but, again, the words refused to gel, which reminded me of St Teresa's dictum "Words clash when the spirit isn't right". As the fast day wore on I found myself sinking into a deep depression that I couldn't shake off. Several times I felt so gloomy I was compelled to leave the house and walk to Silver Strand, just to try and get away from myself. When I got back to my room after my final stroll, I automatically took John of the Cross's *Dark Night of the Soul* from a book shelf and read through a number of underlined passages that often give me comfort when I'm feeling rock-bottom. One of them in particular impressed me so much I jotted it into my song journal. The gist of it, I remembered, suggested that intense periods of depression like I was going through often precede periods of creativity (something I could verify from past experience). During the following days my mood improved and I got the idea of applying the melody that had failed to ignite the bird song to an idea for a song based on Victoire's and other abortion survivor's stories. While I was reflecting on how to get started, I received a serendipitous email from Kathy Sinnott (a fervent Christian protagonist and anti-abortion lobbyist) with a link to a newspaper article by John Waters on the subject of the repeal of the 8th Amendment, which referenced a song by Graham Parker with a graphic description of an abortion operation back in the 1970s or 80s in which a forceps is compared to "talons of steel". This stark image of one of the tools of abortion of that time prompted me to watch a YouTube video of a more up-to-date foetal termination procedure and, while watching it, I pictured the French girl, Victoire, observing the gruesome operation and reflecting on the fact that the infant being terminated might have been herself had her mother not withstood family pressure to abort her.

While mulling over the creative process that had given birth to *Could Have Been Me*, part two of the TV debate ended and part three began, without mention of any singing performances. The intensity of the discussion deepened and, as the verbal exchanges became more and more inflamed, I began to grow uneasy, wondering how my song was going to be received. I recalled a few hostile responses I'd already had to live performances of *Could Have Been Me* during a recent tour of art centres. After one show a young woman came up to me with burning eyes and said that I shouldn't sing such songs on stage. Her expression was so anguished I felt like sympathising with her, for I figured that personal tragedy lay behind her anger. Following another concert, a man attacked me verbally while I was still on stage. I tried to reason with him by explaining that the song wasn't a piece of propaganda but was based on true stories of people who had almost been aborted and felt blessed to be alive, but the man shouted me down and went and demanded and received his entrance fee back at the box office.

As the deadline for the end of the TV debate approached and there was still no sign of songs being introduced, a conspiracy theory began to hatch in my over-taxed brain that political interference might lay behind the suppression of my song. Reflecting back on it, I recalled that every radio station I'd sent files of the song to had refused to play it on the grounds that their hands were tied by broadcasting authority restrictions. All effort to counter this spurious claim went unanswered, even when I pointed out to one radio boss that he and his cohorts hadn't minded breaching BAI regulations on the amount of Irish music they play (or rather don't play) in their schedules.

Claire Byrne eventually brought the show to and end without offering an apology or explanation for why the songs had been dropped from the schedule, which fuelled my paranoia even more. Crestfallen, I knocked off the set and turned out the lights and went upstairs to voice my suspicion to Joan, but found her fast asleep. Retreating to my workroom, I brooded on the many failures that had hampered the song reaching an audience in the weeks gone by and I began to question my motivation for writing it, wondering why the higher powers hadn't got behind me. To check my bona fides on the matter, I went to my song journal and located my awakening interest in the subject of the repeal of the 8th Amendment, which went right back to a piece of doggerel I wrote in March 2017.

In The Soup

In pagan Ireland human sacrifice was acceptable,
and now in post Christian Ireland it may be introduced again.

Old Nick is in the kitchen, stirring up the pot, with a pitchfork for a spoon. Try to savour his broth and you fail, for there's little substance in each scoop. Still, he has the nation on tenterhooks, with the media advertising his ingredients in all the organs of the State. One scoop would have us believe all nuns are Nazis in disguise who systematically plotted the disposal of unwanted babies to be rid of their unmarried mothers' curse. Ironically, while this is being consumed, the same media are dishing out the dirt on the 8th Amendment, insisting it be repealed so we can swallow the swill that abortion can be sanitised. The stew is on the boil. Old Nick is ladling the slop, stirring up the stock of the unsavoury meal, and the nation is swallowing the poison with each sop.

I realised that this humorous take on a very serious subject was over the top, so I didn't attempt to turn it into a song, even when a friend suggested I try. Though I went on taking a keen interest in the forthcoming referendum during the following year, it wasn't until the crow and seagull incident on Silver Strand that I began to develop the notion of writing a song on the issue. To confirm this, I fast forwarded in my song journal to Shrove Tuesday 2018 and came upon the entry about the two birds that fired me up:

A crow flew out of a black cloud over Galway Bay and perched ominously on a rock in front of me (a shadow of a dark mood that had me gripped in its talons). I turned towards the western horizon for relief and found little colour in the oyster shell-grey sky, till a lone gull came gliding into view, offering promise that the hidden source of the opal light above its outstretched wings was the pearl-like orb of the sun.

The melody that failed to ignite these words into melodious rhyme gave wing a few days later to *Could Have Been Me*. According to my song journal, I completed the song on the 4 March 2018. Above the hand written lyric I had jotted a quotation by Leo Tolstoy taken from a book of his I was rereading at the time, *What is Art? "The business of art is to make that understood and felt which in the form of an argument might be incomprehensible and inaccessible."*

Recalling that I'd recited this quotation to camera as part of my prerecorded spot for *The Claire Byrne Show*, I regretted the missed opportunity of displaying to a wide audience its iron-cast truth, which is the heartbeat of *Could Have Been Me*.

After reading over the history of how I came to write the song, I said a prayer and went to bed, satisfied that the motivation behind the composition was not self-serving.

A little over a week after the show, on the 25 of May 2018, the Irish nation went to the polls and made history by voting overwhelmingly to allow the Irish government free reign on repealing the 8th Amendment and replacing it with whatever abortion laws it deems fit to insert into our Constitution in the future. Since then, media pundits have been speculating that what swung the vote for the repeal side was the many tragic stories widely circulated of teenage girls forced to make the lonely trip to London for abortions because their own country was too cruel to cater for their crisis pregnancies. If true (and please remember that the final verse of my song deals with this same sympathy, but with a crucial twist) then such sympathisers should be asked the rhetorical question a wise friend put to me while such speculation was circulating: "Would the Irish government consider legalising crack-cocaine and heroin if supplies of these drugs were blocked from coming into our country and our drug users and addicts started complaining about having to make the long lonely journey to the UK to source their drugs?"

In the article I wrote for *The Sunday Independent* on the motivation behind my song, I ended the piece with this summation:

> *Could Have Been Me* is a depiction of near-death experiences and not just some piece of propaganda. It's a real song, with true artistic values. If some find the potency and poignancy of the lyric disturbing, then that's regrettable but not a valid reason to suppress the song. My main aim in writing the work was to celebrate the lives of survivors who, against the odds, came through the hazard of near extinction to experience the miraculous wonder of being alive in our world through the pure power of love.

Though I fully stand over these words, I recently received a piece of criticism from one of my most vehement detractors who focused on the bridge section of *Could Have Been Me* and suggested that, contrary to my claim, it contained one line of subtle propaganda: "It could have been any one of a few lining up in a voting queue." While reflecting on this questionable fault-line, an alternative bridge section came to me out of the blue and took my breath away, as it went straight to the shores of the heart of my most popular song, *The Voyage*.

It could have been me, it could have been you;
It could have been anyone of our crew,
Or one of your crew too.